Brennan claimed relevance of the traditions for women in the twentieth century.

The second chapter suggests that Mark's auditors were cosmopolitan, dissenting, "anti-twelve," and open to woman assuming leadership positions within the community. In the same vein, the third chapter discovers a tradition of dissension.

Mark 5:24–34 may have been preserved because it stood in dissension with the ancient purity system. A thorough analysis of terms describing menstruation illustrates that the writers of both Leviticus and Mark used the same euphemisms. The second chapter covers the origin and meaning of purity laws and their supposed effects upon worshipers, and demonstrates that woman was excluded from the central workings of the cult because of her biological differences.

The fourth chapter identifies the home of Mark's auditors to be somewhere outside Jerusalem, within the Greco-Roman world. Greek traditions about menstruation are compared with those of the Jewish writers. Although menstruation was not completely understood, Greco-Roman society rarely penalized woman for her differences in biology.

The last chapter interprets Mark 5:24–34 in relation to all of the linguistic, social, and cultural research summarized in the previous chapters. It concludes that the writers of Mark believed that it is woman who legitimately perceives, recognizes, and intuitively understands the voice of God. She is seen to be more capable and honest than the Twelve and as exhibiting the kind of faith in herself and her god needed by the emerging communities.

Woman, Cult, and Miracle Recital

Woman, Cult, and Miracle Recital

A Redactional Critical Investigation on Mark 5 : 24–34

Marla J. Selvidge

Lewisburg
Bucknell University Press
London and Toronto: Associated University Presses

Associated University Presses
440 Forsgate Drive
Cranbury, NJ 08512

Associated University Presses
25 Sicilian Avenue
London WC1A 2QH, England

Associated University Presses
P.O. Box 488, Port Credit
Mississauga, Ontario
Canada L5G 4M2

The paper used in this publication meets the requirements
of the American National Standard for Permanence of Paper
for Printed Library Materials Z39.48-1984.

Library of Congress Cataloging-in-Publication Data

Selvidge, Marla J., 1948–
    Woman, cult, and miracle recital: a redactional critical
investigation on Mark 5:24–34/Marla Jean Selvidge.
        p.   cm.
    Bibliography: p.
    Includes index.
    ISBN 0-8387-5143-1 (alk. paper)
    1. Bible.   N.T.   Mark V, 24–34—Criticism, Redaction.   2. Woman in
the Bible.   I. Title.
BS2585.2.S4   1990
226'.306—dc19
                                                                    87-46439
                                                                    CIP

PRINTED IN THE UNITED STATES OF AMERICA

To:

Professor Frederick W. Danker

Profound words speaker
caretaker
Sharer of truths
Inspirer
and
Grand Thinker.
Mentor.

With gratitude for your neverending
Confidence in Me.

Contents

Contents

Preface

Women's influence and importance in biblical times, however mute over the past two millennia, stands preserved in almost every writing of the New Testament. Endless controversies and theologies were thoroughly investigated by church scholars, while woman and her relation to the events and doctrines was virtually ignored. Recent scholarship has begun the task of sorting out the traditions about women by targeting Paul's works and the Gospels.[1]

The Gospel of Mark awaits scholarly discussion on the topic of woman. This study attempts to begin the investigation into Mark's view of woman and cult by exegeting Mark 5:24–34. This miracle story about a hemorrhaging woman has been chosen because it presents to the reader a variety of seemly unanswerable questions. Why does the woman touch Jesus? Why is there so much emphasis on touching? How can her illness be diagnosed? Why does she kneel before Jesus? Why do the disciples seem oblivious to the healing situation? Who was this woman? Who does she represent? Why does the woman seem to have the ability to appropriate the healing power that is associated with Jesus? Why does Jesus single her out and speak to her? These are just a few of the questions that need to be answered through some type of systematic research.

Methodology

This study is an outgrowth of traditional historical-critical exegetical practices.

LINGUISTIC-SOURCE ANALYSIS

Key words within Mark 5:24–34 have been compared with similar and cognate words found throughout the LXX with the purpose of determining if the miracle story had its source or foundation in the Old Testament Hebrew Bible or Apocrypha.

Key phrases, including cognates and synonyms used to describe the woman's illness, have been compared with other Hellenistic and Greek literature in order to determine if the source for the miracle story or the specific vocabulary used as euphemisms for *menstruation* were employed by these Greek authors.

HISTORICO-CULTURAL INFLUENCES

With a view to determine the relationship of a woman's biology to her role in cult responsibilities, both the major cults and religions during Greco-Roman times have been investigated, including Judaism.

AUDIENCE

The Gospel has been scrutinized in order to ascertain what type of communal situation existed during the redaction of the work. Sociological models were consulted.

MARK'S PERSONAL VIEW OF WOMAN

Every instance in which the female gender is implied or mentioned explicitly has been listed. Every word within Mark 5 : 24–34 has been compared with the remainder of the Gospel in order to ascertain any philological links between this pericope and others involving women.

SURVEY OF SCHOLARSHIP

Every noteworthy interpretation of this passage has been consulted in order to determine how various scholars have viewed this story over the past two thousand years.

Presuppositions

Mark's Gospel preserves traditions that were handed down (orally and possibly in a written form) to the growing Christian communities.[2] This Gospel predates both Matthew and Luke, and thus was used as one of their sources.[3] Its final redaction came during or after the destruction of the temple, around 70 C.E.[4] The Gospel reflects a community in transition and under reconstruction necessitated by the then recent devastating historical events surrounding the fall of Jerusalem.[5] Mark captures and preserves oral and written traditions that attempt to meet the needs of this emerging group. Central to that inquiry is the relation of woman to cult.

Preliminaries

In addition to Kurt Aland's Greek text, two translations of the Bible are used in citations: *The New International Version* is used for the New Testament, and *The Jerusalem Bible* is used for quotations in the Old Testament/Hebrew Bible. Occasional translations are duly noted.

Generally speaking, the chapters are an outgrowth of this methodology. Chapter 1 traces the miracle story through two thousand years of interpretation. Chapter 2 suggests that Mark's auditors were cosmopolitan (both Jew and Hellenist), dissenting, and looking for new leadership. Chapter 3 considers Mark's Judaic heritage of purity laws as they relate to woman. Woman is excluded from the central workings of the cult because of her differences in biology. Chapter 4 demonstrates that menstruation, or woman's biologic differences, rarely hindered her in participating and assuming central roles within the Greco-Roman cults. Chapter 5 interprets Mark 5:24–34 in relation to all of this evidence. Woman becomes a significant community member, role determiner, and voice of God to the emerging communities.

Acknowledgments

With many thanks to Angela M. Janulis, Christina Cummings, and Debbie K. Currin, for their efforts at the computer

Woman, Cult, and Miracle Recital

1
Survey
Interpretations and Discussions Centering on
Mark 5 : 24–34

Interpretative studies focusing on Mark 5:24–34 remain both monocular and diverse. No consensus of opinion has ever been reached on the meaning and significance of this miracle story. Although this story deals with a physical problem that could have vital significance for over half of every congregation, it never found its way into any major theological debates.

The Ancients

The earliest interpretations of Mark 5 : 24–34 compare it with Hebrew law. The most noted mention of the curtailment of the activity of women because of their menstrual cycle, came in approximately 247 C.E., when Dionysius, archbishop of Alexandria, wrote a letter to Basilides. His words were later adopted by the Council at Trullo in 496 C.E.[1] The Greek church regarded this council as ecumenical. The following canon, originally attributed to the apostles,[2] and the observations of Theodore Balsamon, a Greek Scholastic, are of great moment.

Basilides had questioned the archbishop as to the problem of women who were in a menstrous state. Should they enter the church, and should they be allowed to participate in the sacraments? The council answered, with official apostolic authority, "Menstrous women ought not to come to the Holy Table, or touch the holy of holies, nor to the churches but pray elsewhere."[3]

This canon potentially banished women from cultic activities during their menstrual cycles. The social results of this canon are unknown, but it must have dealt a heavy blow against Eastern women in the formative years of the early church.

Almost a thousand years later, Balsamon commented on this canon.[4]

> Balsamon notes how the canon educes the example of the woman who had had an issue of blood for 12 years and who therefore did not dare to touch the Lord, but only the hem of his garment. He also notes that the question proposed, was whether Christian women should be excluded from the church and need follow the examples of the Hebrews who when the menstrual flux was upon them sat in a solitary place by themselves and waited for seven days to pass, and their flux be over. The answer given is as above.[5]

This canon and its subsequent applications and interpretations highlights the central issue that Mark preserves and resolves in Mark 5 : 24–34. In the formative years of the primitive Christian communities, were women categorically discriminated against because of their inherent biologic differences? Or did Mark preserve evidence to the contrary that ignored Levitical law and legitimated new social relationships within the primitive communities?

Not every ancient interpreter approached menstruation and the healing of the hemorrhaging woman in this manner. Most recognized her state to be "unclean," based on the Jewish levitical law codes.[6] Jerome viewed the woman in the pericope as a type of Gentile.[7] He fully recognized and acknowledged the jurisdiction of the Jewish law concerning menstrous women. "As long as she was hemorrhaging she could not come into His presence; she was healed and then came before him. . . . Peace is yours, do not be troubled for the people of the Gentiles have been healed."[8]

As a type of Gentile, the heroine lost her identity. Jerome ignored the meaning and significance of this passage for Mark's earliest auditing and reading publics.

Augustine interprets the passage literally, but also insists that it has to have an underlying meaning. The woman becomes a type of the church from among the Gentiles.[9] Ambrose is not so particular in his interpretation, claiming that the woman represent the entire church.[10] "The likeness of thy church is that woman who went behind and touched the hem of thy garment saying within herself, 'If I do but touch his garment I shall be whole.' So the church confesses her wounds but desires to be healed."[11]

Other interpreters discovered a host of polemics in 5 : 24–34. The woman is viewed as the supreme example of faith. There is no one, not even Peter, who could stand in her brilliance. In a comparison of Peter and the hemorrhaging woman in his *Commentary on Matthew*, Origen[12] comments on unbelief as the reason for Jesus' inability to perform miracles. "And to Peter, when he began to sink it was said, 'O thou of little faith, wherefore didst thou doubt?' But, moreover, she who had the issue of blood, who did not ask for the cure, but only reasoned that if she were to touch the hem of His garment she would be healed, was healed on the spot."[13] Clearly, the woman becomes a positive example of faith.

Chrysostom takes a particular interest in the wisdom of the heroine of Mark 5 : 24–34 by drawing parallels between the Samaritan woman and the Syro-Phoenician women.[14] In comparing the woman with Jairus and the apostles, she loses none of her stature.

Chrysostom recognizes that her illness is judged unclean, according to the law. He does not challenge the rationale behind such a statement and thinks that the woman came toward Jesus because she had "heard . . . that He heals women also."[15] According to Chrysostom, this woman has the honor of being the very first woman who ever approached Jesus publicly. The result of that daring adventure was health. The key to the miracle story must be found in her public confession of that health.

> For what intent doth He bring her forward? In the first place He puts an end to the woman's fear, lest being pricked by her conscience, as having stolen the gift, she should abide in agony. In the second place, He sets her right, in respect of her thinking to be hid. Thirdly, He exhibits her faith to all, so as to provoke the rest to emulation; and His staying of the fountains of her blood was no greater sign than He affords in signifying His knowledge of all things. Moreover the ruler of the synagogue, who was on the point of thorough unbelief, and so of utter ruin, He corrects by the woman. Therefore to correct his weakness beforehand, he brings forward the simple woman.[16]

Chrysostom recognizes the status of the woman as "simple" and raises her to a place of importance within the church. She sets an example that should be followed by the communities. Again, and again, he points to the positive. "Do you see the woman superior to the ruler of the synagogue? . . . for though she was bound by her affliction, yet her faith had given her wings."[17]

In another sermon, Chrysostom singles out the same woman by comparing her with the apostles. "What is this, O Woman? Hast thou then greater confidence than the Apostles? More abundant strength? Confidence and strength says she by no means, nay I am full of shame. Yet nevertheless my shamelessness do I put forward for entreaty. He will respect my confidence."[18]

Similar appreciation for the woman is found in Saint Athanasius[19] as well as in Ephraim[20] of the fourth century. She is to be an encouragement to all Christians. Ephraim comments, "For if from the hem of his garment, healing like this was secretly stolen, could he not assuredly heal when His word distinctly granted healing."[21]

To judge from Eusebius' observations, the fame of this woman or a similar woman appears to have spread throughout the coast of Palestine.

> For they say that she who had an issue of blood, and who as we learn from the sacred Gospels found at the hands of our Savior relief from her affliction, came from this place, and that her house was pointed out in the city, and that marvelous memorials of the good deed, which the Savior wrought upon her, still remained. For [they said] that there stood on a lofty stone at the gates of her house a brazen figure in relief of a woman, bending on her knee and stretching forth her hands like a suppliant, while opposite to this there was another of the same material, an upright figure of a man, clothed in comely fashion in a double cloak and stretching out his hand to the woman; at his feet on the monument itself a strange species of herb was growing, which climbed up to the border of the double cloak of brass, and acted as an antidote to all kinds of diseases. This statue, they said, bore the likeness of Jesus.[22]

Eusebius' account is important for two reasons. It recognizes the menstruating woman and her relation to Jesus as special. And it gives some credence to the notion that the story about the woman in Mark 5 : 24–34 was well-known and had influenced Christian as well as non-Christian communities.

Saint Athanasius testifies to the knowledge about the woman who was healed in Mark 5.[23] In the *Life of St. Anthony* he relates a story about a healing miracle that grounded itself in the miracle story about the hemorrhaging woman. A paralyzed young girl exhibited all sorts of physical disorders. "Her parents having heard of monks going to Anthony, and believing on the Lord who healed the woman with the issue of blood, asked to be allowed, together with the daughter to journey with them."[24]

The young girl was eventually healed. Her parents looked up to a God who healed women. Their God recognized the needs of the opposite sex. They reasoned that if God could heal such a hopeless woman, how much more could He heal their daughter?

Tertullian and Irenaeus are unique in their approaches to Mark 5 : 24–34. The former, in his jurisprudencelike manner, only considers if the woman had broken the law. His presuppositions, of course, are based on his acceptance of the status of woman under Jewish law systems. She was judged unclean. Why did Jesus allow the woman to touch Him? "But in this case He acted as an adversary of the law; and therefore as the law forbids contact with a woman with an issue. He desired not only that this woman should touch Him, but that He should heal her."[25] But did she not break the law and should she not be punished?

> She therefore, not without reason, interpreted for herself the law, as mean-
> ing that such things as are susceptible of defilement become defiled, but
> not so God, whom she knew for certain to be in Christ. But she recollected
> this also that what came under the prohibition of the law was that ordin-
> ary and usual issue of blood which proceeds from natural functions every
> month, and in childbirth, not that which was the result of disordered
> health. Her case, however, was one of long abounding ill health, for which
> she knew that the succour of God's mercy was needed, and not be re-
> garded as having discerned the law, instead of breaking it. This will prove
> to be the faith which was to confer intelligence likewise.[26]

Tertullian draws two exceptions. First, the woman does not come under the auspices of Old Testament/Hebrew Bible regulations concerning women after childbirth or during their menstrual time; the woman's illness is an exception because it is lengthy. Secondly, Jesus' could not be polluted by her touch. The reason given is that He was "as very God." By admitting an exception to the rule in special circumstances and even defending it, Tertullian was obviously unable to separate himself from a Jewish heritage. He recognized her discernment of the law, but would not make a general statement that would include all women. He admitted the problem and only solved it by the use of Midrashic hermeneutics.

Irenaeus makes reference to the woman found in Mark 5 : 24–34 in the context of his literary battle against the Gnostics in the later part of the second century. He does not interpret the story. He merely relates how the Gnostics used this story as they attempted to explain the origin of the universe.[27]

> The same thing is also most clearly indicated by the case of the woman
> who suffered from an issue of blood. For after she had been thus afflicted
> during the 12 years, she was healed by the advent of the Savior, when she
> had touched the border of his garment and on this account the Savior said
> "Who touched me," teaching his disciples the mystery which had occur-
> red among the Aeons, and the healing of the Aeon who had been involved
> in the suffering. For she who had been afflicted 12 years represented that
> power whose essence, as they narrate, was stretching itself forth, and flow-
> ing into immensity; and unless she had touched the garment of the Son,
> that is Aletheia of the first Tetrad, who is denoted by the hem spoken of,
> she would have been dissolved into general essence. She stopped short,
> however, and ceased any longer to suffer. For the power that went forth
> from the Son (and this power they term horose) healed her, and separated
> the passion from her.[28]

This account recognizes that the woman is used as an example to teach the disciples. Her importance in Gnostic theology is further evidence that the story about her experience was well-known and used by others outside the normative worshiping Christian community.

The Middle Years

Significant contributions to the thought and interpretation of Mark 5:24–34 from approximately 500 c.e. through the Reformation years are lacking. Victor of Antioch compiled a catena of works on Mark and succeeded in writing the first commentary between 500 and 600 c.e.[29] Bede,[30] Thomas Aquinas,[31] Zigabenus,[32] and Theophylact,[33] among others,[34] mention the pericope, but contribute little fresh understanding.

Luther[35] and Calvin[36] give their own opinions about the woman. Calvin thinks the woman possesses a sinful nature and emphasizes the fault and error of the woman, while implying that the error is superstition concerning the hem of Jesus' garment. "Now we must draw an analogy, from the health of the body to the salvation of the soul. As Christ attributes it to faith that the woman was freed from her disease, so it is certain that by faith we obtain the remission of sins, which reconciles us to God."[37]

Equating the woman with the sinful nature did little to encourage women during the Reformation. Luther agrees with Calvin and says, "She considers herself unworthy, that she should speak with Him or look upon Him; for she knows, that she has deserved nothing, and has never done anything for the Lord."[38]

Unlike Chrysostom and other Eastern scholars, neither Luther nor Calvin see this woman as a positive, life-giving symbol. Their interpretation ignores the centrality of the woman in this miracle story.

Recent Developments

The bulk of contemporary scholarly investigation in Mark centers in structural analysis, form, redaction (thematics), source, sociorhetorical, composition, and feminist criticism. Commentators, like the traditions they represent, are varied in their approaches and interpretations of Mark.

H. Van der Loos, viewing the Gospels as historical documents, attempts to explain the inconsistencies and discrepancies evidenced among the Gospel writers.[39] At times he outlines Mark's special interests, but does not consider Mark 5 : 24–34 in relation to the Marcan auditors (hearers). He neglects to question why this miracle of all miracles was included and preserved in the traditions of the primitive church.

Others are interested in geography,[40] faith,[41] or the question of power.[42] Some emphasize the woman's touch and its devotional aspects.[43] Yet others view the woman metaphorically, either as a symbol of "outflowing wisdom,"[44] or as a "type of the power of God in Scripture."[45]

Some scholars recognized Mark as an author who was promulgating a $\theta\hat{\epsilon}\iota\sigma\varsigma$ $\mathrm{'}\alpha\nu\acute{\eta}\rho$. Jesus, as a Hellenistic miracle worker, is legitimated by this miracle story about the woman.[46] Still others recognize Mark's subtle references to the Old Testament/Hebrew Bible and its purity laws.[47] This recognition produces varied opinions on her state of being. Many judge her to be "unclean."[48] Some view her as a victim because of her sex. J. Bowman offers a sympathetic interpretation. "I think the circumstances of the New Testament narrative render the inference almost certain that this account was meant for the consolation of those multitudes of stricken women, in all ages, who seem to be afflicted with sorrows in unusual measure, compared with the stronger, and so generally also the more depraved sex."[49]

On the other hand, others maintain that she is a victim of society. The social system was at fault. Matthew B. Riddle says she inherited a negative social condition.

> In those days such diseases especially would be poorly treated and treated without tenderness, first because the patient was Levitically unclean, second because she was a woman. Our Lord's conduct was a protest against both these. Just in proportion as His influence permeates society, is woman not only elevated, but tenderly dealt with, especially in the matter of delicate diseases.[50]

To some, "The demand of the ritual law is no longer valid."[51] Woman was freed from the cultic demands that shackled her.

Allan Menzies shies away from such personal matters and sees the pericope as an etiological apology for the church. It was collected and preserved in order to explain the origin of the church.[52]

Commentaries rarely address current important issues. Thematic studies help fill the void left by these commentaries. Recent scholarship exhibits interest in Mark's own peculiar apologetic-theological tendencies. Scholars show an appreciation for Mark's ability not only as an editor, but also as an author.

One of the earliest writers to report on the authorship of the Gospel of Mark was Papias. According to Eusebius: "For neither did he hear the Lord, nor did he follow him; but afterwards as I said (attended) Peter who adopted his instruction to the needs (of his hearers) but had no design on giving a connected account of the Lord's oracles. So then Mark made no mistake, while he wrote down such things as he remembered them."[53]

Mark was not a dictating machine. The draft was composed from memory. The purpose was not to write a detailed historical account of Jesus and His words. Eusebius recognized the goal of every interpreter as he sees Peter adapting his message for the hearers. It is only logical that this statement would have included the writer of Mark who supposedly walked in Peter's steps.

Wilhelm Wrede, early in the nineteenth century, endeavored to isolate a theological motif that he called the "messianic secret."[54] His goal was to find a "theological gestalt that would explain the four following motifs in the Marcan Narrative":[55]

1. Jesus' silencing of the confession of demons
2. Jesus' command to those healed to seal their lips with regard to their healing
3. Jesus' secret instruction to his disciples
4. The disciple's failure to understand Jesus[56]

He concluded that the Messianic secret motif was a construct of a confused post-Easter community. The Gospel writer was answering a community that failed to understand the Messianic implications of Jesus's life. Scholars disagree on the significance of Wrede's book,[57] but most recognize him to be one of the first scholars to suggest that Mark was not "pure" historical data.[58] The Gospel was composed by a person who had definite theological tendencies, which are revealed in a Gospel attempting to cope with the needs of a changing Christian community.

Since Wrede, authors have discovered other themes in the Marcan complex. E. Lohmeyer[59] and R. H. Lightfoot,[60] for example, attempt to demonstrate that Mark has a preference for the regions of Galilee. Jerusalem, not Galilee, was the central place of the return of Jesus. Their outlines of the Gospel suggest that Jesus' main activity centered in Galilee and would return there.[61]

Etienne Trocmé[62] takes their work one step further. He sees Mark's Galilean emphasis as primarily Hellenistic. It represents an interloper group similar to the Hellenists cited in Acts 7. They did not recognize the ultimate authority of the Jerusalem establishment. "So it may be legitimately inferred that the evangelist was the spokesman of the enterprising movement, which having broken with the mother church at Jerusalem, had launched a mission among the ordinary folk of Palestine and in so doing was armed with the enduring conviction that it thereby conformed with the ecclesiological orders of the living Lord, as well as with the example of the earthly Jesus."[63]

Philipp Vielhauer argues that Mark emphasizes υἱὸς θεοῦ.[64] He compares the Gospel to an Egyptian enthronement ritual. The enthronement scene climaxes at Golgotha. Ralph P. Martin summarizes his argument. "For Mark, who has Christianized this story it becomes a narrative of the son of God, declared to such by a heavenly voice who treads a lonely path fraught with misunderstanding, conflict and rejection, eventually to be put to death. Death is not the end since he is taken up to God and acclaimed as divine son."[65]

Howard C. Kee, admitting the presence of many themes in Mark, finds Mark's literary and theological ideas revolving around the exaltation of Jesus.[66] "The one architectural feature that stands out Mark has placed at the center of his gospel (9 : 2ff), the eschatological vision of Jesus' exaltation at God's right hand."[67] However, Kee is even more concerned about the constituents of that Marcan community. For Kee, the key to the Gospel lies not in the mind of the writer, but in the community that received his words.[68]

Theodore J. Weeden, noticing the negative remarks about the sacred twelve in Mark's Gospel,[69] thinks one of Mark's purposes was to totally discredit the disciples. The disciples are the antithesis of what should be the cornerstone of the Christian community. He suggests that this group of twelve represents an incisive group, which he labels θεῖος ἀνήρ. They seek to legitimate their authority within the community through miracles and special gifts like speaking in tongues. "The interlopers talk about Jesus as a great miracle worker, as one who imparted secret teachings about God and himself, . . . they argue that authentic faith is evidenced in a person by a demonstration of great miracle-working ability and by his ability to have pneumatic experiences of the exalted Lord."[70] According to Mark, the "true" way of Jesus was not excessive showmanship, but humility, suffering, and even death.

These thematic studies are representative of one avenue of investigation into the Gospel of Mark. Although there have been thematic sutdies about Jesus' relation to the woman mentioned in the Gospels,[71] to date, there have been no published thematic studies centering on Mark 5 : 24–34 as it relates to Mark's references to woman and inferences about them in the remainder of the Gospel.

Another popular discipline scholars are applying to the Gospel of Mark today, is called Form Criticism. The goals of the form critics lie in two basic pursuits. First, they intend to isolate units or forms of popular tradition that developed among the peoples of the Christian communities. Secondly, they attempt to determine the "laws which operate as formative factors"[72] in the development of these units. They view the writers of the Gospels as collectors and not as authors of tradition.[73] "The composers are only to the smallest extent authors. They are principally collectors, vehicles of traditions, editors. Before all else their labour consists in handing down, grouping, and working over the material which has come to them."[74]

In an era that was still in hot pursuit of the "historical Jesus," K. L. Schmidt paused for a moment to think about the literary structure of the Gospels.[75] His book, *Der Rahmen der Geschichte Jesu,* [76] analyzes the Gospels, using a literary-compositional point of view. Individualized traditions are linked together with his own thoughts. He saw these traditions developing within the context of Christian worship.

Martin Dibelius, who carried Schmidt's work one step further by attempting to establish laws whereby units or forms developed, classifies Mark 5 : 24–34 as a "Tale."[77] He thinks the healing of Jairus' daughter and the woman circulated together[78] and did not originate with the editor of Mark.[79] Dibelius does not consider the relevance or significance of the woman in this passage of Scripture. He believes that the tale could only have one purpose and that was to testify to the miracle-working ability of their God.

Rudolph Bultmann labels Mark 5 : 24–34 as a "Miracle Story."[80] He agrees that both the healing of Jairus' daughter and the woman are woven together. He recognizes typical stylistic features of the miracle story in this passage.

1. The record of the sickness
2. Emphasis on the fruitless treatment
3. Greatness of the miracle
4. Physical contact[81]

Although both Dibelius and Bultmann claim to pursue the *Sitz im Leben* of each form, it appears that they have neglected Mark 5 : 24–34. They classify it and do not consider its nature, purpose, and function within the early Christian communities other than to legitimate Jesus as a Messiah or wonder worker.

Additional research is exploring the "form" of the entire book of Mark. Can it be labeled an "Heroic story?" an aretalogy,[82] a history,[83] a sermon,[84] a series of lections,[85] a Passover Haggadah,[86] or a new genre called a Gospel? Kee discusses the question of aretalogies.

One aspect of the current resurgence of scholarly interest in the interrela-
tions between the culture of the late Hellenistic world and that of the New
Testament has been the investigation of possible links between aretalogies
and the gospels, especially Mark. Discussion of this subject has been
obfuscated and the emergence of anything like a consensus on the subject
has been hindered by the lack of terminological clarity in treating of
"aretalogy."[87]

Of course, any breakthrough in scholarly consensus concerning the
genre and purpose of the total Marcan statement would affect the
interpretation of Mark 5:24–34. But it appears that this consensus is
not on the horizon.

Two additional and very interesting theses have been suggested by
P. Carrington and R. H. Harrisville. Harrisville[88] postulates that
Mark is a sermon containing a structure and purpose modeled after
the hymn found in Phillippians 2:6–11. He calls it a humiliation-
enthronement hymn. The Gospel of Mark obviously presents a humi-
liation, but the enthronement is questionable. Harrisville does not
deal extensively with Mark 5:24–34 and its meaning within the context of the "hymn."

Carrington, basing his work on certain indicators or marks found in
the margins of particular families of manuscripts, suggests that Mark
was so composed or arranged to be placed in sequence Sunday after
Sunday in order to match the Jewish calendar. Mark is a series of
lections.[89] Although this theory is possible, it does not further the
understanding and interpretation of the Marcan complex. The result
of his work is to place Mark in the center of a Christian-Jewish worshiping community. Mark is to be interpreted against the background
of Judaism.[90] While it is true that there is definitely a Jewish element
present within Mark's statement, there is also evidence of Hellenistic
influences as presented by Dibelius and Bultmann.

Since the advent of form-criticism, the parallel discipline of source
criticism has flowered. Its establishment has been slow in Marcan
studies due to a lack of any remaining extant works used by the author
of Mark. Yet a few scholars have attempted to employ this discipline
upon Mark 5:24–34. P. J. Achtemeier[91] articulates a theory that he
calls the "Pre-Marcan Miracle Catena."[92] Accordingly, there were
two catenae with parallel stories that circulated together before Mark
incorporated them into the Gospel.

Catena I
Stilling of the Storm (4:35–41)
The Gerasene Demoniac (5:1–20)

The Woman with the Hemorrhage (5 : 25–24)
Jarius' Daughter (5 : 21–23, 35–42)
Feeding of the five thousand (6 : 34–44, 53)

Catena II
Jesus Walks on the Sea (6 : 45–51)
The Blind Man of Bethsaida (8 : 22–26)
The Syro-Phoenician Woman (7 : 24b–30)
The Deaf Mute (7 : 32–37)
Feeding of the four thousand (8 : 1–10)[93]

The most likely background out of which the catenae were formed is
to be found in (Hellenistic) Jewish traditions about Moses; the groups
that formed the catenae drew from those traditions in ways similar to
those that Paul's opponents in Corinth drew upon them; the catenae
were formed as part of a liturgy, that celebrated an epiphanic Eucharist based on bread broken with the θεῖος ἀνήρ, Jesus, during his
career and after his Resurrection, and Mark sought to overcome that
view of Jesus and of the Eucharist by the way in which he used the
catena in his own narrative.[94]

Achtemeier's study is important to the study of Mark 5 : 24–34 because of two conclusions he draws about the women in the pericopes.
First, he links the woman with the hemorrhage with the Syro-
Phoenician woman. Secondly, he admits the possibility of having
these two miracle stories read at a Eucharistic setting. He actually
links the healing of the unclean woman to a liturgical event in primitive Christianity, which is in complete opposition to the Canon of
Trullo. Catena or epiphanic Eucharist, the story about the women,
are considered of such significance that they would have circulated
with narratives that legitimated the power and authority of Jesus.

This chapter concludes here with a brief summary of recent
developments in Marcan studies. Jean-Thierry Maertens'[95] study,
which applies the methodology of structuralism to the Synoptic Miracle Accounts, is excellent. His center of inquiry is not Mark 5 : 24–34,
but his conclusions are most relevant when interpreting this passage.
Note his concluding remarks.

Thus the ground of the miracle accounts is the Christian community
which through the parameters of inside vs outside, old vs new, identity vs
otherness, seeks to define the concrete relationship within itself of Jew and
pagan, pure and impure.

Any outside threat to a society's existence generates a solidarity among its
members and creates rites clearly separating "us" from "them." And any
society which faces dangers from within (women, children, the sick) insti-

tutes a ritual for identifying the "pure" and punishing the "impure." These rites of inscription effect "holiness" (Hebrew: separated and so—misleadingly—complete in oneself). They dispense us from the "confusion" of having to live with the impure.

Hence Jesus' signs upset this ideology of purity and this ritualism of we vs them. Rites of belonging can and do separate, but—and this is the fate of whatever marks the human condition—how can they make perfect and holy? Hence they must draw their power from Jesus' non-space, his no-share.[96]

This recognition of the pure/impure relation that is found within the miracle narratives is particularly important when interpreting Mark 5 : 24–34. He recognizes the *Sitz im Leben* of the miracle story as the outgrowth of a reaction to a confining religion. Miracle becomes an explanation for a new relationship among peoples.

Vernon K. Robbins has pioneered an analytical method, termed *socio-rhetorical*. Against the literary background of Hellenistic miracle stories and texts, Robbins claims that the phrase, "Go in Peace," suggests that the woman's audience was both Jewish and Hellenistic because similar phrases are found in each literature.[97]

Redactional-critical studies by David Rhoades, Donald Michie,[98] and Elizabeth Malbon Struthers[99] categorize the woman of Mark 5 as an important character in the story. For Rhoades she is one of the little people who truly understands the meaning and significance of Jesus' life and death. For Struthers she is one of the failed disciples. All fail Jesus in the end.

Gerd Theissen, using the method of composition criticism, sees this story as a "commenting-repeating narrative in which the commenting parts present a completer narrative sequence, and the evaluations, thoughts, and sayings form its inner perspective, which the narrator deliberately stresses as the important part."[100]

In a most unusual article by John J. Pilch,[101] Mark 5 is analyzed with reference to a social science grid. He considers the health care system present in the book. Categories such as the professional sector, popular sector, individual, family, social network, taxonomy of sickness, and folk sector are a few of his concerns. Mark 5 is important in two areas. The writer did not respect the professional doctor. The woman could not be healed by anyone. He says this about the woman. "The hemorrhaging woman is especially noteworthy since she symbolizes the power of womankind in the universal pattern in human society: public: domestic: Man: woman. Menstrual blood is a positive symbol of women in the domestic domain, but a taboo in the public domain. Jesus checks her power-run-wild so that she could once again assume a positive position in society."[102]

Linguistic studies by J. Duncan Derrett and Marla J. Selvidge investigate possible Jewish sources for Mark's original text. Derrett finds linguistic parallels in the prophets Ezekiel, Hosea, Habakkuk, and Zephaniah in Mark 5, which he calls a Sacred Marriage.[103] After a thorough study of all euphemisms for *menstruation* in ancient Greek literature, Selvidge discovered that the two phrases, "flow of blood" and "spring of blood," are only used by the writers of Leviticus. She claims that this story was written to free early Christian women from the social bonds of *niddah*, "banishment" during a woman's menstrual period.[104]

Recent feminist scholars like Winsom Munro,[105] Leonard Swidler,[106] Constance F. Parvey,[107] and Irene Brennan,[108] interpret this story as a banner for equality of women within church and society. She becomes a disciple, and for Alice Buchanan Lane she is one of the thirteen women who correspond to the thirteen male disciples.[109]

In conclusion, it has only been in recent years that the academic community has rediscovered the positive and life-giving, liberating side of this ancient miracle story. For hundreds of years it was used by religious officials to cloister women from the confines of church and altar, or it was neglected by writers who could see no worth in the woman who took matters into her own hands and effected her own healing.

2

The Audience of Mark

It is not necessary to substantiate the significant place that Mark 5:24–34 had in the historico-socio-development of the primitive church. The very fact that it remains ingrained in the traditions preserved by three Gospels and accepted as part of the canon since the early church writers, testifies to its socio-cultural-theological importance. To discover its precise place within Christian history, the lifestyles, theological bents, hopes, and dreams of those who propagated the miracle story, is almost an insurmountable task. Data and methodology are both scant and imprecise. To uncover the communal situations underlying Mark's account is at best a shot at hypothetical reconstruction and may never lead to conclusive evidence. Nevertheless, the adventure in attempting to reconstruct the communities through an analysis of the internal confines of the Gospel, must be undertaken if scholars are to penetrate the milieu that gave birth to the traditions so long preserved.

The aim of this chapter is to articulate evidence in the Gospel of Mark that will elucidate basic characteristics of the Marcan community or communities. The data indicate that Mark's auditors (readers) are in the main dissident, anti-twelve, cosmopolitan, and therefore open to leadership possibilities found within the women of the community.

Communal Situation: Dissension

After a thorough analysis of recent and past sociological studies[1] centering on religious and political sectarianism, Robin Scroggs suggests that Christianity began as a sectarian movement. He lists seven criteria that must be present in order to label any religious movement "sectarian."

1. The sect begins as a protest.
2. The sect rejects the view of reality taken for granted by the establishment.
3. The sect is egalitarian.
4. The sect offers love and acceptance within the community.
5. The sect is a voluntary association.
6. The sect commands a total commitment from its members.
7. Some sects are adventist.[2]

Scroggs finds the Gospels to be the most likely primary sources for his initial study. He dismisses the Acts as tendentious and the Pauline works as a reflection of an individual writer.[3] He also recognizes that analyzing the origins of the data is extremely difficult if not impossible. "It would be comforting to have a consensus about which traditions are authentically Jesus, which come from the agrarian setting of Palestinian Jewish Christianity, and which reflect the urbanization of the church, already an accomplished fact prior to Paul. Such comfort is not to be had."[4]

Twentieth-century sociological endeavors can at best only project shadows of ancient cultures. Contemporary methodologies are imprecise and present conflicting points of view. Scrogg's terminology is inappropriate. The term *sectarian* connotes bigotry, narrow-mindedness, and schism, all of which were not universal characteristics of the early Christian communities. Perhaps a more accurate term would be *Renewal Movement*, as suggested by Gerd Theissen.[5] The Gospels certainly portray a Jesus who attempted to stay within Judaism; his aim was not to overthrow the superstructure. They reveal a person who desired to renew and revitalize the traditions, not to destroy them. The center of activity for Jesus, and even for the evangelists of the early church, localized in the synagogue. The results of such efforts produced a dissenting group whose aim was to overcome oppression. Yet Scrogg's approach and suggested criteria do have merit as a kind of heuristic device or tool that helps to organize the data. He concludes:

> Thus, in my judgement, the earliest church meets all the essential characteristics of the religious sect. . . . The church becomes from this perspective not a theological seminary but a group of people who have experienced the hurt of the world and the healing of communal acceptance. The perspective should enable the interpreter to be more sensitive to the actual life situation within and without the community. . . . It helps us to see that the church in its own way dealt with the problems individuals faced in repressive social conditions.[6]

Scroggs centers his inquiry upon the people of the Gospels, rather than on a particular theology. Oral religious traditions were passed on and communicated to various peoples. In order to understand their theology, the interpreter must first understand the situation of the peoples themselves. Since Mark is probably the earliest attempt at preserving such oral traditions that have survived,[7] then it stands to reason that Scroggs' criteria should be present in this first adventure in communicating the good news in an organized, written form.

The Dissenting Group Begins as a Protest

Social inequality, economic depression, care for the poor, and attack on the leaders of the establishment (i.e., those who are the maintainers of traditional and rigid Jewish social and religious practices), are some of the core problems of any group that exhibits dissension. Throughout the Gospel of Mark, the leaders of the traditional religion, are targets of criticisms, mockery, and condemnation by the writer.[8] The Teachers of the Law "devour widow's houses and for a show make lengthy prayers" (Mark 12 : 38). "Watch out for the yeast of the Pharisees and that of Herod" (Mark 8 : 11). Protest over marital practices resulted in the untimely murder of John the Baptist by the house of Herod.[9] Oppression is evident when Mark warns the readers about governmental practices. "You know that those who are regarded as rulers of the Gentiles lord it over them and their high officials exercise authority over them" (Mark 10 : 42).

The rich and the poor are singled out. There is a definite inequality among different economic groups. Taxes are a primary concern. Should the foreign government be supported?[10] The masses often followed Jesus with no spare food on hand.[11] A prerequisite for discipleship seems to be a kind of just poverty. To a potential follower· Jesus is characterized as saying: "One thing you lack. . . . Go sell everything you have and give to the poor and you will have treasure in heaven" (Mark 10 : 21). The rich are targets for Marcan indictments. "It is easier for a camel to go through the eye of a needle than for a rich man to enter the kingdom of God (Mark 10 : 25).

Protest surfaces as Mark describes physical abuse at the hands of both the political and religious establishment. "You will be handed over to the local councils and flogged in the synagogues" (Mark 13 : 9). Unrest also surfaces as the masses appear to be changeable. The religious leaders fear the crowds and plan to murder Jesus. "But not during the feast, or the people may riot" (Mark 14 : 2).[12] There are tumults of uneasy people everywhere.[13] At times the crowds even pressed against their teacher Jesus.[14]

The climax of the protest centers on the betrayal, arrest, and murder of Jesus. The ultimate payment for any religious or political protest against the establishment is the forfeiture of life.

The Dissenting Group Rejects the Establishment's View of Reality

Mark challenges the Jewish Sabbath and purity laws. The temple is singled out and condemned for its negative influence.[15] Women, children, the ill, and unclean, are no longer outcasts, but become models of the new faith.

Jesus is said to have challenged the stringent "no work" rules on the sabbath. He heals a man. "Which is lawful on the Sabbath, to do good or to do evil?" (Mark 3:4). He defends his disciples for harvesting small amounts of grain on the Sabbath.[16] "The Sabbath was made for man, not man for the Sabbath" (Mark 2:27). Things were changing and Jesus' words, according to Mark, suggest a new regime. The old is passé. "You can't patch an old garment with a piece of new shrunk cloth" (Mark 2:21–22).

The powerful rule because of their authority. Their use of authority controls those people who are not privileged to be one of the ruling establishment. The leader of the emerging dissidents challenged this authority by his teaching, his attitudes, and his life. "The people were amazed at his teaching, because he taught them as one who had authority, not as the teachers of the law" (Mark 1:22). "He is a prophet, like one of the prophets of long ago" (Mark 6:15). The Marcan Jesus assumes the responsibility of the priesthood and even of God. He forgives sins.[17] If the people's sins can so easily be forgiven, what need do they have of a priesthood? With this pronouncement by Jesus, the religious establishment's power over the people dwindles.

Marriage, divorce, and purity laws are all reinterpreted and redesigned by the leader of the new renewal movement of dissidents. "What then God yoked together, let no person separate" (Mark 10:2). Marriage is an important social relationship. The Resurrection, according to the Marcan Jesus, recognizes sexual differentiation and equality. "When the dead rise, they will neither marry nor be given in marriage; they will be like the angels of heaven" (Mark 12:25). Status and relationships seem to be obliterated. God becomes the God of the living not the dead.[18]

The Pharisees came to be known as the bruised and bleeding ones

Lev 11, 13, 15

because they constantly bumped into objects as they tried to avoid looking at or touching unclean people in the marketplace.[19] As the book of Leviticus dictates, many things can potentially make a person unclean before God.[20] The disciples of Jesus defy this ritualistic approach to life. They ate without performing the proper hand washings. "Why don't your disciples live according to the tradition of the elders instead of eating their food with unclean hands?" (Mark 7:5). The answer that is given smacks against the religious rituals performed by Jews of the day.[21] "These people honor me with their lips; but their hearts are far from me. They worship me in vain; their teachings are but rules made by men" (Mark 7:6–7).

The Marcan Jesus is portrayed as talking with women, touching a woman, and letting a woman touch Him.[22] He even ventured to grasp the hand of a dead person, also a female.[23] He ate with outcasts.[24] "I have not come to call the righteous, but sinners" (Mark 2:17). A dedicated member of the ruling classes would certainly avoid such associations and liaisons. These outcasts were contagiously unclean.[25]

Not only does the writer of Mark portray Jesus and his group rejecting the view of reality taken by the establishment, but there are also hints that the establishment rejected Jesus' view of reality. Many question his identity. Some see him only as the son of a working-class person.[26] The Scribes see him as aligned with Beelzebul,[27] that is, anti-God. Establishment forces feel that they represent the true God to the people.

Policies within the dissenting community require or have already produced family dissolutions. Peter asserts, "We have left everything to follow you" (Mark 10:48). Mark writes in an eschatological tone: "Brother will betray brother to death, and a father a child. Children will rebel against their parents and have them put to death" (Mark 13:12). This separation from kindred was certainly against the Jewish tenets of replenishing the race.[28]

The emerging dissenting group led initially by Jesus, reacted, reinterpreted, and redefined their own concepts of religion and how that religion would be practiced in their lives.

The Dissenting Group Is Egalitarian

The new approach to worshiping God offered membership to anyone who was willing to follow the teachings of Jesus. According to Mark, the followers and listeners of Jesus were not limited to Galilee or its neighbors. "Many people came to him from Judea, Jerusalem, Idumea, and the regions across the Jordan and around Tyre and

Sidon" (Mark 3 : 7).[29] Jesus' message suggests that Mark was not ethnocentric. Mark contends that all people deserve an opportunity to hear about the new religion. "And the Gospel must be first preached to all nations" (Mark 13 : 10, 10 : 9). Jesus himself was purported to have "traveled throughout Galilee" (Mark 1 : 38–39), an area heavily influenced by Greco-Roman culture.

No person was turned away because of race, sex, or physical ailment. All were welcome. At the opening of Mark's Gospel, Jesus is portrayed as healing whomever came to him. "That evening after sunset the people brought to Jesus all the sick and demon-possessed. The whole town gathered at the door" (Mark 1 : 32–33). The blind,[30] the deformed,[31] the unclean and possibly mad,[32] the chronically ill,[33] and even the dead,[34] were touched by the leader of the emerging dissenting group. The new community even welcomed female Gentiles, such as the Syro-phoenician woman.[35] Jesus is portrayed eating with sinners, men and women alike.[36]

Family is no longer defined according to bloodline or family name. The new alignments within the community are based on a redefined relationship centering in a reinterpreted God. "Who are my mother and my brothers? Here are my mother and my brothers. Whoever does God's will is my brother and sister and mother" (Mark 3 : 33–35). Many traditional family relations are not the material needed for cohesion of the new community. The writer attempts to show that Jesus' appeal to community transcends the auditors' closely knit society. The emerging community will become, or already is, a family.

Service within the community is not limited to a select few. The twelve were chosen as special emissaries with orders ". . . to proclaim and to have authority to expel demons" (Mark 3 : 15–16). Mark admits that there were others doing comparable things. John proposed the question to Jesus about someone who was casting out demons in Jesus' name.[37] Without hesitation, the people, or specifically, the person, is not condemned by Jesus. "Do not stop him. . . . For whoever is not against us is for us" (Mark 9 : 39). This open access to service is apparent throughout the Gospel. Although the twelve seem to be everpresent companions of Jesus, right behind them are the masses of people who constantly followed Him.[38] Among those followers were a group of women, who according to Mark, never abandoned Jesus.[39] They were the few who managed to remain solid. "In Galilee these women had followed him and cared for his needs. Many other women who had come up with him to Jerusalem were also there" (Mark 15 : 40–41). These very same women, according to the Gospel, were entrusted with the divine proclamation, "He is risen" (Mark 16 : 6). Among the followers and those who served Jesus, Mark chooses to remember the woman who anointed Jesus' body.[40] Her service to the founder of the community and possibly to the community itself became part of the Gospel message. "I tell you the truth, wherever the gospel is preached throughout the world, what she has done will also be told, in memory of her" (Mark 14:1–8).

Women were not the only serving members of the community. Bartimaeus, a blind beggar, became a follower,[41] as well as tax collectors and sinners.[42] The religious community assumes a broad supracultural base. Believing, serving, and following are open to all.

The Dissenting Group Offers Love and Acceptance Within the Community

Universal acceptance within the community is evidenced by the different types of people Jesus healed, conversed with, and called. Specific examples using the Greek words for *love* are not so evident. It is no secret that the masses felt comfortable with Jesus and his select group. Mark recognizes their presence at every turn. Marcan statements on love center primarily around three pericopae. It is Jesus who is the beloved. On two occasions a theophanic voice announces to the world, "You are my son whom I love" (Mark 1:11; 9:7). On another occasion the beloved son is the center of a vicious parable of death.[43] Love originates with the voice from heaven. Only once does Jesus explicitly admit His love for a specific person.[44] In an emotional response to a potential follower the text reads, "Jesus looked at him and loved him."[45] Although the person could not find it within himself to surrender his wealth to the poor (a definite act of love as well as surrender of his privileged status), he was loved by the Marcan Jesus.

The key passage on love it located in Mark 12. Jesus is challenged to recite the most important commandment. "Love the Lord your God with all your heart. . . . The second is this: Love your neighbor as yourself.[46] There is no greater commandment than these" (Mark 12:30–33).

The community is to be centered in love. Their worship and daily life should center around a situation of sacrificial giving. The example of love is not to deny access of God or the community to anyone. "Whoever welcomes one of these little children in my name welcomes me" (Mark 10:14).

The bonds of love are cemented together by the principle of forgiveness. "When you stand praying, if you hold anything against anyone, forgive him. . . ." (Mark 11:25). The community protects, cares for, and attempts to harmonize all life situations for anyone who elects membership.

The Dissenting Group Is a Voluntary Association

"Come follow me. . . ." (Mark 1 : 17–18). Nowhere in the Gospel of Mark are there any legal precepts or rituals prescribed for membership in the community. No one is compelled or forcibly taken into an association with the founder or any of his followers. The choice of a relationship with Jesus and thus a community was up to the individual. "He who has ears to hear, let him hear" (Mark 4 : 9).[47] Of course, once a commitment was indicated, Mark does recognize the appointment of the twelve for a special mission.[48] The very fact that Mark claims that all twelve fled when Jesus was arrested, demonstrates that the bonds of the community were based upon a free association.[49]

The Dissenting Group Demands a Total Commitment from Its Members

This total commitment was not only to a complete faith in the Marcan Jesus and his reinterpretation of religious living, but it also extended to marriage, affluence, persecution, and personal security. Jesus' life was a model for future believers. Mark demands that faith in Jesus extends so far as to believe that Jesus controls the natural elements.[50] Unbelief can hinder the progress of the healing nature of the church.[51]

The Marcan Jesus demanded a rigorous asceticism of the itinerate twelve. The words echo, "Take nothing for the journey except a staff—no bread, no bag, no money in your belts. Wear sandles, but not an extra tunic" (Mark 6 : 8–9). This mandate, even two thousand years ago, was practically impossible to uphold.

Affluent living seems to be negated by the new religion. "Go sell everything you have and give to the poor . . . then come follow me" (Mark 10 : 17–21). The followers are encouraged to look forward to the future world for their material satisfaction. Peter exclaims almost defiantly, "We have left everything to follow you" (Mark 10 : 28). Even family relationships are questioned.[52]

The Marcan Jesus, and thus the dissenting group, demands a total giving of self. This demand approaches masochism in these words, "If anyone would come after me he must deny himself and take up his cross and follow me" (Mark 8 : 34). What does it mean to deny oneself? Are these words to be taken literally? Is the individual lost in the cause of the community? Some earlier worshipers believed that they were called to die. Again the Gospel of Mark reiterates, "For whoever wants to save his life will lose it, and whoever loses his life for me and the gospel will save it" (Mark 8:34). A commitment even to death, was certainly demanded by associating with the rebels of the dissenting group.

Rejection by their own communities is evident. "All will hate you because of me, but anyone who stands firm to the end will be saved" (Mark 13:13).[53] How much of this comes from an actual historic situation will never be known. Mark's statements are difficult to understand and even more difficult to implement. Perhaps the writer used hyperbole or profound exaggeration. Whatever the case, the bottom line reads the same. The dissenting movement demanded allegiance. Nothing in this life was too precious to give up: not home, family, wealth, health, friends, or even one's own life.

Some Dissenting Groups Are Adventist

When the oppressed or those in the lower ranks of society have little control over government or religious practices, they will frequently develop a futuristic cosmic interpretation of their situation.[54] Their hope and "salvation" is found in the tomorrows. "The imminent expectation of the eschaton is consistently there."[55] This attitude is certainly expressed in the Marcan complex, primarily in the images surrounding the Son of Man.[56] "At that time people will see the Son of Man coming in the clouds with great power and glory."[57] God's kingdom will somehow break into the mundane and obliterate all sorrows, pain, and degradation. The oppressed will rise up in order to rule again. This happening could take place at any moment. "I tell you the truth, some who are standing here will not taste death before they see the Kingdom of God come with power" (Mark 9:1). Somehow this hope served to lessen the tensions the dissidents experienced at the hands of the traditionalists.

The Gospel of Mark, then, meets Scroggs' criteria by preserving traditions that suggest that the auditors (hearers) emerged as a dissenting movement.

Communal Situation: Hostility Toward the Twelve

With surprise, one realizes that Mark has little "good" to say about the twelve.[58] Their role within the Gospel is very important, yet only in a negative sense. The example of the twelve, their actions, thoughts, desires, ambitions, and relationships, are all repudiated by Mark. They never offer a real foundation for the Christian movement. They stand ridiculed and cajoled in almost every episode they enter. Peter's name, however important or venerated, in early Christian circles, finds no legitimation in Mark. Peter unconditionally denies Jesus and is never found at his feet again. It would almost seem that Mark considers the twelve to be similar to, or part of, the establishment that seeks to control the communities' religious activity. This attitude ultimately raises the questions: "Why does Mark abuse the traditions of the twelve?" Why is the scared entourage discredited? The answer must lie within the author's intentions and purposes for composing the Gospel.

Etienne Trocmé, in *The Formation of the Gospel According to Mark*,[59] sees the negativism as a partisan attitude. Galilean Christianity is legitimated while the Jerusalem hierarchy is negated.[60] "[Mark] . . . was the spokesman of an enterprising movement which having broken away from the mother church of Jerusalem, had launched out into a large scale missionary venture among the common people in Palestine and in so doing felt that it was obeying the command of the risen Christ and at the same time following his earthly example."[61]

Trocmé sees the Jerusalem church as crystallized, denying the entry of Gentiles and discriminating against the Hellenists as pictured in Acts 1–6. The Gospel offers the emerging community an alternative to the administration and dominance of those who walk in the footsteps of the twelve.[62] "The author of Mark thus sees the Christian mission as a call to a religious revolution among the Jews of Palestine."[63] It is a movement that aims at seizing the religious government of Israel in God's name and winning over the neighboring peoples at the same time.[64]

The twelve have neglected this revolution. Trocmé concludes, "It is obvious, indeed, that the author of Mark mistrusts the pride and exclusiveness of the twelve. . . ."[65] The leadership of the developing church is in the hands of the Galilean country people. And for Trocmé, those leaders come from a Jewish heritage.[66] Trocmé admits the need of a mission to the Gentiles, but at the point of time of writing Mark, the Gentiles are not in control. He does not seriously consider the interspersed passages that relate to women and their role within the upcoming community. He sees the new group in terms of generalities, movements, and personal issues.

Another provocative study centering on Mark's negative treatment of the twelve was produced by T. J. Weeden's *Traditions in Conflict*. Taking a somewhat stronger stand against the twelve, Weeden outlines three stages in the developing attitude of the twelve.

1. Unperceptiveness
2. Misconception
3. Rejection[67]

He catalogs a host of verses that demonstrate this negative response and relation to the leader of the new religious movement. This negation has not gone unobserved by various other scholars.[68] "I am convinced with Tyson and Schreiber that a careful analysis of Mark's presentation of the disciples supports the contention that Mark is engaged in a polemic against the disciples. . . ."[69]

David J. Hawkin considered the same question and concluded that the readership of Mark is not encouraged to identify with the disciples. "Only by understanding what the disciples failed to understand can the catechumen be initiated into the mystery of Christ."[70]

According to T. J. Weeden, "Though the disciples are the carefully picked confidants of Jesus, heroes of the early church, authorities for authentic christology and discipleship, ironically they emerge in the Markan drama with extremely poor performances both in terms of their perspicacity about Jesus' teaching and ministry and in terms of their loyalty to him."[71]

Weeden sees this negation of the twelve rooted in a Christological dispute coming from his own community.[72] For Mark, true messiahship or discipleship is suffering discipleship.[73] There appears to be a group of people who are challenging this point of view. Weeden terms their camp as espousing a *divine man* Christology. For them, Jesus is seen in terms of a divine Hellentistic miracle worker. Legitimation of the true leaders of the community come through a demonstration of pneumatic gifts.[74] "They described Jesus as a great miracle-worker who had bequeathed to the church a legacy of secret teachings about God and himself and who can be experienced as the exalted Lord if the Christian cultivates his personal life to the high pitch of spiritual ecstasy."[75] The twelve represent this group so opposed to the self-denying teachings that Mark advocates.

Although the words *divine man* never appear in the Gospel of Mark, Weeden maintains that they can be inferred from the text. Appropriately recognizing the negativism toward the twelve, some scholars disagree with Weeden's theorization of the pneumatic group. They conclude that he relies more on theory than the text of Mark.[76] Like Trocmé, Weeden makes the mistake of ignoring the role of others who play an important part in relation to the disciples. Both scholarly opinions neglect the role of women. Weeden states unequivocally that their role is not central to the point of the story until the addition of the instruction from the angel.[77] Careful scrutiny of the remainder of the Gospel will prove this statement to be false.

Mark's Characterization of the Twelve

Prior to the appointment of the twelve[78], Mark identifies a group of followers of Jesus who are termed *disciples*.[79] Apparently, out of this group of general disciples Jesus chose the twelve. The text reads "... and called to him those he wanted and they came to him" (Mark 3:13). The writer separates the twelve from "the ones around him" in Mark 4:10. Again in chapter 6 the twelve are singled out for a special mission.[80] They are personally taught humility and service,[81] and Jesus even instructs them about His own personal destiny.[82] The twelve followed Him from the regions of Galilee southward to Jerusalem and to a secluded place in Bethany.[83] The writer makes no apology as testimony is given to the fact that the betrayer Judas was one of the sacred twelve.[84] The last meal is spent in discussion concerning which one of the twelve would eventually betray Jesus.[85]

The role of the twelve, which includes Peter, James, and John, is by no means completely negative. To be chosen by the Marcan Jesus was certainly a great honor. They were among the few who received privileged information and served as constant followers of Jesus (Mark 4:34). In their role as disciples (which probably included others), the twelve become intermediaries between Jesus and the Jewish establishment[86], and between Jesus and the masses.[87] At times the writer of Mark even presents them as healers effecting a positive influence on the community.[88] Their activity defies the Jewish establishment as they ignore Sabbath laws.[89] The writer of Mark cannot deny the historic influence and continuing effect of the twelve upon the Christian communities at large. Yet for all the "good" they have done in the past, Mark systematically denies that they should have precedence and influence in the future,[90] i.e., the present situation in the emerging congregation. Both the twelve, and especially Peter, are singled out as antithetical to the purposes and programs of the Marcan communities.

The twelve saw Jesus as a tool for their own personal self-gratification. James and John privately made a request to Jesus to give them important positions in the regime.[91] Their exclusivism, perhaps even ethnocentrism, extended even to children,[92] and to others who were doing similar service.[93] There appears to be a real division between the twelve and Jesus. Mark 9:38 states, "We saw a man driving out demons in your name and we told him to stop because he was following us." Jesus turns the tables and notes that it did not matter whether they were following "us," it was the fact that they were doing the miracle in Jesus' name that was of consequence.[94] James and John appear to detract from the leader. The writer of the Gospel immediately centers the reader's attention upon Jesus.

There is no doubt that the twelve were followers of Jesus.[95] Yet how committed was their allegiance? According to the author, they doubted Jesus' supernatural abilities,[96] his true identity,[97] and questioned his view of reality.[98] Jesus took them into his confidence. "He did not say anything to them without using a parable. But when he was alone with his own disciples, he explained everything" (Mark 4:34).

If anyone should know what it meant to be an authentic practicing disciple, the twelve should. Yet, even with this privileged status they understand very little of Jesus' true intentions, projections, and purposes. "Do you still not see or understand?" (Mark 7:17).

When a test of the twelve's own authority came and Jesus' presence was conspicuously absent, the disciples failed. They lacked the ability to appropriate authority to heal and discernment to know how to heal.[99] Their failure even extends to the person of Jesus himself. It is not the masses, not the religious establishment, or the government that finally selects and points the finger at Jesus. His downfall came at the word of a personal disciple, one of the elite twelve, Judas.[100] Even until the death of Jesus the disciples remained self-seeking and self-centered.

Peter

One disciple rises above the others. Peter's name must have held a special place within the community. He is singled out eighteen times by Mark. It is Peter who is the first to openly proclaim Jesus as Christ,[101] and yet it is also Peter who is the one to deny and negate his relationship with Jesus the loudest and the longest.[102] His companions, James, John, and Judas, stand as one-time leaders in the movement. Weeden gives his assessment of the twelve in an appropriately caustic manner. "I conclude that Mark is assiduously involved in a vendetta against the disciples. He is intent on totally discrediting them. He paints them as obtuse, obdurate, recalcitrant men, who at first are unperceptive of Jesus' messiahship, then oppose its style and character, and finally totally reject it. As the coup de grace, Mark closes his Gospel without rehabilitating the disciples."[103]

In general, the examples set by the twelve should not be followed, imitated, or emulated. They were influential in the past, but their type of leadership does not meet the needs of the emerging community, says Mark.

If the leadership of the community is not in the hands of those who follow the twelve, then whom does Mark legitimate as proper examples in the community? Perhaps a hint is given in the Gentile outlook of the Gospel. The world of the twelve had been abolished with the holocaust of 70 C.E. The emerging mass of peoples evidenced a cross-cultural fertilization. Perhaps the visionaries of the new community would arise from this new group who had prospects of living in a very, very, different world.

Communal Situation: Cosmopolitan

V. Taylor states unequivocally, "The sympathies of Mark are Gentile in their range, but his tradition is Jewish Christian to the core."[104] Frederick C. Grant agrees with Taylor. "Some time before the Marcan gospel was compiled, the new sect had been cut loose—or had cut itself loose from Judaism, and was launched upon the broad seas of the Hellenistic world with its many competing cults and religions. . . . Thus the Gospel of Mark, though deriving its tradition from Palestine, was the sacred book of tradition of the early Gentile church."[105]

For these reasons, and others to be discussed, this chapter identifies the community of Mark as "cosmopolitan" in nature. It is comprised of a diverse people including both Jew and Gentile.

The dichotomy of the Jewish-Gentile influence upon the Gospel of Mark is recognized by most scholars. Tradition has never ascribed the Gospel to an exclusively Jewish locale, even though the Gospel possesses obvious Jewish influences and traditions. Some scholars, including C. C. Torrey,[106] E. Nestle,[107] J. Wellhausen,[108] and A. Deissman,[109] see an Aramaic original.[110] Allan Menzies lists the Aramaic words employed by the author of Mark.[111] It appears that the Gospel does have a semitic coloring. According to V. Taylor, "[M]onopoly of asyndeton in narrative, . . . excessive use of the paratactic construction, and . . . the Aramaic proleptic pronoun in narrative may consciously be construed as evidence of the kind of Greek which an Aramaic speaking Jew would write."[112] The "Jewishness" of the Gospel is also evidenced by the dissenting characteristics listed in the first part of this book.

In spite of the Jewish linguistic, and sociocultural overtones of the Gospel, most scholars recognize Mark's audience to be primarily Gentile in nature.[113] As early as Clement of Alexandria[114] and Chrysostom[115] Mark's treatise was linked with Rome and Alexandria, respectively.[116] Antioch has also been suggested as its place of origin.[117]

The non-Jewish nature of the Gospel, and thus of the community, is apparent as Mark explains Jewish customs like washing one's hands before a meal,[118] and the activities that are involved on Jewish holidays.[119] The author translates Aramaic words for the readers[120] and appears not to understand the coinage of Palestine.[121] Sometimes Mark even explains geographic areas.[122]

Throughout the book, various Latin transliterations or Latinisms are employed by the author.[123] Both this and the evidence of persecution from Roman officialdom point to a Gentile, possible Roman influence.[124] Mark even seems to describe a Roman style house (Mark 4:21), Roman watches (Mark 13:15), Roman measures (Mark 12:15, 42), and the Praetorium (Mark 15:16).[125]

Further evidence of the Gospel's Gentile orientation may be viewed within Mark's own theological themes. The Gospel consistently underscores that the good-news means openness to the non-Jewish segment of society.[126] This is especially evidenced in the characters who are chosen as examples of the Gospel and the emphasis placed upon geography. The Syro-Phoenician woman,[127] the centurion,[128] and the Gerasene demoniac,[129] are just a few of the non-Jews, who were welcomed with open arms into the narrative and thus into the worshiping community. Mark does show some interest in geography. The reader is constantly aware of Jesus moving from place to place and from people to people.[130] Mark points out that those who came to Jesus were from different locales,[131] from as far away as Tyre and Sidon. "They have come a long way," is a phrase attached to the context of the feeding of the 4,000. According to F. W. Danker, it serves "to enunciate the gentile orientation."[132] One should take notice also that the feeding of the 5,000 takes place in Jewish territory[133] and the feeding of the 4,000 seems to take place near Tyre.[134]

C. Roth has argued that the cleansing of the temple (Mark 11:17) by Jesus is a direct reference to the Gentiles. "My house shall be called a house of prayer for all nations."[135] R. Scroggs suggests that the community is ecstatic and has separated from Judaism and begun a mission to the Gentiles.[136]

The communal situation of Mark was certainly varied. It denied the exclusivism of Judaism, and as it found itself in conflict it began a transition to a more Gentile-oriented community. This is the period that is evidenced in the Gospel of Mark. It is a time of transition and reconstruction. It is a time of fear and persecution,[137] but it is also a time when the community is demonstrating that it is socially aware, open-ended, and certainly tending toward antiritualism, as viewed by Mark's negative attitudes toward purity laws restricting food consumption and associations with non-Jews. They are in the midst of building a counterculture. According to W. Stark, this is a time of transvaluation of values.[138] They have rejected formal Judaism, and according to Mark, doubt the leadership ability of those who have ministered in direct line with the twelve. It is a new world, and Mark seeks to point out that leadership qualities can be found in others who historically have been faithful to the Jesus movement since the days when he lived. Chapter 5 will enunciate Mark's view of those who are the best qualified and most appropriate people to lead the movement and to act as legitimate examples of authentic Christianity. Chapters, 3 and 4 will give a historical-critical background of that group in relation to the constituency of this Jesus-centered community.

3

Cultic Status of Woman:
Judaic Heritage of Mark

Purity Legislation and the Jewish Woman

The Marcan corpus did not develop within a vacuum. Chapter 2 articulated various evidences of cross-cultural cosmopolitan influences upon the traditions preserved in the Gospel. It was suggested that the new religious movement, at its most primitive inception, began as a reaction to certain tenets within Judaism. Christianity emerged as a group of dissenting people. This movement sought freedom from a burdening system and promoted egalitarian ideals, suggests Mark.

Mark 5 : 24–34:
A Dissension to the Levitical Purity Mandates

In the classic form of a miracle story, the writer of Mark preserves a tradition centered in dissension. Mark 5 : 24–34 had particular significance for the women in Mark's own communities. Why was it preserved? One answer is found in its relation to the Priestly purity laws found in Leviticus. The miracle story of the hemorrhaging woman stands preserved because it stood as a definitive answer to the purity laws that historically had attempted to control women in their cultic and social expression within the community. The specifics and ramifications of these codes will be detailed in this chapter.

If this miracle story stands in dissension to the purity system, it would stand to reason that there would be marked similarities in vocabulary between Leviticus and Mark 5 : 24–34. After a close comparison of all the significant words found in this passage, it was determined that twenty-five of the forty-eight key words were employed by the writers of the LXX translation of Leviticus. The following is an abbreviated summary of the most important similarities.

The physical problem of chronic hemorrhaging exhibited by the woman in the Marcan pericope was not an uncommon ailment. Greek and Roman writers often discussed women's gynecologic problems. The Greek physicians and writers never employ the two phrases used by Mark to describe the woman's illness: η‘ πηγῆ τοῦ αἵματος and ἐν ῥύσει αἵματος (Mark 5:25). Soranus, in his first-century monumental *Gynaeciorum*, lists three words used to describe menstruation: καταμήν, ἐπιμήν, and κάθαρσις.[1] Plutarch, a contemporary of Soranus, labels the monthly flow as ἐμμηνοις η‘μερῶν περιόδοις and ἐμμήνοις καὶ καθαρσίους.[2] Hippocrates refers to it as ῥοῶ γυναικείω,[3] and in another work poetically calls menstruation γυναικείων ἄγωγον.[4] Diodorus characterizes it as τὰς κοιλιάς τὰς ῥεούσας φαρμάκῳ.[5] In the context of illness Aristotle uses αἱμορροΐς[6] and σφόδρα αἱμτώδης.[7] Normal menstruation is termed αἱμα του περιτώματος and μηνιώδους περιττωμάτος.[8] Aelian,[9] Demosthenes,[10] and Pliny the Elder,[11] use a combination of these words. No Greek author employs exactly the same language used in Mark 5:24–34. Although ῥεώ is used with a noun, αἱμα occasionally, πηγή is never used to describe abnormal or normal menstruation. Comparison with the LXX version of Leviticus yields very different results. The Greek translation of Leviticus seems to exhibit a preference for the vocabulary used in Mark to describe or diagnose the condition of the woman in Mark 5:24–34.

Of the seventeen times ῥύσις is used in the LXX, fifteen are found only in Leviticus. ῥύσις plus αἱμα are linked together in two instances. A from of the verb ῥέω plus αἱμα is found in Leviticus 15:19. All of these references are made exclusively within the context of legislation attempting to control sexuality. ῥύσις is classified as unclean ἀκαθαρσία[12] and usually associated with a discharge from the body.

Leviticus is the only book in the LXX to directly use ἡ πηγῆ τοῦ αἵματος to refer to menstruation. The word πηγή is normally used of water, or as a symbol for the source of wisdom, life, God, and so forth.[13] The Song of Solomon 4:12 comes very close in its use of πηγή as a euphemism for participation in sexual intercourse. Jeremiah 51:36 states with reference to Israel's enemy, "I will dry up her sea and make her fountain dry." Although this is an allegorical statement, it does use the word πηγή as a symbol of female fertility that could refer to a woman's menstrual cycle. In conclusion, both phrases used by Mark to designate the woman's condition are exclusively employed by Leviticus (in the LXX) within the context of purity regulations. No other major Greek writer employs these phrases as normal euphemisms for *menstruation*.

Other major similarities in vocabulary are also found within Mark 5:24–34. The writer of Mark does not name the woman (Mark 5:25). She is called γύνη and θυγάτηρ (Mark 5:34). Although θυγάτηρ has been interpreted as an endearing term,[14] the writers of Leviticus do not use it in this way. Mark's use of this term is in remarkable contrast to the impersonal approach of Leviticus. Of the thirteen times the word is mentioned in Leviticus, it is always used in reference to family. γυνή אִשּׁ is a common term. Comparison of this term within Leviticus turned up some significant emphases of the book. Of the thirty-four times γυνή אִשּׁ is mentioned, twenty-five of these instances are in the context of attempting to control a woman's sexuality and sexual expression within the community and cult.[15] There have been various studies on the social and religious status of women in the Old Testament. Not all agree as to her participation and influence in cultic activities. They do agree upon the androcentric emphasis present in the Old Testament/Hebrew Bible. Caroline M. Breyfogle concluded that P (compiler and editor of Leviticus) "places a lower estimation upon women in general (Lev. 27:2ff)."[16] W. A. Meeks claims, "No where in Judaism do we hear of any real tendency to harmonize social roles of male and female."[17] Woman had very little direct contact or influence in the functioning of the Hebrew cult. Her biological differences prevented any Jewish woman from assuming a central position within the cult.

The only office or occupation other than childbearer, sex object, or cook, which is recognized by Leviticus for women is Necromancer ἐγγαστρίμυθος or magician ἐπαοιδός. The word ἐγγαστρίμυθος literally means "one that prophesies from the belly."[18] It is related to a ventriloquist. Both of these offices or occupations were outlawed in Israel because they were of central importance to the non-Jewish cults.

The word γυνή is never applied in Leviticus to a person having any official office or responsibility in cult activities. This negative summation clearly points to a repressive social-cultic condition. A woman's life was controlled from birth until death. She had virtually no control over her social life, her body, or her cultic associations and responsibilities.

The Gospel of Mark, like the book of Leviticus, shows a preference for using the verb ἅπτω.[19] The woman is said to have "touched his garment." Leviticus uses this term approximately 28 times. No other Old Testament book approaches this usage. The verb ἅπτω is found almost exclusively in the context of causing uncleanness due to touching or being touched.[20] The state of holiness can also be transmitted by touch.[21] Touching and the activities of a woman are linked

11 out or 28 times in Leviticus.[22] Leviticus also preserves a phrase of special interest that warns only women after childbirth. "She must not touch anything consecrated nor go to the sanctuary until the time of purification is over" (Leviticus 12:4). Neither her touch nor her presence was welcome in cultic affairs during this infectious time.

The woman in Mark 5:24–34 touched the garment of Jesus. $\iota\mu\alpha\tau\iota o\nu$ is never used directly of a woman's clothing in Leviticus.[23] The Priestly work uses $\iota\mu\alpha\tau\iota o\nu$ to describe the priest's garments, and anyone who performs priestly functions.[24] Lepers,[25] those who have eaten improperly killed meat,[26] and those having bodily discharges,[27] are told to wash their clothes. Clothing, in the Levitical legislation, is a sign of office or an extension of the person.

The woman came toward Jesus because "she had heard the things concerning Jesus."[28] One hundred percent of the references in Leviticus to $\alpha\kappa o\nu\omega$ deal with hearing some type of evidence.[29] Appropriately, the woman in Mark made her decision to seek Jesus because of the evidence, $\tau\alpha$ $\pi\epsilon\rho\iota$ of Jesus. The usage of the word in both books is exactly the same.

Various forms of the verb $\lambda\epsilon\gamma\omega$ are used throughout the pericope in Mark[30] as a conversation takes place between Jesus and his disciples and Jesus and the woman. Leviticus uses a form of this verb fifty times. It is used exclusively by the editors of Leviticus to characterize a direct dialogue between $\kappa\upsilon\rho\iota o\varsigma$ and the leaders of Israel, i.e., Moses and Aaron, and an indirect dialogue between the $\kappa\upsilon\rho\iota o\varsigma$ and the sons of Israel.[31] The Priestly $\kappa\upsilon\rho\iota o\varsigma$ never speaks directly with a woman.[32] In the Marcan episode Jesus does not hesitate to do so.

Mark records that $\epsilon\gamma\nu\omega$ $\tau\omega$ $\sigma\omega\mu\alpha\tau\iota$ $o\tau\iota$ $\iota\alpha\tau\alpha\iota$[33]. Leviticus used various forms of the verb $\gamma\iota\nu\omega\sigma\kappa\omega$, but always within the context of discovering uncleanness or wrongdoing.[34] The woman's knowledge is extended to her body $\sigma\omega\mu\alpha$ בשׂר. Seventeen out of the twenty times this word is used by Leviticus within the context of uncleanness.[35] In an almost ironic situation, the woman discovers her healing, not her uncleanness.

The woman was cured. Two words are used in the Marcan pericope to signify health.[36] Leviticus does not use $\sigma\omega\zeta\omega$, but $\iota\alpha o\mu\alpha\iota$ is mentioned twice. In one instance it is used when describing the healing of a leper,[37] and in another it links physical illness with the state of uncleanness. "...Declare the house clean, for the infection is cured."[38]

According to the story, Jesus knew that something had happened. $\Delta\upsilon\nu\alpha\mu\iota\varsigma$ had left Him.[39] He wanted to see or know $\tau\eta\nu$ $\tau o\upsilon\tau o$ $\pi o\iota\eta\sigma\alpha\sigma\alpha\nu$.[40] The feminine gender of the participal lets the reader know that Jesus knew that a woman had touched him. $\pi o\iota\epsilon\omega$ is used

sixty-two times in Leviticus and usually is linked with the performance of some activity. The priests do sacrifices,[41] and people do
good or evil.[42] Although the use of the term in Leviticus is ambivalent,
this is not true of Mark. The woman is engaged in touching the Holy
One. She is the one who reaches out to the Holy One. In Leviticus the
verb ποιέω is juxtapositioned to the activities of the priest,[43] who
alone has the right to touch holy things. Women are never linked to
such activities in the Priestly document.

The woman fell down before Jesus. Her state was fear (φοβηθεῖσα)
and trembling.[44] Seven out of the eight times that fear is used by the
writers of Leviticus, it is linked with the cult. Either one should fear
God or the sanctuary.[45] Only in one instance is it used in the sense of
"respect."[46] Mark uses the term in the same sense as in the book of
Leviticus. The woman is standing before something holy.

Leviticus records only one use of the word εἰρήνη. Jesus' farewell
greeting was "Go in peace."[47] Irony surfaces again in the Marcan
statement. The woman had ignored the Levitical purity laws by
touching something holy, Jesus. Her reward was peace. Note how
Leviticus uses the word *peace*. "If you keep my laws . . . I will give
peace to the land and you shall sleep with none to frighten you."[48]

The woman is pronounced ὑγιής by Jesus.[49] Ironically, this term is
only used by Leviticus when the priest diagnoses and pronounces a
leper unclean.[50] Mark's use of the term has the opposite meaning,
which points in a positive direction.

In summary, these represent the most important linguistic similarities between Mark 5:24–34 and Leviticus. The miracle story clearly
preserves a tradition that suggests an attitude of dissension toward the
legislation mandated by the writers of the Levitical Code.

The Inequality of the Sexes in Levitical Legislation and in the Old Testament/Hebrew Bible

THE BOOK OF LEVITICUS

The primitive tradition preserved in Mark 5:24–34 dissented to purity laws that date back over five-hundred years.[51] Purity laws served
to separate men from women, community from state, elect from non-
elect, Jew from non-Jew, and God from people. "The writing of the P
traditions belongs to the period when postexilic Judaism was being
firmly established with its strict Habdalah rules."[52] Habdalah is the
principle of complete separation between clean and unclean and holy
and unholy. Some Jewish families chose to return to their desolate

homeland. In order to maintain an identity and keep the community
from becoming acculturated and thereby losing their religion and un-
iqueness, the leaders of the community required rigid discipline from
the returnees. Of prime importance were the purity laws.

The book of Leviticus consistently emphasizes that all areas of life
must be pure or clean. "Yes it is I, Yahweh, who brought you out of
Egypt to be your God: you therefore must be holy because I am holy"
(Leviticus 11 : 45).[53]

Leviticus goes on to list those things, that could cause uncleanness;
certain animals,[54] leprosy or diseases of the skin,[55] discharges of the
body,[56] and childbirth.[57] The Holiness Code[58] goes on to list specific
laws that must be kept by the Jews if they were to remain in a state of
cleanness before Yahweh. Although Leviticus is not explicit about the
relation of these laws to cleanness, it does imply that all the laws must
be kept if one is to stand before Yahweh. "You must make yourselves
holy, for I am Yahweh your God. You must keep my laws and put
them into practice, for it is I, Yahweh, who make you holy."[59]

Not only did the Levitical code attempt to control the lives of Jewish people as they worshiped their God, but also as they lived out their
day-to-day social existence. Their laws extended to marriage,[60]
business,[61] prostitution,[62] interracial and international relations,[63] as
well as to various other cultural peculiarities.[64]

Purity was uppermost in the minds of the Priestly writers. According to the *Encyclopedia Judaica*, purity is

> a concept that a person or object can be in a state which, by religious law,
> prevents the person or object from having any contact with the temple or
> cult. The state is transferable from one object to another in a variety of
> ways . . . and is independent of the actual physical condition.[65]

> Uncleanness is not just a lack of cleanness. It is a power which positively
> defiles.[66]

Leonard Swidler, in his book *Women in Judaism: The Status of Women in Formative
Judaism*, sums up the results of unclean living.

> Thus, though at times the incurring of uncleanness is involuntary, one of
> the main results is to somehow separate onself from God, to be displeasing
> to God. The consequences of ritual impurity can be dire in the extreme. A
> polluted person is always in the wrong. He has developed some strong
> condition or simply crossed some line which should not have been crossed
> and this displacement unleashes danger for someone.[67]

Danger resulted from normal or abnormal discharges of the body.
The Levitical purity laws were designed to control the activity of per-

sons in this condition. The following discussion will center on Leviticus chapter 15 as it compares the purity laws governing women and men.

At first sight there appears to be no inequity in the purity laws.[68] A careful comparison of the verses that apply strictly to men, and the verses that apply strictly to women, yield some surprising results.

SUMMARY OF THE CONTENTS OF LEVITICUS 15

Both men and women are termed *unclean* because of the ῥύσις that comes out of their bodies. If a man has a discharge from his body γονορρυής (Leviticus 15:13), γόνον (Leviticus 15:3) he affects all who touch him, all those he touches, and anything he touches. He is unclean for seven days (Leviticus 15:13). As the term indicates, this discharge was probably due to a physical illness.[69] The man is considered unclean even if the discharge is not in a continuous flow (Leviticus 15:3). At the end of his seclusion, when he is healthy again, he must offer a sacrifice for sin (Leviticus 15:15).

If a man has a seminal discharge ἐξέλθη ἐξ αὐτοῦ κοίτη σπέρματος (Leviticus 15:16) he is unclean only until evening. "Any clothing or leather touched by the seminal discharge must be washed and it will be unclean until evening" (Leviticus 15:17). If he sleeps with a woman, both must wash and are judged unclean until evening (ἕσπερας) (Leviticus 15:18).

The Levitical code also deals with different states of uncleanness for the woman in chapter 15 and a third in chapter 12. A woman who has a normal discharge of blood ἦ ῥ'ἐόυσα αἵματι or ἡ ῥύσις αὐτῆς ἐν τῷ σώματι αὐτῆς (Leviticus 15:19) is classified as unclean for seven days. Anyone whom she touches, or who touches her, or touches anything she has touched "will be unclean until evening" (Leviticus 15:19–23). If a man sleeps with her he will be unclean for seven days also and his contagious condition can be spread to others (Leviticus 15:24).

A woman is also unclean if she has an irregular menstrual cycle or if the flow is prolonged for some reason. "During the time the flow lasts she shall be in the same state of uncleanness as during her monthly periods" (Leviticus 15:26). When the flow ceases, she must wait an additional seven days before she can be pronounced clean. She then offers a sin offering (Leviticus 15:28–30).

Chapter 12 lists another cause for uncleanness in women, childbirth. At the birth of a male the woman is unclean for seven days. Before she can return or reenter into the cultic and social life of the community she must wait an additional thirty days (Leviticus 12:1–

4). If a female is born, the confinement is doubled (Leviticus 12:5–8). Letha Scanzoni and Nancy Hardesty comment upon the differences in the lengths of confinement. "The implication is that by bringing another female into the world she has increased the likelihood of the continuation of the curse, because this child too will one day bear the uncleanness of menstruation and childbirth."[70] At the end of the woman's seclusion she must offer a sacrifice for sin (Leviticus 12:8).

INEQUITABLE TENDENCIES IN THE PURITY LEGISLATION

In comparing the purity laws certain inequitable tendencies emerge. Biologic dysfunctions are treated differently. If a man has a normal seminal discharge he is only unclean until evening. If a woman has a regular monthly period she is banished for seven days. She would be completely out of touch with the cult and society at large for one whole week. He is only penalized an evening.

Uncleanness is treated differently. If a woman sleeps with a man she is only unclean until evening (Leviticus 15:18). If a man sleeps with a woman, who is in her period, he will be unclean for seven days, and she also communicates her contagiousness to him (Leviticus 15:24). A woman is not made contagious by a man. Later legislation in *The Holiness Code* makes sleeping with a menstrous woman a supreme offense. "The man who lies with a woman during her monthly periods and uncovers her nakedness: he has laid bare the source of her blood, and she has uncovered the source of her blood; both of them must be outlawed from their people" (Leviticus 20:18). It appears that women are not contagious to other women.

Additional inequities emerge as the lists of contagious articles are compared for man and woman. The Levitical code points out that it is the woman herself who is contagious. She is put at the top of the list of contagious articles (Leviticus 15:19). The list for the man begins with a contagious object—his bed (Leviticus 15:4). The woman's sphere of activity seems to be more limited than the man's. Leviticus is only concerned about her "bed, seat, or anything on her bed or chair" (Leviticus 15:21–27). Most of these objects would be confined to the home. The list of objects for the man includes "earthenware, wood, a saddle, and other objects" (Leviticus 15:10). Apparently, men even traveled when they were considered to be unclean (Leviticus 15:9).

At times the antidote for uncleanness was a bath. Curiously enough, the text never admonishes a woman to go wash her clothes after being made unclean by the touch of a man who has had a discharge. After sleeping together, both the man and woman are told to wash (Leviticus 15:18).

When comparing the laws concerning who must take a bath or wash his clothes because of coming in contact with someone or something contagious, it appears that the woman is omitted. Leviticus specifically speaks of washing clothes in masculine terms.[71]

The chapter ends with a summary of the laws concerning discharges from the body. The last phrase, ὅς ἄν κοιμηθῆμετά ἀποκαθημεύης, "Anyone who might have slept with a person being unclean. . . ." (Leviticus 15:33) concludes with a statement about an unclean woman. ἀποκαθημεύης is feminine and leaves no doubt that it is the woman who makes the man unclean. The summary does not conclude with a law about a man making a woman unclean. It is not concerned with his contagiousness in relation to her.

This legislation was aimed at controlling both men and women. A woman was more severely restricted because she was a woman. Her biologic processes were different. Seven out of every twenty-eight days a woman was secluded form society and banished from the cult. A woman's menstrual cycle was considered a time of cleansing καθαρσία to the Greeks.[72] The Jews added a negative prefix and called it unclean ἀκάθαρτος 'ακαθαρσιά.[73] A woman's normal biologic rhythms were considered abnormal to the Jews.

Woman was also noticeably absent from cultic affairs at the birth of a child. Her seclusion could extend to eighty or more days. A woman's life had to be centered around her biologic cycles if she was to be a functioning person within the Hebrew cult. She had to plan her cultic life around those times when she would not be contagious. She could not undertake any lengthy project outside the confines of her home. Her monthly cycle prevented her from engaging in activities that would last longer than a twenty-eight-day cycle, or activities that would place her primarily in contact with men.

Death would result if these laws were not followed (Leviticus 15:31). Their actions would actually defile "my tabernacle which is set amongst them" (Leviticus 15:31). The temple was the cultic and social center for the Hebrews. Meticulous purity laws served to organize every area of a Hebrew's life, even her sexuality. If the Jews attempted to keep the command given to Abraham to reproduce (Genesis 9:1), a woman would be secluded at least eighty days out of every year if she was pregnant, and up to ninety-one days if she was not pregnant.

THE OLD TESTAMENT / HEBREW BIBLE AND MENSTRUATION

The book of Leviticus is not the only source for evidence of restrictive ideas and measures placed upon a woman because of her biologic difference from a man. The following is placed here to give additional evidence of the Hebrew's negative attitude toward woman and her menstrual cycles.

Although Exodus does not mention menstruation as such, it does preserve an ancient attitude about woman and her relation to cultic events. "So Moses come down from the mountain to the people and bade them prepare themselves; and they washed their clothing. Then he said to the people. Be ready for the third day; do not go near any woman."[74]

Implied in this statement is the idea that somehow a woman could negate a proper or clean state of being needed in order for a cultic happening to take place. Relations with a woman could potentially prevent Yahweh from descending upon the holy mountain.[75]

The symbol of a menstrous woman is often equated with fallen Israel. The book of Ezra takes a dim view of the people who are presently occupying the Palestinian area. "The land you are entering to possess is a land unclean because of the foulness of the natives of the countries and of the abominations with which their impurities have infected it from end to end."[76]

The MT reads בְּנִדַּת עַמֵּי and אֶרֶץ בְדָּה.[77] The Hebrew word for "menstruation" is כדח.[78] Ezar is especially concerned about who marries whom. He is determined to keep the Hebrew line pure. He attempts to control sexual relations like the Levitical code. "You must not give your daughters to their sons nor take their daughters for your sons. . . ."[79] The emphasis is on the giving and taking of women.

Lamentations characterizes the city of Jerusalem as unclean as it surveys its desolated state.[80]

> Yahweh has summoned against Jacob,
>   foes from every side;
> Jerusalem has become
>   an unclean thing to them.[81]

Jerusalem is compared to an unclean or filthy rag. The MT reads יְרוּשָׁלַם לְכִדָּה and the LXX reads ἐγενήθη Ἰερουσαλημ εἰς ἀποκαθημένην.[82] For the writer of Lamentations, "Her filth clings to the hem of her clothes she has never thought of ending like this, sinking as low as this."[83]

The Chronicler records that Hezekiah commanded the temple to be cleaned by the Levites. "Eject what is impure from the sanctuary."[84] The MT calls this impurity הַבִּדָּה.[85] The LXX labels the same impurity 'ακαθαρσίαν.[86] A woman's normal biologic function is viewed as distasteful and used to describe the worst kind of filth.

Another ancient instance of woman having some kind of influence upon cultic matters is found in I Samuel. "David replied to the priest, certainly, women are forbidden us, as always when I set off on a campaign. The soldiers' things are pure. Though this is a profane journey, they are certainly pure today as far as their things are concerned. The priest then gave them what had been consecrated."[87]

Contact with a woman was the determining factor as to whether the men were clean or unclean. The fact that they may have had murder in their minds as they set out on the journey did not make them unclean, yet the mere touch of a woman could.

Ezekiel details his ideal of a righteous man in negative terms. "The upright man is law-abiding and honest; he does not eat on the mountains or raise his eyes to the idols of the House of Israel, does not seduce his neighbor's wife, or sleep with a woman in her periods."[88] To Ezekiel, a woman is a source of temptation and uncleanness. Her biologic difference can cause a man to be unrighteous.

These are only a few examples of the literature in the Old Testament/Hebrew Bible that exhibit the same distaste and restrictive attitude toward a woman because of her biologic difference and functions. Formative or early Judaism has little to say on the subject. The greater amount of material on attitudes toward menstruation seems to begin with the exilic and postexilic literature.

Purity and Woman: The Intertestamental Period

The negative and restrictive attitudes toward a woman's biologic functions do not end with the writings of the Old Testament/Hebrew Bible. Numerous writings during the Intertestamental period served to preserve this attitude toward woman and purity. The most significant Jewish sect to detail laws restricting a woman because of her biologic differences were the Essenes, situated in the desert community of Qumran. A survey of the Qumran tests reveals similar attitudes toward women as evidenced in Leviticus. The sect emerged some time in the later part of second or early part of the first century B.C.E. (125–165 B.C.).[89]

This separatist congregation set out to keep their isolated community holy. One of their most important objectives was ". . . to distinguish between unclean and clean and to recognize holy from profanity."[90] The congregation believed that this state of clean/ unclean should regulate their everyday lives.

> The foregoing is the rule concerning the various regulations for disting- uishing clean from unclean and for recognizing holy from profane, such as it is to obtain in the urban communities of Israel. It is by these ordinances that the enlightened man may correctly determine his human relations on this or that particular occasion; and it is in this manner that the progeny of Israel is to conduct itself in order to avoid damnation.[91]

They felt that the generation of Jews who were then living in Jeru- salem, were defiled. Defilement came due to the impiety of men and menstrual impurity.[92] The temple was also defiled because of the priests' association with women in their menstrual periods. "In as much as they do not keep separate according to the law but lie with her that sees the blood of the flux."[93]

Although the Qumran documents do not have detailed legislation concerning menstruation created by their community, it is implied that woman could never be a full member of the Qumran sect. "No one who is afflicted by any form of human uncleanness is to be ad- mitted to the community, nor is anyone who becomes so afflicted to maintain his position in it."[94] The Essenes preserve the tradition that uncleanness is contagious. "If any unclean person comes in contact with such water, he merely renders it unclean; and the same is true of water drawn in a vessel."[95]

If a person was in this unclean and contagious condition he could not enter the place of worship. "As for those who come to the house of worship, not one is to come in a state of uncleanness. . . .'[96] Sleeping with a woman in any part of the city where the sanctuary was located would render the man unclean. "No one is to lie with a woman in the city of the sanctuary thereby defiling the city of the sanctuary with their impurity."[97]

The woman prostitute is viewed as alluring and damning in the *The Wiles of the Harlot*.[98] "Alas, she has ever brought ruin on all who pos- sessed her and destruction of all who laid hold on her; for her ways are the ways of death, and her roads are the paths of sin; her trails are the twists and turns of wrongdoing and (her) byways are lawless trans- gression. Her gates are the gates of death, beside her doorway she strides (luring) men to hell."[99]

To the Essenes, the woman was the personification of evil and yet she was also the embodiment of wisdom. She is to be pursued and possessed. In a fragment of Sirach 51 : 13f the Essenes preserve a posi- tive symbolism of women. "[Kept shut though they were,] I forced open her gates, having only in mind to set my eyes on treasures which surely lay hidden behind."[100]

For the Essenes, a woman was a necessary evil. At best their cultic attitude toward a woman was negative. The woman is desired as a lover[101] and yet shunned because of her biology. She could keep him from performing his cultic responsibilities and she could even, by sleeping with him, defile the sanctuary.

The Qumran documents do not list a woman holding an office. Some scholars question the very presence of women on the compound.[102] Women are never directly addressed except perhaps in the opening lines of the *Manual of Discipline*. "All that present themselves are to be assembled together, women and children included."[103]

This Qumran document aimed at preparing the congregation for the future when the sons of light would rule once again. The Essenes recognized that they would need women and even children in the new world.

The oldest copy of the *Book of Jubilees* was preserved in the Qumran library.[104] It was written sometime between 135 and 105 B.C. by a Pharisee.[105] Jacob Neusner sees a marked similarity between Jubilees and the Qumran documents. "Jubilee's and the Yahad's view of purity have in common the obsessive interest in menstrual purity."[106]

The *Book of Jubilees* justifies the purity laws regarding women and childbirth by rewriting the creation account. According to Jubilees the purity laws were instituted when God created human beings.

> In the first week was Adam created, and the rib—his wife; in the second week He showed her unto him; and for this reason the commandment was given to keep in their defilement, for a male seven days, and for a female twice seven days. And after Adam had completed 40 days in the land where he had been created we brought him into the garden of Eden to till and keep it, but his wife they brought in on the eightieth day, and after this she entered into the garden on Eden.[107]

According to Jubilees, a woman waited longer before she entered the garden. There is no rationale given as to why a woman must be secluded after childbirth. Jubilees answers authoritatively. It was written on the tablets; therefore the law must be kept. No discussion on the matter is allowed.

Numerous Jewish writings surfaced during the rise and fall of Hebrew political power in the Interestamental period. Many of these writings chose to transmit the ancient traditions that linked a woman's menstrual period with impurity or uncleanness. Neusner, in his excellent book entitled *The Idea of Purity in Ancient Judaism*, lists most of the Interestamental literature that emphasizes purity and its relation to cultic activities.[108] Those writings that link impurity with menstruation will be detailed here.

The Letter of Jeremiah,[109] written circa 300 B.C.E., warns the Jews about polluted idols. They should stay away from their sacrifices. "The menstrous woman and the woman in childbed touch their sacrifices; knowing therefore by these things that they are no gods, fear them not."[110]

Sometime during the first century before Jesus, the *Psalms of Solomon* was composed.[111] Here again, a woman is seen defiling cultic activities. "They [the priests] trode the altar of the Lord (coming straight) from all manner of uncleanness; and with menstrual blood they defiled the sacrifices, as though they were common flesh. They left no sin undone, wherein they surpassed not the heathen."[112]

The second-century B.C.E. work entitled the *Assumption of Moses*,[113] does not mention menstruation specifically, but it transmits the tradition of the ruinous touch. "Though with their hands and minds they touch unclean things; yet their mouth shall speak great things, and they shall say furthermore, 'Do not touch me, lest thou should pollute me in the place [where I stand].'"[114]

The *Testament of the Twelve Patriachs* emerged around the first century B.C.E.[115] Generally, the idea of purity is limited "chiefly to sexual conduct."[116] The *Testament of Issachar* 4:4 sees the beauty of a woman as a corrupting influence. One should not look a long time at a lovely woman "lest she should pollute his mind with corruption."[117]

The apocalyptic book of *Enoch*[118] places the origin of evil in the hands of fallen angels. The target of the fallen was women, who in turn, spread evil throughout the world. "And all the others together with them took unto themselves wives, and each chose for himself one, and they began to go into them and to defile themselves with them and they taught them charms and enchantments and the cutting of roots. . . ."[119]

Somehow the angels defiled themselves. Is this an illusion to the menstrual state? This state of defilement was supposed to be remedied when the earth was cleansed by the flood. "And cleanse thou the earth from all oppression, and from all unrighteousness, and from all sin, and from all ungodlessness: and all the uncleanness that is wrought upon the earth destroy from off the earth. . . .[120] and the earth shall be cleansed from all defilement."[121]

Purity and Woman: The Christian Period

It is certain that the restrictive attitude toward women found in the Old Testament/Hebrew Bible was passed on through interim Jewish writers, and eventually found its way into the hands of rabbis as well as other literate Jews who prospered during the early Christian era.

The rabbis escalated these myths involving a woman and her menstrual cycle.

The Babylonian Talmud contains ten chapters and a commentary on the laws regulating the menstruant. The tractate entitled "niddah" found in the Mishnah is ten chapters long.[122] Many of these laws that date back into antiquity are kept by the Orthodox Jewish woman today.[123] Leonard Swidler, in his study on the status of Jewish women from 200 B.C.E. to 400 C.E., offers an opinion concerning these laws. "In the Rabbinic period, which began, of course in the late Second Temple period, i.e., first and second centuries B.C.E., the laws relating to the menstrous woman comprise some of the most fundamental priciples of the halakhic system, while a scrupulous observance of their minutiae has been one of the distinguishing signs of an exemplary traditional Jewish family life."[124]

A few quotations taken from the Talmud and the Mishnah serve to illustrate Swidler's opinion. "Our Rabbis taught: There are three who must not pass between [two men], nor may [others] pass between them, viz.: a dog, a palm tree, and a woman. . . . If a menstruant woman passes between two [men], if it is at the beginning of her menses she will cause strife between them."[125] The rabbis continued the tradition that women should be completely secluded during their monthly periods.

> What is the hedge which the Torah made about its words? Lo, it says, also thou shalt not approach unto a woman . . . as long as she is impure by her cleanness. May her husband perhaps embrace her or kiss her or engage her in idle chatter? The verse says, Thou shalt not approach. May she perhaps sleep with him in her clothes on the couch? The verse says, Thou shalt not approach. May she wash her face perhaps and paint her eyes? The verse says, And her that is sick with her impurity: All the days of her impurity let her be in isolation. Hence it was said: She that neglects herself in the days of her impurity, with her the Sages are pleased; but she that adorns herself in the days of her impurity with her the Sages are displeased.[126]

In language that appears to approach hysteria, the Talmud records different types of blood stains and varying degrees of uncleanness.[127] "The Sages distinguished between several types of blood, some clean others unclean that issue from a woman."[128] Finally, at one point the rabbis agreed that "all blood renders a woman unclean."[129]

Ideas about purity and the menstruating woman were not confined to only those who served at the temple or synagogue. Josephus, a Jewish historian of the Pharisaic party, and an Alexandrian Jewish philosopher, continued to propagate the ancient purity system even into the first century of the Christian era. Josephus takes the purity regulations seriously. The temple must be kept pure. "Persons afflicted with gonorrhoea or leprosy were excluded from the city altogether; the temple was closed to women during their menstruation, and even when free from impurity they were not permitted to pass the boundary which we have mentioned above."[130]

Women were not to take part in the cultic activities, which included sacrificing during their periods. "For those afflicted with leprosy or gonorrhoea, or menstrous women, or persons otherwise defiled were not permitted to partake of the sacrifice. . . ."[131]

Moses is credited with the purity laws controlling a woman immediately after childbirth and the seclusion each month.

> Women after childbirth are forbidden by him [Moses] to enter the temple or to touch the sacrifices until forty days have elapsed, if it is a male infant; double that number is prescribed for the birth of a female. But they enter at the end of the aforesaid term to offer sacrifices, which the priest apportions to God.[132]
>
> Women too, when beset by their natural secretions, he secluded until the seventh day, after which they were permitted, as now pure to return to society.[133]

Josephus changed little of the traditions concerning purity and women that were passed on to him. Sometimes he attempts to offer some type of rationale for their existence. The ritual cleansing requirement of Leviticus 15:18 after sexual relations was probably quite bothersome for his generation. Josephus attempts to uphold the law. "For the law regards this act as involving a partition of the soul [part of it going] into another place; for it suffers both when implanted in bodies, and again when severed from them by death. That is why the Law has enjoined purification in all such cases."[134]

Pseudo-philo, a Jewish writing, departs dramatically from the concrete Josephus. Purity regulations to Philo were hypocritical. "We shall be pure from wrongdoing and wash away the filthiness which defiles our lives in thought and word and deed. For it is absurd that a man shoud be forbidden to enter the temples save after bathing and cleansing his body, and yet should attempt to pray and sacrifice with a heart still soiled and spotted."[135] Yet when interpreting the purity laws and women, he chose to maintain the status quo.

> Whenever the menstrual issue occurs, a man must not touch a woman, but during that period refrain from intercourse and respect the law of nature. He must also remember that the generative seeds should not be wasted

fruitlessly for the sake of a gross and untimely pleasure. . . . But if the menstruation ceases, he must boldly sow the generative seeds, no longer fearing that what he lays will perish.[136]

Purity and Woman: Cultic Restrictions

It is one thing to analyze a law code and detail its potential inequalities. It is another matter to demonstrate a relationship between those laws and actual inequalities within the society at large. The following section will attempt to summarize the affects of the menstrual laws upon the lives of Jewish women.

The androcentric focus of the Old Testament/Hebrew Bible is an accepted maxim. The status of women within that focus is by not means evident. Many scholars claim that women, even though their roles in the Hebrew society were different, were equal with men in cultic matters.[137] Others demonstrate that the Hebrew society was indeed sexist.[138] The key question in this study is: "Did woman exercise any authority in cultic matters? Did she ever serve at the altar and represent her people before Yahweh?" There are always exceptions to every system. These exceptions will be surveyed in the next section. Historically, if woman did manage to have a voice in cultic affairs, it was usually in spite of the religious system, not because of it. Clarence J. Vos states without reserve, "It was not her task to lead the family or tribe in worship."[139]

Circumcision

From the moment of birth, woman was differentiated from man in cultic affairs. For some strange reason a female child was considered "contagious" longer than a male child.[140] A Hebrew daughter was considered less desirable than a son.[141] No special ceremony attended the birth of a female. The Old Testament records no initiation ceremony for her to enter the cult. Yet the male child was circumcised eight days after his birth. This ceremony signified that he was a member of the covenant community.[142] "She was a second-class citizen from birth. This fact was symbolically expressed in restricting the initiatory rite of circumcision, which was the sign of the covenant, to males (Gen. 12). Though the woman was a member of the convenant community, she never received the sign which marked one for life as enjoying the rights and privileges of such fellowship."[143]

J. B. Segal suggests that the length of time the male child had to wait until he could be circumcised was due to the unclean state of his mother. "A male infant was circumcised on the eighth day after his birth because he was affected by his mother's uncleanness during the first seven days after delivery. The eighth day was the first on which he could be approached by the male who carried out the ceremony."[144]

In primitive Judaism, it may have been the woman who performed the ceremony. In Exodus 3 : 24–26 it is Zipporah who satisfies the requirements of Yahweh by circumcising her son. Chapter 12 of Leviticus in the LXX could be translated as the woman performed the ceremony.[145]

The Priesthood

There is no feminine term for *priest* in the Old Testament.[146] No woman was ever appointed to the priesthood, according to the traditions. Logically, prominence and influence within the cult came to those people who were situated closest to the sanctuary. The only pathway to influence open to the Hebrew woman was marriage. Yet marrying a priest was not an ordinary matter. The woman must be a virgin, never divorced, or prostituted for money.[147] Woman was never in charge of her own body, according to the legal codes.[148] Her father maintained the right to sell her, or trade her in marriage.[149] The decision was not hers to make.[150] In the Hebrew world, rape was an acceptable way of obtaining an unpromised virgin. The man could choose to pay a fine for his advances or to marry the woman.[151] It was not easy to remain a virgin in a male-oriented male-serviceable society.[152]

Accidence of birth could place a woman within the confines of a high priest's family. Her authority and influence was systematically negated by priestly legislation. "If a daughter of a man who is a priest profanes herself by prostitution, she profanes her father and must be burnt to death."[153]

Woman was left standing at the door at the tent of meeting. She was never granted the privilege of taking the yearly step into the Holy of Holies or preparing sacrifice on behalf of her people. She was required to bring an offering for her own sins; but could not intercede for another.

G. Barrois points to biologic factors as the prime deterrent to woman assuming any office or responsibility in cult. "Biological factors determine clearly the status of the Israelite woman in relation to the Aaronic priesthood."[154] "Feminine activities in Hebrew culture had their normal center in tent life and in the village house."[155]

Since woman was unclean seven out of every twenty-eight days, she could never serve at the altar. Her state of uncleanness could potentially call down the wrath of Yahweh upon all Israel.[156] In describing the investiture of a priest in Leviticus chapters 8–9, the feminine gender is never mentioned. If woman did have any influence in cultic matters, it would be through either her husband or her father.[157]

Woman's participation in cultic activities remained at best peripheral. The male was commanded to attend three yearly festivals.[158] "It was also the recognized duty of the women to be present if it were feasible, but the natural disabilities and inescapable duties made impracticable a stringent law requiring their attendance."[159]

Although there is ample evidence of women attending feasts, they were never respresentatives, nor were they given any special responsibilities at these community functions.[160] "Beer says that in religion the Hebrew women were on an equal footing with men only when the whole community was involved, and that they could not know the secrets of the cult."[161]

Women were allowed to make a cultic vow, that is, if their husband or father agreed. In considering the worth of individuals who made a vow at the temple, the male is valued at fifty shekels and the woman is only valued at thirty.[162] "Thus it appears that a male of any age was more highly valued than a female."[163]

The Synagogue

The segregation of women from centrality in cultic activities led to an even greater separation in the religious lives of postexilic Judaism. Most scholars believe that women were completely segregated from men in the synagogues. Eliezer L. Sukenik gives a discussion and excellent archaeological documentation on the existence of a separate women's section in the ancient synagogues.[164] However, Bernadette J. Brooten challenges accepted archaeological and literary interpretations concerning the status of women in the synagogue. She claims that there is no hard evidence that clearly separates men and women. She thinks that many of the inscriptions calling women synagogue rulers found throughout the Near East suggests that women were leaders and very much a part of the worshiping community. The titles should not be considered honorific, but functional.[165]

A synagogue was formally recognized if there were ten worshiping males in the city, a Minyan.[166] Woman was not recognized as a voting member. Her voice was silent. "Jewish women were not only to be seen as little as possible, they were also to be heard and spoken to as little as possible."[167] Irene Brennan maintains that "no self-respecting Jew, still less a religious leader, would talk in public to a woman."[168] "The accepted social convention, that a man should not speak to a woman in public, was adopted in such an extreme form by certain Pharisees that they were known as the bruised and bleeding Pharisees. These men refused to look about them for fear of looking upon a woman and the subsequent injuries they sustained were thought to be evidence of extraordinary piety."[169]

If woman did not have a voice in the synagogue, then there was no possible way that she could be chosen as a leader. W. A. Meeks, in his noteworthy article, "The Image of the Androgyne: Some Uses of a Symbol in Earliest Christianity," finds no evidence of woman ever serving in a synagogue office.[170] "But at least three women in the Roman Jewish community were honored in tomb inscriptions with the title 'mater synagogue,' corresponding to the more frequent (nine times) 'pater synagogue.'"[171]

The Second Temple

Josephus takes many opportunities to describe the general blueprint of the temple and the woman's place in that plan.

> All who ever saw our temple are aware of the general design of the building, and the inviolable barriers which preserved its sanctity. It had four surrounding courts, each with its special statutory restrictions. The outer court was open to all, foreigners included; women during their impurity were alone refused admission. To the second court all Jews were admitted and, when uncontaminated by any defilement, their wives; to the third male Jews, if clean and purified; to the fourth the priests robed in their priestly vestments. The sanctuary was entered only by the high-priests clad in the raiment peculiar to themselves.[172]

Accordingly, the woman's court was five steps above the Gentiles and fifteen steps below the court of the Jewish men.[173] "A special place of worship was walled off for the women, rendering a second gate requisite. . . ."[174] "For women were nor permitted to enter by the others [gates] nor yet pass by the way of their own gate beyond the partition wall. This court was, however, thrown open for worship to all Jewish women alike. . . ."[175]

G. Barrois says that, when they were impure, women were temporarily assigned to the eastern courtyard, which they shared with male Israelites who were temporarily or permanently impure.[176] Woman was admitted to the outer limits of the sanctuary only reluctantly. When she was found to be in her monthly period, the Gentiles, according to Josephus, had more status within the cult than a Jewish woman. The only time she could confidently and legitimately mingle with male Israelites was when they both found themselves to be impure and in a state of banishment.

Religious Education

If men had very little conversation with women, it stands to reason that it would be very difficult for them to receive a religious education, since only the men retained such traditions. "Very few women were students of the Law: It was not intended that they should be. Yet the highest and most adorable thing in the world was to study the Law. The greatest and purest joy in the world was to fulfill all the commandments and ordinances of the Pentateuch and Rabbinic codes. But women need not and could not observe them all."[177]

Some women did learn the Torah by being tutored by their fathers. These instances were rare because a girl was often betrothed by the age of twelve.[178] "Ben Azzai wanted to teach daughters enough Torah so that they would know that if they performed some meritorious deeds, . . . this would result in postponing the deadly effects of the drinking the 'Waters of Bitterness' by wives suspected of adultery."[179]

If a woman did find a place beside the men in learning the Torah, she would never be allowed to teach it to anyone else.[180] "The Pharisees ruled against woman teachers, and their code would certainly be adverse to any idea of a woman priest. Women had been excluded from the priesthood before the Pharisaic rise to power, but the Pharisee's bias could only confirm a pattern already set."[181]

Legal Witnesses

Since women had virtually no responsibilities in cult affairs that affected the entire congregation, and men were encouraged not to engage a woman in conversation, it is no surprise that her word was not accepted as legitimate testimony in a court of law.

Basically women were not allowed to bear witness in the Jewish society of the rabbinic period. The ancient Mishnah stated the matter quite clearly:

"The Law about the oath of testimony applies to men but not to women."[182]

To the woman he gave nine curses and death: The burden of the blood of menstruation and the blood of virginity; the burden of pregnancy, the burden of childbirth; the burden of bringing up children; her head is covered as one in mourning. . . . She is not to be believed as a witness; and after everything—death.[183]

Woman could participate in some activities of the cult, but she was never a privileged member as her male counterpart. Her birth was not attended by any festivities or intitation rites into the cult. Her biologic difference kept her from the inner confines of the sanctuary and from assuming any central role in cultic affairs. Her greatest achievement, in the area of the cult, would be in marrying a priest, if she could preserve her virginity, or in producing a male heir who might become a priest. She was not required to attend the festivals. Even as the daughter of a priest she could not eat the most holy things.[184]

Woman was segregated from man in both the temple and synagogue. Religious men avoided her on the street. Her education in things religious was minimal, if at all. The sphere of her life centered around her home and childbearing and only incidentally at the altar. Her secluded state offered little opportunity for growth or advancement in social or cultic affairs. If she witnessed a crime, her word was not valid. Her cultic worth as a person, especially during the postexilic period, was half that of a man. It is difficult not to conclude that the Levitical purity laws concerning woman did not potentially influence and even control her life at the altar as well as the marketplace. The writer of Mark inherits a negative and suppressive cultic tradition about women from their Jewish ancestors.

The Exceptions: Heroines of the Old Testament

Prior to the golden age of Israel (circa 1000 B.C.E.) there were legends of great women who influenced whole tribes of Semitic peoples. None of these women were called priestesses. The Old Testament classifies them as prophetesses.[185] Miriam claimed that she had direct contact with Yahweh.[186] The book of Numbers clearly states that Yahweh spoke to Miriam and Aaron.[187] She is also characterized as the leader of a victory celebration after the glorious defeat of Pharoah's army in Exodus.[188]

Deborah, a key political figure during the formative years of Israel, settled disputes in Israel.[189] "Her horizon is not limited by the clannish outlook of villagers snug in their villages; it extends to all the tribes: her function is that of Shophet, a Hebrew name for the charismatic chieftain who sits in counsel, hears the cases of God's people, and leads the tribes in times stress."[190] Although Deborah was married, this did not detour her from her duties as she led with Barak, ten thousand men into battle (Judges 4:4–10).

After Deborah's monumental achievements, five hundred years of silence toward women's activities is found in the Old Testament/ Hebrew Bible. The next prophetess appears under the reign of Josiah (circa 640–609 B.C.).[191] Huldah was consulted as a mouthpiece for Yahweh. Her advice reached the highest office in the land—the king.[192]

Isaiah, years later, claims that the mother of his children was a prophetess.[193] There is a divided opinion as to whether his wife was a prophetess. She could have been a temple prostitute,[194] or a prophetess who was known throughout Israel, [195] or only the wife of a prophet.[196] According to Isaiah, she speaks no oracle of her own.[197]

The prophet Joel promised that in the later days of the Messiah, "your sons and daughters will prophesy."[198] Yet very few of the daughters who lived during Old Testament times were recorded for posterity. Caroline M. Breyfogle believes that there were probably many more great women in Israel's history, but their names were erased due to tendential attitudes. "[The prophetesses of Israel] achieved an objective result recognizable in the community and engraven upon conservative tradition. Perhaps these prophetesses may have been more prominent in history than tradition was allowed to represent in an age characterized by man's dominance over women."[199]

In the rare instances a woman has power in the Old Testament, her biologic difference did not handicap her. "Biological factors play no part in the exercise of the prophetic charism quo charism, because it draws its origin not from the will of man, but the Holy Spirit."[200] Yet there is no evidence of a prophetess functioning as a priest or receiving such ordination.

The הַקְּדֵשָׁה or πόρνη, "religious prostitute," is mentioned throughout the Hebrew texts, usually in negative terms.[201] These women are thought to have had some type of ministry at the door or the tent of meeting. They probably served as sacred prostitutes in non-Jewish religions, but R. De Vaux claims that no one really knows their exact function.[202] Brevard S. Childs suggests that they were some type of cleaning and repairing service; others suggest that they were dancers and singers.[203]

Breyfogle suggests that the Semitic Goddess Istar (called Ashtart, Athtar, Atar, and Ashtoreth) and her worship were common knowledge in Israel.[204] Saul deposited his armor in "a house of

Ashtaroth."[205] A sanctuary was built by Solomon for a Phoenician Ashtoreth,[206] which Josiah destroyed some time later.[207] Non-Jewish cults were known as the Baal and Ashtaroth during the seventh century B.C.E. Numerous other examples can be given.[208] "They infected the worship of Yahweh and their gains swelled the revenues of the temple, and later became the object of Deuteronomic legislation."[209] The threat they presented to Yahwism was great. How great, will never be known, due to the editing by the religious. History will never know if great women did if fact serve at the door of the tent.

Although women never legitimately directed central cultic affairs for Israel, there is ample evidence to suggest that at times they were allowed to participate in certain cultic activities.[210] Both men and women were equally eligible to take the Nazarite vow.[211] Unlike the man, the woman's vow could be broken by her husband or her father.[212] This vow appears to have begun as a kind of social service and later became "an ascetic practice of a temporary nature."[213]

Women like men, were accountable for their sins as prescribed by the laws. She brought her own sacrifice to the priest.[214] Early Israel records a couple, who together, brought a sacrifice to the Angel of the Lord.[215] Women were instrumental in the furnishing of the sanctuary of the Lord.[216] Women prayed, fasted,[217] inquired of the Lord,[218] and named their own children. "In 45 cases in which the naming of the children is recorded in the Old Testament, in 26 it is ascribed to woman, in 14 to men and in 5 to God."[219] Sometimes she ate at the sacrificial meal.[220] In later Judaism, there is evidence in Alexandria that men and women in the Therapeutae sect of Judaism came together in a communal meal after singing in separate choirs.[221] Women also sang and danced and celebrated their god.[222]

Israel's cultic history and woman's participation in that history varied. It would appear that formative Judaism was much more open to the involvement of women in cults than during the postexilic period.[223] A few isolated communities of Jews did exist that allowed some degree of involvement by women in the cult. Her religious activities did not legitimately center at the tent or the temple. Woman's religion, in Judaism, was chiefly a personal religion. She could pray, dance, sing, and even make a vow. Her sacrifices and money were readily accepted by the priests. She was known to be present at some feasts.[224] But she stood always on the outside of cultic activities. Its mysteries were foreign and unknown to her. She never entered its innermost sanctuary.

4

Cultic Status of Woman:
Greco-Roman Heritage of Mark

Purity, Menstruation, and Superstition

The writer of Mark chose to preserve primitive traditions that reflect the beginnings of Christianity. The oldest traditions were primarily Jewish-oriented, probably because the Jesus movement began as a dissenting group within established Judaism. Mark's Gospel was compiled long after these initial conflicts began. The Gospel story grew in a cross-cultural atmosphere dominated by Greco-Roman influences. Mark's auditors were not only a group of Jewish dissenters, but a world of mixed races. "As the Church was separated from the synagogue and gained its own independent foothold, it also incorporated ideas from the many diverse cultures present in the Hellenized Roman world and from the mystery religions popular throughout the empire at the time."[1]

No one knows how little or how much influence the cults of the Roman Empire had upon the growth of Christianity. Yet it is undeniable that they were popular during the time of the inception of Christianity and the birth of the Gospel of Mark.

Chapter 3 demonstrated that Mark 5:24–34 began as a dissension to the purity laws found in Leviticus. Ultimately, these purity regulations led to a segregation of women and denial of any cultic responsibility. Women were never allowed to lead cult activities due to their inherited biology. The question this chapter will attempt to answer is: Is evidence of this restrictive attitude found also in the Greco-Roman state and local cults? Were women in general barred from holding a central position in the cult because of their biologic difference from man?

Mary Douglas, a noted anthropologist, summarizes Greek thought on purity and impurity. "Greek thought seems to have been relatively free of ritual pollution in the period in which Homer describes (if there

71

is such a historical period) while clusters of pollution concepts emerge later and are expressed by the classical dramatists."[2] According to Sarah B. Pomeroy, the earliest known nonmedical reference to menstruation in classical literature is found in Aristophanes. The female genitals were referred to by Aristophanes as *choiros* ("pig"), and he called a napkin for menstrual blood a *choirokomeion* ("pigpen").[3]

Some classical writers show disgust and even fear of a woman's monthly cycle, yet these attitudes do not seem to restrict women from functioning in society and more importantly, in cult activities. The clean-unclean syndrome, which controlled much of the Jewish way of life, finds very little presence in the Greco-Roman world. L. Swidler cites a response made by a woman philosopher, named Theano, to the woman question. "Within the context of the primitive assumption that sexual intercourse makes a person 'unclean,' she asked: 'In how many days after intercourse with a man will a woman be clean? [The answer:] If it is her own husband, she is immediately clean; if it is with a stranger, never.'"[4]

Theano changed the intent of the question by her answer. She saw it as a moral question, not one of superstition. The body, by itself, has nothing to do with being unclean. It is an affair of the mind or of the will. It is an ethical decision. Yet this story does imply that within the Greek world, there were ideas that linked purity and the body.

A hint of a blood-taboo at birth remains in Plutarch's *Moralia*. In describing the birth of a child he states,

> For there is nothing so imperfect, so helpless, so naked, so shapeless, so foul, as man observed at birth, to whom alone, one might almost say, Nature has given not even a clean passage to the light; but, defiled with blood and covered with filth and resembling more one just slain than one just born, he is an object for one to touch or lift up or kiss or embrace except for someone who loves with natural affection.[5]

The ancient superstition of defiling blood, for Plutarch, is overcome by love (φίλουντις).[6]

Superstitions about a woman's menstrual cycle abound in agricultural writings. Columella, a Spaniard, contemporary with Seneca, and a successful farmer, writes in his *De re Rustica*, "A shrub of rue lasts many years without deteriorating, unless a woman, who is in her menstrual period touches it; in which case it dries up."[7]

He continues by banning women from entering his fields during their monthly cycle. "Care, however, must be taken that a woman is admitted as little as possible to the place where the cucumbers and gourds are planted; for usually the growth of the greenstuff is checked by contact with a woman, indeed if she is also in the period of menstruation, she will kill the young produce merely by looking at it."[8]

Aelian, in his book on animals differs with Columella. He welcomes women to his fields. "Caterpillars feed upon vegetables and in a short while destroy them. But they in turn are destroyed if a woman with her monthly courses upon her walks through the vegetables."[9]

Pliny the Elder, a career person in the Roman calvary of the first century c.e., catalogs a list of superstitions about women and their menstrual cycles. At the end of his diatribe he apologizes for having brought up the subject. "This is all the information it would be right for me to repeat, most of which needs an apology from me. As the rest of it is detestable and unspeakable. . . ."[10]

Pliny reports that females have great positive powers due to their menstrual cycles.

> Over and above all this there is no limit to woman's power. First of all, they say that hailstorms and whirlwinds are driven away if menstrual fluid is exposed to the very flashes of lightning: that stormy weather too is thus kept away, and that at sea exposure, even without menstruation, prevents storms.[11]
>
> Many say that even this great plague is remedial; that it makes a liniment for gout, and that by her touch a woman in this state relieves scrofula, parotid tumors, superficial abscesses, erysipelas, bails, and eyefluxes. Lais and Scalpe hold that the bite of a mad dog, tertians, and quartans are cured by the flux. . . .[12]

Unlike the Jews, the Greeks believed that sleeping with a menstruating woman had its beneficial effects. "Icatides the physician assures us that quartans are ended by sexual intercourse provided the woman is beginning to menstruate."[13]

The Greeks also possessed myths about the negative effects of a woman's monthly.

> Wild indeed are the stories told of the mysterious and awful power of the menstrous discharge itself, the manifold magic of which I have spoken of in the proper place. Of these tales I may without shame mention the following: if the female power should issue when the moon or sun is in eclipse, it will cause irremediable harm; no less harm if there is no moon, at such seasons sexual intercourse brings death and disease upon man. . . .[14]

Copper rusts, bees fly away, a mare will miscarry, and mirrors tarnish if touched by a menstruating woman. "Not even fire, the all conquering overcomes it."[15] It turns new wine sour, steel is dulled, and it drives dogs mad.[16] Pliny agrees with Columella that there are certain times when a woman should not be around vegetation. If they walk in the garden at sunrise, "the crop dries up,... the young vines are irremedially harmed by the touch, and the rue and ivy, plants of the highest medicinal power, die at once."[17]

Superstitions about a woman's monthly periods certainly are not lacking in the Greco-Roman world. The sciences also have their opinions about the origin, duration, complications, and diseases, centered upon the biologic functions of a woman. According to Pliny, women have their monthly flows because of "moles in her womb."[18] Plutarch disagrees. The monthly flow is evidence of an overabundant supply of blood in the woman's body. It leaves the body in order to "lighten and cleanse the rest of the body and in season to render the woman fertile ground for ploughing, as it were, and sowing."[19]

By profession, Aristotle, Hippocrates, and Soranus were physicians. In their discussions concerning the biologic functions of women, none of them betray an attitude that would hinder women in society at large or in cultic affairs.

In fact, Aristotle of the fourth century B.C., compares menstrual fluid with semen in man. "Thus much is evident: the menstrual fluid is a residue, and it is the analogous thing in females to the semen in males."[20] Both of these fluids constitute a cleansing of the body.[21] Yet Aristotle also believed that the loss of the monthly fluid by the woman made her physically less capable than a man.[22]

Soranus, of the first century C.E., has written an entire volume on women and their physical problems.[23] His approach is scientific and objective and relates no restrictive attitudes toward women because of their natural biologic functions.

There appear to be no direct links between the Greco-Roman superstitions about a woman's monthly cycle and her assumption of cult activities. It is generally agreed that women's status in Rome as well as Greece had progressed significantly and afforded women more opportunities that her predecessors lacked.[24]

Priestesses and the Greco-Roman Cults

Considering religious activity, women are rarely denied participation in cultic affairs because of their sex, and never because of their menstrual cycle. Unlike their Jewish sisters, all of whom had to remain in an outer court of the temple, the Greco-Roman women were eligible to officiate at the altar. The Jewess worshiped a male diety. The Greco-Romans had their female deities and consorts to worship. The first century C.E. brought with it divinized women under the state-controlled worship of the emperor. The following discussion will center upon the major state and popular cults administered by women. A few exceptions will be noted because some cults barred all women from attending the festivities and becoming members.

W. A. Meeks, in an excellent article on androgynous symbolism in the early Christian period, suggests that women had gained an equal standing with men in many areas that had been closed to her earlier.[25] "In Greece even professional athletes were opened to women of the first century B.C."[26] His article goes on to detail advancement in economics, marriage, philosophical schools, and particular cult activities. "There are in fact signs that in some cultic associations the ordinary social roles were disregarded."[27] He cites an inscription on a shrine honoring Agdistis in Philadelphia, Lydia. "The commandments given to Dionysius [the owner of the house] (by Zeus), granting access in sleep to his own house both to free men and women and to household slaves."[28]

In most of the cultic entrance or initiation ceremonies, "women were initiated on a par with men, just as distinctions of origin, family, class or servitude, were put aside."[29]

State Cults

The most noted official cultic office held by women in the Empire was the Vestal Virgin. The word *vesta* means "candle" and her sacred emblem was the sacred fire. "They were dedicated to the worship and service of the goddess of fertility."[30] The Virgins' main duty was to attend to the Temple of Vesta and never let the sacred fire burn out. Other duties centered around their presence at all major religious ceremonies of the state and some of the more popular cults.[31] "In all the public duties performed by them a reference can be traced to one leading idea—that the food and nourishment of the State, of which the sacred fire was a symbol, depended for its maintenance on the accurate performance of their duties."[32] J. P. V. D. Balsdon adds, "It also depended, of course, on their remaining virgins without spot or blemish."[33]

Only young women between the ages of six and ten were selected. During the Republic they came only from the wealthier and influential families; later daughters of freedman were admitted in the early years of the first century C.E.[34] The length of service was until the age of forty. According to Sarah B. Pomeroy, the Vestal Virgins were the most liberated women in all of Rome because they were not bound to any one man.[35] Balsdon characterizes their activities as "pleasing privileges."[36] Pomeroy sees this freedom as a sign of emancipation.[37]

> Further evidence of the freedom from the restrictions of ordinary women is to be found in the privileges enjoyed by the Vestals. They were the only women permitted to drive through the city of Rome in a carpentum, a two-wheeled wagon, which conferred high status on its occupant. Like magistrates, priests, and men of certain distinctions, they were preceded in the streets by a lictor (attendant) who cleared the way before them. . . . The Vestals retained places on the Imperial podium. These privileges had such implications of status that the "rights of the Vestals" were often conferred upon female members of the imperial family, who were frequently portrayed as Vestals on coins.[38]

Their allegiance, honesty, and trustworthiness can be seen in their duties of guarding important documents, wills, and carrying letters for the emperors.[39]

Early in the Republic, aristocratic young ladies stood in line in order to be considered for the cultic honor. Later the attitudes changed. The upper classes had dwindled and women in general seemed to be less prone to promise their daughters to at least thirty years of celibacy.[40] Immorality, or sexual relations with a man, could end in condemnation, scandal, and loss of the office. For many the risk was too great.

The cult of Ceres, whose Latin name means "to produce," or "to grow," was the only other state cult to be administered exclusively by priestesses.[41] Ceres was thought to protect wives from their husbands. She protected their rights. Toward the later part of the third century B.C.E., Ceres became Hellenized and adopted the name of Demeter. "The cult of Hellenized Ceres was exclusively in the hands of women. Greek priestesses were brought from Naples or Valeia (Elea) to supervise the new cult."[42]

Popular Cults

Women seemed to have excelled in the cultic realm during Hellenistic times in the Greco-Roman Empire.[43] The Empire only recognized official state cults; the others it tolerated. Among the most influential cults of the time was Isis; following close behind was Dionysius.

During New Testament times, by far the most attractive cult was Isis. Isis was born in Egypt where women's rights and worth had blossomed. "Isis was a wife and a mother, but she also had been a whore."[44] Therefore, she attracted women from every strata of society. Her influence elevated the status of women. "Diodorus Siculus reported that because of the example of Isis; the Egyptian Queens had more honor than the kings, and that among commoners the wives ruled the husbands."[45] A hymn to Isis, probably recorded in the second century C.E., had a refrain that is sung, "She made the power of women equal to that of men."[46]

The Romans praised social order, but Isis would close her doors to no one. She was not class conscious; all could enter her sanctuary. The priesthood was open to both men and women. "Both men and women could hold high office within the cult."[47] Frescoes of Herculaneum and Pompeii reveal women performing all duties of this sacred cult.[48]

Isis represented the individual and she became so popular that Rome could not suppress her growth within the Empire. Eventually she was represented in every major city throughout the Mediterranean world.[49] Above all, the banner Isis carried was imprinted with the phrase, "Equality of Women."

The cults of Attis, Cybele, and Dionysius became inextricably bound during the Roman period. Attis and Dionysius are male deities who pass through various stages of life, from childhood to old age. Both are "closely associated with the earth-mother goddess Cybele."[50] Dionysius was primarily the god of women. Jack T. Sanders maintains that the origin of the Dionysiac worship was within the context of a matriarchy in pre-Hellenistic times.[51] Walter F. Otto agrees that this Dionysiac cult attracted primarily women.

> We should never forget that the Dionysiac world is, above all, a world of women. Women awaken Dionysius and bring him up. Women accompany him wherever he is. Women await him and are the first ones to be overcome with his madness. . . . Much more important than the sexual act are the act of birth and the feeding of a child. . . . The terrible trauma of childbirth, the wildness which belongs to motherliness in its primal form, a wildness which can break loose in an alarming way not only in animals . . . all these reveal the innnermost nature of the Dionysiac madness: the churning up of the essence of life surrounded by the storms of death.[52]

Dionysius of Halicarnassus, while describing the rites of Cybele says, "A man, Phryx, and a woman, Phrygia, performed for her the priestly rites."[53] Hugo Hepding assembles a great deal of evidence in proof of a woman priesthood at the altar of Cybele.[54]

There were many other state and local deities, and gods and goddesses of the mystery religions, which were served by women priestesses or dedicated to women patrons. For over two thousand years the cult of Eleusis dominated Greece and reached its peak during the

Roman Empire. The Eleusinian mystery religions began with the worship of a goddess of agriculture and fertility, Demeter. Women were central to the cult and maintained her temples.[55] Woman was worshiped because of, not in spite of her different biologic frame. The female reproductive powers were idolized in the cults of Bona Dea and Fortuna.[56] Fortuna was "the guarantor not only of the fruits of the earth but also of women's physical maturation and sexual fulfillment."[57] Unlike the Bona Dea cult whose festivities excluded the presence of men,[58] Fortuna welcomed men who were "interested in her promise of virility, material success and economic prosperity."[59]

The worship of Aphrodite, Ishtar, Diana, and their equivalents, echoed throughout the Empire.[60] Woman's voice was heard at the altar and worshiped in the temple. The first century C.E. ushered in a new age of divinized woman. Wives of the emperors, and women of state were legally proclaimed goddesses. Drusilla,[61] sister of Gaius, was the first woman to be consecrated a goddess on September 23, C.E. 38.[62] Claudius' grandmother, Augusta; as well as Claudia Augusta, daughter of Nero and Poppaea; and Flavia Domitilla, the daughter of Vespasian, soon had cults named after them upon their deaths.[63]

Christianity grew in the midst of a culture that recognized and promoted the capabilities of woman at the altar. Her person and biologic difference rarely kept her from participation in religious activities. Yet some of the cults denied access to women. Among these cults were Mithras and Hercules.[64] In the cult of Hercules no other god was mentioned as a consort or to be worshiped as an equivalent. Women and dogs were not admitted.[65] Mithras, the god of light, was worshiped mainly by the Roman armies, with a few devotees among the Asians. Its rites were so secretive that they have been forgotten. Monuments to the cult are found largely near seaports and garrisons.[66]

One of the most important functions of women during the Classical period in Greece was that of oracle. "The primary meaning of oracle is the response of a god to a question asked him by a worshipper."[67] Unlike the book of Leviticus that characterizes Yahweh speaking only to males, here the gods chose to speak through a woman. For example, the Delphic Oracle was the most well-known in Classical times. It presided over Apollo. It is true that a male prophet or priest asked the question. But the question was directed toward the Pythia. The Pythia was a young woman, who, in a frenzied state, would speak for Apollo.[68] Oracles to various gods were found throughout the Near Eastern world.

The Greco-Roman world preserved remnants of purity superstitions in the writings of its poets, philosophers, and scientists. Although menstruation was not completely understood, society rarely penalized a woman for her difference in biology. Woman was never barred from accepting responsibility in cults because of her menstrual cycle. In fact, she was chosen to represent the state, and later she was divinized for her caretaker role. The cults flourished as women adopted central roles in the worship of Isis, Dionysius, Eleusis, Aphrodite, and others. Unlike her Jewish sisters, the Greco-Roman women, with the exceptions of a few male-only cults, had relative freedom in all areas of cult activities.

5

Woman: Significant Member, Role Determiner, and Voice of God to the Community

Cosmopolitan, under reconstruction, and oriented toward a broader-changing world, are just a few of the characteristics of the Marcan readers (auditors). Evidence of dissenting groups and non-Jewish influences mingle and linger, while at times dominating certain sections of the work. Out of this network of traditions, Mark 5:24–34 stands out as a banner making a candid and timely statement about women within the developing Christian communities. My aim in this chapter is to examine and interpret this miracle story in detail. Consideration will be given to important verses, individual words in their relation to the immediate context, parallel statements, and related traditions about women as preserved by Mark.

Preliminary Considerations

According to R. Bultmann[1] and Martin Dibelius,[2] Mark 5:24–34 follows the classical form of the miracle story (novelle or tale). It exhibits the length of sickness, characteristics of disease, difficulty of healing, ineffective treatment of physicians, doubt and contemptuous treatment of the healer, and at last, the healing.[3] This form, like all forms, developed as the community grew and was changed as the need arose. When Mark chose to preserve this story by committing it to writing, it became, at least in one point in time, fixed.[4]

This story interrupts another miracle story about the healing of a daughter in the family of Jairus. In at least five other instances within the Marcan statement, a story is found inserted into another story.[5] Benjamin W. Bacon, K. L. Schmidt, and H. Van der Loos postulated that historical facts prompted the insertion.[6] Mark is supposedly giving the audience a play by play description of the life of Jesus. E. Wendling sees the number twelve as the shaping factor in the stories.

Coincidentally, both stories centered around the number twelve and were thus linked together,[7] although some scholars would agree with H. A. Guy that "there is no obvious relation between the two stories."[8] S. E. Johnson recognizes the radically differing styles of the two stories. He suggests that Mark inserted the story about the woman into the Jairus story in the process of constructing the Gospel. "Differences in language between the two stories tend to show that they were not connected in the tradition. The narrative of the woman is in standard though simple Hellenistic Greek, with periodic sentences and numerous participles, while the other story contains an Aramaic word, simpler syntax and such expressions as θυγάτριον, and ἐσχάτως ἔχει."[9]

According to Paul J. Achtemeier, "There is no compelling reason, then, why the stories had to be combined by the traditions in order for either of them to be understood."[10] Yet in his commentary on Mark he allows for a distant relationship of the two stories in terms of their similar statements about faith. "Mark 5:21–43 is an example of two miracle stories which have been combined in a very simple way. The story of the woman with the flow of blood has simply been inserted into the story of the raising of Jairus' daughter, perhaps to let the statement about faith in the inner story interpret the meaning of the story into which it has been inserted."[11] Achtemeier views the two stories as originating separately. They circulated independently and were probably employed in eucharistic services.[12]

There is ample evidence to suggest that there are definite similarities between the two miracle stories. Both women are termed *daughters* (Mark 5:23, 34); both report the number twelve (Mark 5:25, 42). Both deal with the healing of females (Mark 5:23, 26). Both women had what seemed to be incurable diseases (Mark 5:23, 26). Both Jairus and the woman approached Jesus from out of the crowd (Mark 5:22, 27). Both healings had as their object salvation (Mark 5:23 σωθῇ, 5:28 σωθήσομαι). Both miracles involved faith (ἡ πίστις in Mark 5:34 and πίστευε in 5:36). Both believed in the efficacy of Jesus' touch (Mark 5:23 ἐπιθῇς τάς χεῖρας and 5:28 ἐαν ἄψωμαι note that the subjunctive is used in each case). Both Jairus and the woman fell before Jesus (πίπτει in Mark 5:22 and προσέπεσεν in 5:33). Jesus is said to have spoken with both the young girl and the woman at the end of the healing (Mark 5:34, 41). Jesus gave both of the women a command to commence an activity (Mark 5:34 ὕπαγε and 5:41 ἔγειρε). Both of the healings were witnessed by Jesus' disciples (Mark 5:31 οἱ μαθηταὶ αὐτοῦ and 5:40 τοὺς μετάὐτοῦ and 5:37).

Some would maintain that the similarities point to a complete Marcan creation. "It was not a compilation of popular anecdotes, evolving over a long period of time, careless of the reality of the facts. It was a three-fold historico-apologetic composition, written by definite authors, in a hierarchical community, at a time when witnesses of the events were still alive and aflame with zeal to propagate or annihilate the new religion."[13]

It is very difficult to ascertain the exact point in history when the two stories became intertwined. The important fact for this study is the author's choice to preserve these traditions rather than any others. They may be solely a Marcan creation or an outgrowth of primitive Christian living. Whatever the case, the stories do stem from at least one, and possibly several communal situations, and Mark uses them to communicate what God's will is for future Christian living.

Purpose of the Miracle Story

Two thousand years of historical and exegetical reflections upon the miracle story have traditionally centered inquiries in the person performing the miracle, Jesus. The unusual happenings reported in miracle stories are variously viewed as signs of the heavenly realm intervening into the realm of the mundane;[14] "symbolic demonstrations of God's forgiveness in action";[15] or a "special form of revelation in which the power of God is manifested in a new reality."[16] There is an omnipotent message present in each story that points toward a new era. They are a sign of redemption.[17]

Some recent scholars, among them Theodore J. Weeden, center their inquiries upon the person of Jesus as the legitimator of a new religious movement. "The author (or authors) of the Signs source persuaded his reader that Jesus was the Christ by narrating one sign after another until the reader was forced to conclude what the author intended him to conclude: the Jesus of the signs, like theios aner from Nazareth, is the Christ."[18]

Achtemeier takes a different approach by viewing the miracle story in relation to a worshiping community. "The stories were shaped, therefore, to show that the power which could perform such wonders during Jesus' earthly career was still persent for those who, through their faith in him, incorporated themselves into a fellowship whose Lord he continued to be."[19]

According to G. W. Allport and L. J. Postman, oral tradition (rumor) always circulates in order to meet the needs of the community. They would agree with Achtemeier's emphasis on the community. "[W]e know that rumors concerning a given subject matter will circulate within a group in proportion to the importance and the ambiguity of this subject matter in the lives of the individual members of the group, and the principal reason why rumor circulates is because it serves the twin functions by explaining and relieving emotional tensions felt by individuals."[20]

The present inquiry will follow the lead of Achtemeier and others of related viewpoint and center on the people (and therefore the primitive church) involved in the miracle stories, rather than on the person or the theology of the person of Jesus. Miracle stories are viewed as communicative vehicles that serve to meet the needs within the community. Stories are preserved because they reveal important concepts to community members. Mark 5:24–34, it will be demonstrated, served the needs of its communities by presenting a miracle story that freed woman from a restrictive cultic and social roles within society, and freed her to a new, demanding, creative, and healing role, within the worshiping communities.

Situating the Story

Mark 5:24–34 is located in the teaching section of the Gospel.[21] It is situated near the Sea of Galilee. No specific city is mentioned. The twelve have been chosen and are at Jesus' side amid the thronging crowds. Mark had revealed the character and authority of Jesus, but his mission will not be divulged until chapter 8.

Woman: Significant Community Member

The miracle story of the hemorrhaging woman touches at the core of the cultic discrimination within the Hebrew cult. She stands as a symbol for all Hebrew women. Biologic differences prevented her form experiencing initiation rites,[22] from serving at the sanctuary, and even from participating in the feasts. Her religious activity appears to be only personal except in cases of mourning, dancing, and praying.[23] This healing story focuses upon the woman and consciously details that she has physical, emotional, and social worth to the community and the cult. Her involvement with the divine is no longer peripheral, but central.

Physical Worth

Out of the anonymous masses the woman emerges (Mark 5:27). This is the same crowd that has followed Jesus since He began his missionary trek. They provide a constant audience for his works and teachings.[24] The woman has no name. Mark refers to her simply as "woman" (Mark 5 : 25). She has no real class distinction or authority. She is a nameless face, unlike Jairus whom Mark calls a synagogue chief (Mark 5 : 22). Later traditions attached to her the names of Bernice and Veronica.[25] Her introduction to Jesus came through rumor. "Hearing the things concerning Jesus. . . ." (Mark 5 : 27).

Mark constantly emphasizes "hearing" as a vehicle whereby people come to belief.[26] Men as well as women were responsible for hearing the words and recognizing the deeds of Jesus. A voice out of the heavens spoke to all. "Listen to Him."[27]

Mark is concerned about the woman's physical and emotional dilemma and their resulting socio-cultic disruption. The healing takes on a double entendre. Using the present tense ($o\check{v}\sigma\alpha$), which implies continuous activity, Mark describes the woman's physical problem. He diagnoses the situation as $o\check{v}\sigma\alpha\ \dot{\epsilon}\nu\ \dot{\rho}\acute{v}\sigma\epsilon\iota\ \ddot{\alpha}\iota\mu\alpha\tau o\varsigma$ (Mark 5 : 25).[28] Her condition is chronic, lasting over twelve years, and shows no signs of abatement. Soranus in his first-century work on gynecology describes a similar condition.

> According to the ancients, as Alexander Philalethes says in the first book "On Gynecology," the flux is an increased flow of blood through the uterus over a protracted period." But according to Demetrius the Herophilean, it is a "flow of fluid matter through the uterus over a protracted period" since the flux may not be sanguineous only, but different at different times.[29]
>
> As a general rule, however, we shall diagnose the flux from the fact that the genital parts are continually moistened by fluids of different color, and that the patient is pale, wastes away, lacks appetite, often becomes breathless when walking, and has swollen feet.[30]

A comparison of Mark's description of this woman's illness with Matthew's and Luke's account, reveals that Mark spends more time discussing the woman's problems. Matthew omits all of her medical history, and Luke only briefly touches upon it.[31] Luke summarizes her background. ". . . She could not be healed by anyone."[32] Mark escalates and interprets the ailment of the woman. She is not only physically oppressed because of her disease, but is socially oppressed because of the lack of insight and ineptitude of the physicians. Their trade has increased her bodily discomfort. Heraclitus, in about the sixth century B.C., writes about such medical healers as "[p]hysicians who cut and burn, demand payment of a fee, though undeserving, since they produce the same (pains as the disease)."[33]

The types of remedies used for female illnesses reveal a widespread general ignorance. "One remedy consisted of drinking a goblet of wine containing a powder compounded from rubber, alum, and garden crocuses. Another treatment consisted of a dose of Persian onions cooked in wine with the summons, "Arise out of your flow of blood." Other physicians prescribed sudden shock, or the carrying of the ash of an ostrich's egg in a certain cloth."[34]

The *Mishna* asserts that "the best of physicians deserved hell . . . ."[35] Soranus suggests the use of mild potions as good medicine.

> Such potions are: an infusion of sawdust from the lotus tree, either alone or with two obols of Samian earth in two cyaths of water (and if opportunity allows with tart wine too); or together with it, the rennet of a hare, calf, lamb, or deer (for this has a coagulating faculty); or ground grapestones, or myrtle berries, or pomegranate peel, or pine bark of something similar, sprinkled upon the potion do the amount of two drachms; or a decoction of Theban dates or quinces and apples."[36]

It is not difficult to understand the rationale for Mark's escalation of negative remarks toward the ἰατροί in relation to woman's diseases (Mark 5:26). Ironically, Mark writes earlier, "It is not the healthy who need a doctor but the sick" (κακῶς) (Mark 2:17). Various authors have attempted to identify the ethnic background of the physicians as either Gentile or Jewish, and specifically Pharisaic.[37] In view of the specific similarities of vocabulary found between this pericope and the book of Leviticus,[38] it would stand to reason that the woman's problems were compounded by ancient outrageous and dehumanizing sacral-physical practices. Yet this does not preclude an attack against the Hellenistic healers.[39]

The woman is more than victimized physically. She has lost her monetary base. Indirectly this passage admits that women did own some type of personal property during the time of the Marcan communities. Note: τὰ παραὐτῆς πάντα (Mark 5:26). No husband or male referent is mentioned. It must be assumed, therefore, that Mark is indicating that she managed her own estate, however poorly. She was the target of money-seeking adventurous healers. The word δαπανήσασα is used rarely in the New Testament and only once in Mark. The word denotes expenditure, ordinarily of money, and here connotes payment of expenses.[40] Paul uses it in the sense of using or spending himself for his congregation at Corinth.[41] Mark is very aware of money-seeking individuals throughout the Gospel. They not only come from the area of physical healers, but also from within the established cult. Recognizing that women do gain property at the death of their husbands and thus become prey for conniving religious people, Mark states: "Watch out for the Teachers of the Law. . . . They devour widow's houses and for show make lengthy prayers."[42]

The woman's encounter with the physicians "profited her nothing" (Mark 5:26). ὠφελήθεισα is again used by Mark in the context of discipleship. "For what profit is it for a person to gain the whole world and lose his own soul" (Mark 8:36). She profited neither physically, emotionally, or financially. Perhaps Mark is also hinting that her physicians, in the event they were Jewish, brought her no closer to God.

Mark's concern for the physico-emotional health as evidenced in Mark 5 of woman, is found throughout the Marcan complex. In the immediate context of this story, Jesus raises a young girl from apparent death (Mark 5:34–41).[43] One of the first miracles performed by Jesus in the unfolding Marcan narrative is upon Peter's mother-in-law. She was "fever stricken."[44] Mark even records Jesus' interest in the well-being of a non-Jewess: the daughter of a woman from the area of Syria and Phoenicia was cured of demon possession.[45] The phrase, "How dreadful it will be in those days for pregnant women and nursing mothers."[46] evidences a keen awareness of a woman's physical being. For Mark, a woman's health was very important. In a community that cared little about its women, there would be very little or no emphasis upon keeping them well. Mark chose to reproduce, preserve, and articulate miracle stories and sayings about women that made them and their male counterparts aware of their physical-emotional nature. Physical health is just one step in being a well-functioning community member. Mark accepts a woman as "other" as well as her biologic differences. Maintaining women in good health is, and should be, one goal of the community, suggests Mark.

Socio-Cultic Worth

Mark not only emphasizes a woman's worth in the areas of physico-emotional, but the author also sees the need and worth of a woman within society and the cult.

In the matter of divorce, Mark admits that women have been divorcing their husbands.[47] Although the author objects to such practices, it is noteworthy that the woman's side of the issue is mentioned in the matter. Matthew views divorce only from the man's point of view.[48] Luke admits that some women are divorced, but in his account they do not take the initiative.[49] Kee correctly observes, "The very fact that women's rights are taken into account shows that this logion has been adapted by the Markan traditions to meet the needs and life style of the non-Jewish communities."[50]

Woman's worth is also strongly articulated as Mark views the lineage of Jesus through Mary. "Isn't this Mary's son? . . ."[51] His father is never mentioned by Mark. Within this social interest of woman, Mark also makes a candid statement about her cultic relation and function within the communities.

In a reaction to the purity laws penned by the editors of Leviticus[52] and passed on by other Jewish writings, Mark skillfully and purposefully preserved this miracle story. A Jewish woman was restricted from holding a central place in cult activities due to her biologic processes. Blood made her ceremonially unclean and therefore she was excluded from any contact with the Divine.[53] Woman's essential worth to the socio-cultic community is articulated as Mark narrates this healing story. She moves from anonymity to family member, from an impersonal relationship with Jesus to a personal one, from complete disruption in her personal, social, and cultic life to a total state of wholeness. The breach between man and woman, and woman and cult, is closed.

Mark is concerned about purity laws and their negative effects upon people. Throughout the Gospel these negative opinions are expressed in miracle stories and controversy stories. Here, in Mark 5:24–34, this critical polemic against purity regulations reaches a climax for woman. In two instances (Mark 5:24, 29) the woman's condition is termed a μάστιξ. According to Mark, both the woman and Jesus view her condition in the same vein. It is not a mere physical ailment. Mark uses this term only once again in 3:10. "For he had healed many, so that those with diseases (μάστιξ) were pushing forward to touch Him." There are marked philological similarities between this verse and Mark 5:24–34. Luke uses the term μάστιξ as one of the diseases that Jesus healed.[54] Hebrews and Acts use the term to mean "whips" or "scourgings."[55] "The reference in the first verse (Acts 22:24) is to Roman torture. In the second passage (Hebrews 11:36), which enumerates the sufferings of the martyrs, the reference is to stripes received in the synagogue."[56]

The central idea of this word can be articulated in the words *disaster*,[57] *punishment for sin*,[58] and a general emphasis on something that is difficult or hard coming constantly into an individual's life. It can also be translated as sickness,[59] which may or may not originate with God.[60]

For centuries the Hebrew woman was discriminated against because of her physical otherness. The visual of μάστιξ is one of being beaten to the point of no resistance. The woman in the miracle story was beaten because of her physical ailment. She was taboo to all.[61] She could have no intimate relations with men,[62] nor could she, as a responsible Jewess, with a good conscience, be milling about among the masses. Tradition stands firm on the matter, according to the *Mishnah*. "Heedlessness of the laws of the 'menstruant' was one of the three trangressions for which women died in childbirth."[63]

The woman was considered to be unclean, which necessitated a disruption between her and her community, her cult and God, and herself. She needed a cohesiveness in her life. In desperation she reached out to the only person left who might be able to help her. Her ultimate healing come as a result of her own initiative in the meeting and touching of Jesus.

As discussed in chapter 3, the phrases $η$‘ $πηγὴ$, $τοῦ$ $αἵματος$, and $οὖσα$ $ἐν$ $ῥύσει$ $αἵματος$ show a dependence upon traditions, and therefore terminology used by the writers of Leviticus. In addition to the laws secluding woman, Mark finds other aspects of the Jewish purity system unacceptable. In listing the things that make a person clean or unclean, Mark 7:20 never mentions menstruation, leprosy, death, or certain foods as being impure and therefore unclean.[64] Rather than such an external set of separating laws, Mark argues for an internalized ethical system. "What comes out of a person is what makes that person unclean. For from within, out of people's hearts, come evil thoughts. . . ." (Mark 7:20–23). For Mark, the washing of hands to affect some type of cleanness, is irrelevant. While discussing the issue of eating with clean or unclean hands, Mark uses contemporary traditions as an opportunity to denounce the present accepted Jewish practice and to make the universal point that all foods are clean.[65] Mark will not tolerate ethnic snobbery or separateness. The physical separateness that results from observing laws relating to ritual purity or holiness embraces all people who participate in the Jewish traditions. "Holiness requires that individuals shall conform to the class to which they belong. All holiness requires that different classes of things shall not be confused. . . . Holiness means keeping distinct the categories of creation. It therefore involves correct definition, discrimination and order."[66] This separatistic emphasis in cultic living involved the sexes, foods, the living from the dead, as well as a host of other categories. Mark's Gospel breaks down those categories and thus the barriers.[67]

"The important space devoted to setting aside the ritual laws of Jewish separateness (7:1–20) both in precept and in action shows that this was an issue for Mark's community: the community was open across social, economic, sexual, and ethnic barriers."[68]

Further evidence of Mark's tendentious treatment of purity laws can be viewed in the healings of the leper, the daughter of the woman who lived in a Gentile area, as well as the cleansing of the temple by Jesus.[69] The leper's healing resulted from the touch of Jesus.[70] He was instructed to report back to the local priest, but ignored the message and instead began to tell the story to anyone who came along.[71] The Marcan community offered healing and community to people who had the most distasteful and antisocial diseases. There was no segregation. There was no negative reaction by Mark in the episode that deals with Joseph of Arimathea, a leading citizen, who actually prepared the body of Jesus for burial.[72] Mark further records that others were involved in such activities. The women watched and the next day set out to finish the job that Joseph had begun.[73] Mark, as is common elsewhere in the narrative, does not endorse any type of sacrifice or ritual ablutions in order to fulfill purity legislation.[74] According to Mark, Jesus himself had no misgivings about touching a dead person. With him he took the three and the mother and father into the apparently dead girl's room (Mark 5 : 35–41).

Our story of the woman with the flow of blood and the story of the healing of the daughter of the Syro-Phoenician mother have much in common. One author claims that in a pre-Marcan stage they circulated independently as parallel stories.[75] By preserving them Mark not only shows concern for the physical well-being of woman, but points out that the preaching activity of Jesus broke down hundreds of years of prejudice toward people of a different ethnic origin. In considering the miracle performed by Jesus to the daughter of the Gentile woman, Mark uncovers a social separation and attitude that is seen to be unbecoming for members of the emerging community. The text glaringly points out that she was a non-Jew, a Greek ('Ελληνίς).[76] She appeals to Jesus' sense of equality.[77] Jesus does not hesitate to speak with the woman. There is a conversation, a merging of the worlds. T. A. Burkill observes correctly,

Accordingly, a careful scrutiny of the gospel persuades us that Mark 7 : 24–31 follows directly from the design of the evangelist: he wishes to illustrate the Lord's freedom from the purity regulations and to demonstrate that the apostolic mission to the Gentiles was prefigured in the earthly ministry; and he infers from the traditions reference to the woman's Syro-phoenician connections that the journey beyond Palestine was an excursion into the region of Tyre and Sidon—totally disregarding the possibility that she may have been thought of by the tradients as an emigree resident in Galilee.[78]

Both A. Dermience and Burkill[79] correctly view this woman and her daughter as symbolic of the inclusion of non-Jews into the Christian community. But while it is true that she and her daughter are symbolic of the masses of people who are classified as impure because of an accident of birth, Mark appears to have a broader interest. Along with the emphasis on the participation of Gentiles in the new adventure, the author purposefully perserves a tradition about a Gentile woman. A woman has a place within the inner circle of Christian believers. Her presence is needed and desired. She is important. According to Howard C. Kee, "Her lack of cultic cleanliness was no barrier to her participation in the powers of the New Age at work through Jesus."[80] She is more than "a symbol and prototype of the faithful gentiles."[81] She is symbol and prototype of woman serving and functioning within the cultic worshiping community.

Cultic discrimination is most obvious in a woman's relationship with, and proximity to, the temple.[82] The purposes of the temple revolved around setting an example "of rigorous exactness in all that concerned cult."[83] She was always on the fringes of the sacral official activities. She was kept separate: first, because she was a woman; and secondly, because of her monthly cycles. Mark shows no respect for this system of separateness.

"My house will be called a house of prayer for all nations. . . ."[84] *Irony* is the only word that can be used for the historic development of the temple and its functions. "The sanctuary, which had been intended as a place where God would dwell and be accessible not only to Israel but to all nations, had become a place of greedy, busy commerce."[85]

It was reported that the money changers situated in stands outside the temple courts actually, exchanged for a price, impure money for pure money for the pilgrims, so that they could pay their temple dues.[86] With no emotional attachment Mark tells of the fall of the temple.[87] Its destruction was monumental to the Jewish cult, but meant little to the newly forming community. It had stood as a reminder to separateness and socio-class distinctions. Its disappearance placed everyone on the same level before God. There was no heavy curtain that kept anyone from seeking God. "The curtain of the temple was torn in two from top to bottom" (Mark 15:38). All, no matter who they were, had open access to the Divine. No shadow, priest, rite, or tax could keep anyone from worshiping their God. "[T]hroughout Mark, the point that is made in both subtle and overt ways that there are no social or eithnic prerequisites for admission to the convenant community: it is indeed the 'outcasts of Israel' who are welcomed into membership."[88]

The woman with the flow of blood, the daughter of Jairus, the Syro-Phoenician woman and her daughter, and all women who attempted to worship at the temple are among those who were potential outcasts of the Hebrew cultic community. All are welcomed as members, and the author intimates that their role is, has been, or should be much more important than just membership.

An Invitation to the Hemorrhaging Woman

Mark reiterates unequivocally that Jesus' mission was not to the establishment or to those who would classify themselves as δίκαιοι.[89] "I have come to call (καλέσαι) the righteous, but sinners (ἁμαρτωλούς)" (Mark 2:17). For Mark the sinners are those people who do not systematically keep the laws mandated by the Jewish establishment. They are non-Jews[90] or those who choose not the live according to Jewish mandates. The desperate woman of Mark 5:24–34 could easily be classified as a sinner, especially with reference to the Levitical purity system. According to Mark it was to her kind of person that Jesus' life and ministry gravitated. The word ἀκολουθέω[91] is used within the Gospel of Mark in the sense of discipleship. Jesus called James and John, and they followed him.[92] In a true sense, Mark 5:24–34 represents the call of this very ill person. Because of her own initiative she circumvented the established system of rules and headed toward the god-figure of Jesus. Mark clearly points out that she touched Jesus' garment.[93] (Perhaps the author is intimating that she touched his very person.) This is the only complete miracle story perserved by Mark that records a person who initiated the touch and received healing.[94] Others attempted to touch Jesus because they believed that his touch would bring healing.[95]

Matthew and Luke differ with Mark. Perhaps they were offended by the notion that a woman actually touched Jesus' personal garments.[96] Both emphasize that it is only the fringe of Jesus' garment that made contact with the woman.[97]

According to Mark, there is definite personal contact between the hemorrhaging woman and Jesus. The disciples do not recognize it, but Jesus is aware of it (Mark 5:30–31). The woman's primary goal was to bring healing (σωθήσομαι) to herself (Mark 5:28). σώζω is inextricably bound up with the requirements of discipleship. Marcan discipleship presents a double-bind situation to Jesus' followers. "For all who wish to save (σῶσαι) their lives will lose them, but all who lose their lives for me and the gospel will save (σώσει) them" (Mark 8:35; my own translation). The immediate result of touching Jesus' garments did not bring σωτηρία and thus discipleship. It brought healing (ἴαται) from her μάστιξ (Mark 5:29). In Greek thought, ἰάομαι has the idea of restoration, making good and release from physical suffering. Mark uses ἰάομαι only once. The context is the alleviation of this woman's physical-emotional suffering.[98] In both instances that the verb ἰάομαι is used in Leviticus, it is found in the context of healing someone who is considered unclean.[99] Mark seems to be indicating that the woman experienced two levels of healing, that is, the physicoemotional and the cosmic or spiritual. According to Johannes Weiss, the miracle stories were designed to teach more than just what the surface stories indicated. "They taught how in the idea of healing (ἰᾶσθαι) and of the savior (σώζειν, σώτηρ), the release from bodily suffering and death and the release from sin are closely connected. . . . Thus in these stories proclaimed the twofold gospel of the savior of the body and the soul."[100]

On the physical plane, Mark describes the healing of the woman's illness in natural, metaphoric terms. "And immediately the fountain of blood of her was dried up. . . ." (Mark 5 : 29). Usually the words *dried up* have a negative connotation. For instance, Mark tells the story about a man who had a hand that was withered or dried up,[101] and plants and trees wither and die.[102] Here in this miracle story the word has the positive meaning of cure. If the community's source of water "dried up," this would be a very grave situation. The woman's spring is dried up, but she has regained her health.

Matthew and Luke hesitate to use Mark's description of the woman's problems and her healing.[103] Luke changes πηγή to ῥύσις and uses a form of the verb ἵστημι.[104] Mark's characterization of her healing seems to stem from an agricultural type of existence, or at least a culture that used earthly euphemisms and other metaphors to describe physical illness.

According to Mark, Jesus recognized immediately that a physical healing had taken place. The woman had touched him. According to Jewish tradition, she had potentially defiled him. "He shows no indignation at the ritual defilment, but ignores it; for the woman is seen not as an unclean object but as a human being suffering. . . . He does not attack the demands of the cult worship directly, he merely ignores them as irrelevant when they distract from the essential relationship between man and God."[105]

The woman's life was to be saved (σωθήσομαι). She received ἴασις. Mark records a conversation between Jesus and the woman (Mark 5 : 33). Jesus' parting words to her are, "Daughter, your faith has made you well (σέσωκεν); go in peace, and be healed (ἴσθι ὑγιὴς) of your disease" (Mark 5 : 34). Jesus engaged in a conversation with, and gave a command to, a woman. According to the *Talmud*, "As long as a man engages in too much conversation with women, he causes evil to himself."[106] By speaking with the woman, Mark contends that Jesus, and thus the community, should recognize her as an important human being. She is not just property, as viewed by Old Testament civil law found in Exodus[107] and Deuteronomy.[108] She is a person and deserves to be recognized as such by the entire community. She is no longer just a woman who has emerged from the nameless masses. She becomes a "daughter." She is considered to be one of the family members. Mark demonstrates here that all ethnic or social barriers barring membership to the community should be obliterated.[109] "Whoever does the will of God, that one is my brother and sister and my mother" (Mark 3:35). Thus Jesus recognizes and pronounces the woman's new state of being and relationship to the community, to herself and to her god. "Your faith has saved you" (Mark 5:34). Her original goal of $\sigma\omega\theta\acute{\eta}\sigma o\mu\alpha\iota$ has been achieved in a way that she had not anticipated. She now becomes an integral member of the community. This membership materialized because of her own courageous will and initiative. She did not have to be called, cajoled, or coered. Her own free will brought her in contact with Jesus and his teachings and thus the power he represented.

"Wholeness" ($\dot{v}\gamma\iota\acute{\eta}s$) and "peacefulness" ($\dot{\epsilon}\iota\rho\acute{\eta}\nu\eta$) (Mark 5:24) were the results marked by the verbs $\iota\hat{\alpha}\sigma\theta\alpha\iota$ and $\sigma\acute{\omega}\zeta\epsilon\iota\nu$. The disruption that was caused by her illness ended. She is now a whole person after twelve long years. Her relations with the opposite sex can legitimately resume. Her relations in the community are restored. She has found a completeness of life because her status has changed.[110] The Greeks understood the goal of the healing activity of the gods as human happiness.[111] Her new state of being can be characterized as happy in direct opposition of $\epsilon\dot{\iota}s$ $\tau\grave{o}$ $\hat{\epsilon}\hat{\iota}\rho o\nu$ $\dot{\epsilon}\lambda\theta\sigma o\nu\sigma\alpha$ (Mark 5:26).

"Go in Peace" is a familiar Old and New Testament saying.[112] In the LXX it can mean a "state of rest." It is also used as a greeting and presents an alternative to war. It signifies prosperity and lack of suffering.[113] Often it is used to describe relations between peoples, the state of the soul, relations with God, relations with God, as well as the eschatological salvation of the whole person.[114] Generally speaking, the New Testament reflects the same ideas of "peace" as those found in the Old Testament (LXX).[115] The rabbis see שלום as a "gift of God to his people."[116]

This spoken word of peace to the woman with the flow of blood is also spoken to Bartimaeus,[117] and to no one else in Mark's Gospel. Mark recognizes the particular struggles of this woman and the outcast Bartimaeus. The author thus acknowledges all women and people who have been outside the confines of the centralized cult worship. Jesus speaks with, commands, and encourages the woman to worship him openly. The woman came and "fell down before him" (Mark 5:33). The word used in the text is $\pi\rho o\sigma\epsilon\acute{\pi}\epsilon\sigma\epsilon\nu$. This word is always used in the sense of worship in Mark. In the context of 5 : 24–34 it is Jairus also who falls before Jesus. The text says, "He fell to his feet" (Mark 5 : 22). Since αὐτου is masculine, there is some question as to whether Jarius fell to his own feet or before Jesus. Some manuscripts add "to his hands," indicating an act of humility or worship. Mark is obviously comparing the activity of both Jairus and the woman. There is no mistake. The woman fell directly before Jesus (Mark 5 : 33). The manuscript C changes προσέπεσεν to προσεκύνησεν and recognizes her worshipful act. Other manuscripts change the reading, "She fell before him," to ἐμπρόσθεν πάντων, "she fell before all," and emphasizes the community aspect of her testimony.[118]

Through a personal encounter with Jesus whom Mark terms "the son of God,"[119] a woman in general finds a new state of being within the community. Her life is healed. Her future is peaceful. She is legitimated by Mark as worthwhile member of the community of the elect. Her worship, speech, and person, can be healing.[120] The woman ascends from a nameless face in the crowd to a significant community member whose functions involve peace and healing.

Woman: Authentic Role Determiner for the Communities

In the miracle story of the hemorrhaging woman, Mark preserves an example of a woman who would not give up. She is the active one throughout the narration. It is to her faith that Jesus attributes the healing (Mark 5 : 34). He recognized, according to Mark, the totality of her faith. According to Lane, "It was Mark's chance to show a radical faith."[121] Scholars have generally accepted the special example of faith found in this woman.[122] From Origen to Bornkamm, interpreters have centered their questions either upon Jesus himself or upon the faith of the woman.[123] Some scholars have recognized the implicit comparison that Mark makes between the woman and the twelve who did not exhibit such a faith. Ephraim sees the woman shaming all those who were not healed by a similar faith.[124] Chrysostom views her faith as something to provoke the rest to emulation.[125] Her faith is superior to that of Jairus. "Do you see the woman superior to the ruler?"[126]

Bulwark of Faith

In the context, both Jairus and the woman fall before Jesus. The man, being a high official of the Jewish synagogue (Mark 5:22–23) was impotent. He could do nothing to save his dying daughter (Mark 5:36). Jesus encouraged the man. "Don't fear, only believe" (Mark 5:36). The woman needed no external stimuli; it originated from within her. Her faith activity pursued the power that resided in and through Jesus (Mark 5:30). She precipitated a supernatural happening. The ruler did little but watch Jesus in action (Mark 5:40).

Bartimaeus is also commended by Mark for his faith. His persistent call to Jesus resulted in his healing.[127] Bartimaeus does not touch Jesus, nor is the healing affected indirectly. Jesus directly pronounces the man healed. Bartimaeus, like the ruler, is responsible for the healing only in the sense that they both sought out Jesus diligently. The woman and Bartimaeus are similar characters in that they are both ill, both aggressive in their relationship to Jesus, and both are seen as the precipitating cause of their own healing.

Chrysostom also compares the faith of the woman with the faith of the apostles. "Hast thou greater confidence than the Apostles? more abundant strength?"[128] None of the twelve ever feel or experience the healing touch of Jesus. In a frightening episode on the lake they exhibit their lack of faith by showing their fear.[129]

For Mark, the disciples, and specifically the twelve, are an "unbelieving generation." The Marcan Jesus recognizes a lack of allegiance in his disciples and the people of his own home town.[130] "And he was amazed at their lack of faith" (Mark 6:6). "O unbelieving generation how long shall I stay with you? How long shall I put up with you?" (Mark 9:19).

The woman, on the other hand, stands as a bulwark of faith. She exhibits the emotion of fear (Mark 5:33), but is not paralyzed by it. She has an active faith that overcomes such obstacles. Others, like those of Jesus' own home town and the general group of disciples have difficulty exercising this kind of faith. All three Gospels agree that the faith of the woman was the initial cause for her healing.[131]

This theme of faith overcoming the impossible is an important one for the Marcan statement. In times of trouble and economic and political disaster[132] it is faith that makes things happen. "Therefore I tell you, whatever you ask in prayer, believe that you will receive it and it will be yours" (Mark 11:24). "Everything is possible for the person who believes" (Mark 9:23). The community must rely on their own faith since Jesus is no longer with them physically. This belief should be directed toward God.[133] It should be centered in the Gospel.[134] Mark points to woman as possessing this strength of faith. It is to her the community should look to find the kind of faith needed in the new age.[135]

Faith Healer

The faith of the hemorrhaging woman was so strong that the healing appears to be an involuntary act (Mark 5 : 30). According to W. E. Bundy, "The cure is by auto-suggestion: the woman heals herself by her own faith without the conscious cooperation of Jesus."[136] The woman was aware of her physical healing before or at least simultaneously with the report that Jesus felt δύναμιν ἐξελθοῦσαν (Mark 5 : 30). Her healing experience is the only instance of its kind in the Gospel of Mark. For centuries, scholars have similarly attempted to explain away Mark's declaration in this story. Some see magic lurking in the background.[137] The early Gnostics, according to Irenaeus, attached cosmic significance to the touch of this woman. An aeon had been healed by her touch. They felt that she was in grave danger when she touched Jesus because she could have been dissolved in an instant.[138]

The word "power" (δύναμις) is a special word for Mark, exhibiting transcendent and even celestial qualities. It is used for the unusual or supernatural things that happen at the hands of Jesus.[139] The kingdom of God is described as powerful.[140] Using the perfect tense of ἔρχομαι, Mark intimates that the kingdom of God is already present and is continuing into future time (Mark 9 : 1). Cosmic significance surrounds the son of the man who promises to come with great power.[141] The idea of tapping into supernatural strength is definitely at the core of understanding the term δύναμις.[142]

Mark admits that there are other people outside the circles of Jesus who are doing wondrous things called δυνάμεις. Jesus' answer to these workers is, according to Mark, "No one who does a miracle in my name can in the next moment say anything bad against me, for whoever is not against us is for us" (Mark 9 : 39–40). Mark is aggressively pointing out that "power" is not only available to the known worshiping community and the descendents of the twelve but to others also. "Although the conduct of the strange exorcist of Mark 9 : 38ff. par is rooted in a superstitious use of the name so far as he himself and those around him are concerned, Jesus endorses him. His answer implies neither approval nor condemnation of the superstition. With the patience of the truly great He is seeking to lead the disciples out of their self-seeking narrowness."[143]

According to Mark, "Jesus performs miracles διὰ τῶν χειρῶν" (Mark 6 : 2), and "John the Baptist was said to have ἐνεργοῦσιν δυνάμεις ἐν αὐτῷ."[144] Here in Mark 5 : 24–34 it is the woman who faithfully accepts the power. Using the same verb ποιέω as Mark 6 : 5, the Marcan Jesus recognizes the activity of a woman. She is active; he appears to be more passive. He does not touch her; she touches him. She does not continue to seek him out; he looks for her in the crowd (Mark 5:31–32). In Leviticus (LXX), ποιεώ is almost exclusively used of performing sacral duties. Yahweh orders Aaron and sons to do rites like sacrifices and perform atonement for the congregation.[145] In this story the woman performs. There is a mutual happening between the woman and Jesus, and perhaps something beyond Jesus. H. Van der Loos calls it a "divine mystery."[146]

T. J. Weeden compares the woman to the disciples who witnessed the healing activity of Jesus.

> In Mark 5:25 the woman with the hemorrhage recognizes at first sight the healing powers of Jesus which no other physician has—powers so great that even by touching his garments one can be healed (5:28–29). But the disciples, who have accompanied Jesus through all his miraculous activity, are unaware of his power (5:30–31) and respond uncomprehendingly to Jesus' discovery that someone has touched his garments to be healed.[147]

Marie J. Lagrange also points out the ineptitude and shallowness of the disciples who followed Jesus. "La réflexion des disciples n'est pas très respectuese pour Jesus; elle part d'un gros bon sens qui ne pénétre pas l'intention du Maître."[148] The role of the woman is conspicuously positive in relation to the role of those with Jesus. She becomes a recipient and vehicle for "power."

Perhaps Mark is legitimating the role of faith healer within the community. The woman with the flow of blood is an ideal example of one who appropriates power through faith to effect a healing. Jesus' answer to John's question about others performing "powers" other than the accepted circle, enlarges the possibilities of service.[149] The relative pronoun ὅς designates anyone who claims to perform (Mark 9:39). Mark demonstrates an open attitude toward serving members of the community.[150] The woman alone knew the power and its affects upon her body. She had privileged information. She possessed a secret knowledge.

There is ample evidence of faith healers in the New Testament. In the Corinthian list of gifts, χαρίσματα ἰαμάτων is near the top and right underneath is ἐνεργημάτα δυνάμεων.[151] Perhaps both of these qualities or gifts could be attributed to the woman as she drew upon the power within the sphere of Jesus. The twelve were given healing powers, according to Matthew.[152] Mark claims that they anointed the sick.[153] Yet Mark also claims that failure resulted from their attempts to use this healing ability.[154]

Touch is the way that the Marcan Jesus reached out to the sick, demon possessed, and helpless.[155] The woman touched Jesus and became a person who could appropriate the divine power in a positive manner.[156] The worshiping community would always value such people. Jesus' message was, "Go in peace" (Mark 5:34). Mark legitimates a woman with the potential of being an example of a faith healer to the community.

Authentic Model for the Community

THE MODEL OF THE TWELVE IS REJECTED

Mark thinks the twelve failed Jesus. The privileged group produced one traitor, Judas[157] and one who openly denied his relationship with Jesus, Peter.[158] Mark uses the verb $\dot{\alpha}\nu\alpha\theta\epsilon\mu\alpha\tau\dot{\iota}\zeta\epsilon\iota\nu$ with reference to Peter and his relationship with Jesus.[159] "In 8:35 and 38 we learn that whoever would save his life (at the expense of the gospel) will lose it and that whoever is presently ashamed of Jesus will become an object of shame at the last judgement. By these criteria, should not the eleven be finally condemned? For at 14:50 they forsake their Master and flee for their lives and at 14:71 Peter is ashamed of his past association with the Messiah."[160]

If the twelve failed Jesus and did not carry out the intended program, then who is Mark legitimating as model and role determiner, as well as project director, for the developing community? Answers to these questions will ultimately be found by isolating positive remarks made about women within the Marcan complex.

The twelve, according to Mark, do not understand Jesus' earthly intentions. His life of suffering and death are rejected by the group.[161] James and John lobbied for a political favor from Jesus. They wanted to administer to the new realm at his side.[162] Jesus negated their ambitions and his reply was, according to Mark, "These places belong to those for whom they have been prepared."[163] It is not clear whether Mark is advocating a change or that a change has already taken place within the community. The author is confident of at least one thing; the community is in a state of flux and the people need a new mindset in order to continue. The author emphasizes the positive nature of belief throughout the Gospel. "Believe that you will receive and it will be yours" (Mark 11:24). The present time is the beginning of a new age.[164] There are indications that the contractions of birth have already begun.

The newly formed group that was emerging within the community of Mark included women. Mark mentions this at the beginning and the end of the Gospel.[165] This inclusio sets the pace for the entire Gospel. A woman is always near, yet not always at the center of, activity. She is there in the crowds, as disciple, as healed and healer, and as grave-preparer. She becomes the authentic model for the emerging community.

Woman: Teacher of the Twelve and Others

The primary teaching example for the community is Jesus Himself. Women above all others, follow the teachings of Jesus and are found to be the proper examples of His life and traditions. Mark 5 : 24–34 is only one instance used by Mark to teach his audience that women follow in the teaching steps of Jesus.[166] What is the teaching role of Jesus? "In giving Jesus this role as prophet-teacher, . . . Mark presents him as the one who interprets the will of God to the convenant people. The new convenant demands a new appropriation of the Law (Jer. 31 : 33) by God's new people to whom he grants a new understanding ('new heart')."[167]

Mark located 5 : 24–34 within the teaching section of the Gospel.[168] The miraculous happening to the woman is situated before the general group of disciples (Mark 5 : 31) with the inner three (Mark 5 : 37), a thronging crowd (Mark 5 : 21, 27), people who knew Jesus (Mark 5 : 35), and the presence of a synagogue chief named Jairus and his servants (Mark 5 : 22). The only representative groups that are absent are the Pharisees and the rest of the Jewish establishment.

Jairus[169] is an important character in the story of this woman. "The name Jair occurs in the Old Testament. (Num. 32 : 41; Judges 10 : 3f) In Esther 2 : 5 the LXX uses the Hellenized form that we have here. The suggestion that the name was chosen for its symbolic appropriation to this story (he enlightens—or he awakes) is most unlikely, for it is not Jairus who either awakens or is awakened."[170]

C. E. B. Cranfield is in error at this point. Jairus is indeed an appropriate name. It is he who is the enlightened one and his name fits him well. Jairus begs Jesus to come and heal his daughter (Mark 5 : 22–23). The apparent death of the girl is the result of her illness (Mark 5 : 35). Jairus, even with such stature as a synagogue chief, did not know how to tap into the power that was associated with or within the person of Jesus (Mark 5:21–23). In this sense he is not enlightened. The woman, who would have been an outcast in his own synagogue because of being ritually defiled, is the one who appropriates the healing power for herself. The ruler is immediately recognized in the narrative; the woman must aggressively seek out Jesus. She is healed secretly and does not desire public recognition. The ruler needs the personal touch and presence of Jesus in order for a healing to take place. The woman reaches out and takes of the power within Jesus. It is Jairus who learns. The woman already knows.

The pericope details that Jesus brought the woman forward. He recognized the feminine touch (Mark 5:32). "She fell at his feet and told him the whole truth" (Mark 5:33). She is an example of faith to everyone. Her work of faith was displayed before the entire community. All watch her as an example of a faithful follower.

In a characteristic Marcan style,[171] teaching takes place through example and activity. Unlike Matthew and sometimes Luke, Mark does not explicitly tell the audience what to think or believe. The author tells a story and uses the characters in that story as a means of communication. What each character does is important to the interpretation of any narrative.[172] A woman's life should be watched and followed. The woman with a flow of blood aggressively reached out. She is not shy.[173] Mark characterizes her motives as open and not self-seeking. She has no dream of restoring her lost income. She has no ideas of revenge, although the tradition does exhibit hostility toward the sacral-medical field. After the healing, according to Mark, she does not center the attention upon herself. She resumes her place in the thronging crowd. The community should be well aware that this beaten woman was one of the most unlikely candidates for inclusion into the circles of Jesus. She had no rank, riches, or political power. If she had any gift at all it must be found within her own self. She is an example of all those who seek entrance into the Christian community who can only offer themselves as a service to the rest.

WOMAN AS PROCLAIMER OF TRUTH

The honesty and sincerity of the woman is characterized by Mark as she volunteers to tell Jesus the whole story. Jesus seeks out the woman. This is very uncharacteristic of Jesus' activities in other stories. This περιεβλέπετο legitimates the woman in the community (Mark 5:32). The congregation witnesses the Divine reaching out to the woman. She, according to the text, "told him all the truth" (Mark 5:33). Some religious leaders would question whether any woman was capable of truth.[174] Indeed, Matthew omits this whole section of the woman speaking personally with Jesus before the crowd.[175] Luke attempts to interpret what $\pi\widehat{\alpha}\sigma\alpha\nu\ \tau\grave{\eta}\nu\ \dot{\alpha}\lambda\acute{\eta}\theta\epsilon\iota\alpha\nu$ is for the Lucan congregation. "She declared in the presence of all the people why she had touched him, and how she had been immediately healed" (Luke 8:47). What did the woman say to Jesus? What is the content of $\dot{\alpha}\lambda\acute{\eta}\theta\epsilon\iota\alpha$? Mark does not tell the audience. Other than this passage, Mark only uses $\dot{\alpha}\lambda\acute{\eta}\theta\epsilon\iota\alpha$ and $\dot{\alpha}\lambda\eta\theta\acute{\eta}\varsigma$ with reference to Jesus. The content of the word must be found in the person of Jesus. "Teacher, we know you are a man of integrity . . . you teach the way of God in accordance with truth" (Mark 12:14). A scribe testifies to the truth-speaking nature of Jesus.[176] The writer to the Ephesians agrees with Mark's opinion of Jesus' person. "You, however, did not come to know Christ that way. Surely you heard of him and were taught in him in accordance with the truth that is in Jesus."[177] The woman in this miracle story, is following the example set by the leader of the emerging group, Jesus.

The readers of Mark's work would associate truth with Jesus. But what is the essential meaning of truth? $Ἀλήθεια$, to the Hebrew mind, would suggest in certain contexts the elements of a "reality that is binding,"[178] such as trust, confidence, genuineness, veracity, and reliability. It is also a legal term.[179] The person who is righteous is therefore truthful.[180] The prophet Hosea complained that he could find no truth in the land.[181] He maintains "that in every sphere of life truthfulness grows out of unerring knowledge of God's will, and that such knowledge is for its part an actualisation of truthfulness."[182]

For the Hellenist, $\dot{\alpha}\lambda\acute{\eta}\theta\epsilon\iota\alpha$ would bring to mind nonconcealment.[183] It was the "actual state of affairs." "The only one thing which is truly $\dot{\alpha}\lambda\eta\theta\acute{\epsilon}\varsigma$ is that which always is, the divine. . . ."[184] The Gospel of John would agree as the writer attempts to convince the audience that Jesus is "the Way, the Truth, and the Life."[185]

Mark is confident that the woman is capable of such lofty expectations. She was in contact with the divine.[186] She spoke to the divine. Her response could be no less. Were the twelve capable of such honesty? Certainly Judas would have failed this test and Peter, according to Mark, actually lied.[187] Trustworthiness is found within the person of Jesus and within the speech and life of the healed woman. She is an example to the community. Her life can be trusted. Constance F. Parvey speaks of the new role of women within the Christian community. "As Jewish culture held onto its traditions regarding woman, and as Hellenistic culture was carving out new definitions, these converged into a new configuration in the primitive church. Because of this sense of the urgency of the end times, a new and radically equivalent role of woman and men together in Christ was forged."[188]

WOMAN AS GENUINE SERVANT

The verb "to serve" ($\delta\iota\alpha\kappa o\nu\acute{\epsilon}\omega$) constitutes an important theme in Mark's outline of the life of Jesus. The Gospel begins, reaches a climax, and ends on a note of service.[189] Service is the key to admission in the new regime begun with Jesus.[190] Service can be summed up by three central concepts repeated often throughout the Gospel: suffering ($\pi\acute{\alpha}\sigma\chi\omega$), following ($\dot{\alpha}\kappa o\lambda o\upsilon\theta\acute{\epsilon}\omega$), and denying ($\dot{\alpha}\rho\nu\acute{\epsilon}o\mu\alpha\iota$).[191] The authentic followers of the leader of this new dissenting movement must embody these qualities. The key verse of the Gospel is as follows: "For even the son of man did not come to be served, but to serve and give his life a ransom for the many."[192] "The route to power is here seen as utterly paradoxical: the role of $\delta\iota\acute{\alpha}\kappa\theta o\nu o\varsigma$ or $\delta o\hat{\upsilon}\lambda o\varsigma$—acting not merely in a servile function but as a slave—which leads to death on behalf of others."[193]

The ideal example of a servant is found in the person of Jesus. Jesus was a servant in a variety of ways. He was quick to please both his own disciples and potential followers. Mark's Jesus says: "What do you want me to do for you?"[194] to both Bartimaeus and two of his chosen disciples, James and John. The two brothers' attitudes toward serving emphasize the stark difference between Jesus and themselves. They desired political power. Jesus' humble question demonstrates the proper approach to Christian living. Instead of desiring political clout, the community should desire to help one another, to give to one another, and even to heal one another.

The opposite of service and therefore the opposite of those who claim allegiance with Jesus is expressed in Mark 10:42. "You know that those who are regarded as rulers of the Gentiles lord it over them and their high officials exercise authority over them" (Mark 10:42).

"Lording it over them" ($\kappa\alpha\tau\alpha\ \kappa\upsilon\rho\iota\epsilon\acute{\upsilon}o\upsilon\sigma\iota\nu$),[195] implies subjugation, dominion, and mastery. This is not the way of those who claim to follow Jesus. "Not so with you. Instead, whoever wants to become among you must be your servant, and whoever wants to be servant must be slave to all" (Mark 10:44).

The words *to serve* resound with meniality. Greeks desired to be served not to serve. "How can a man be happy when he has to serve someone?"[196] Dignity was forfeited if one stooped to the level of serving tables. "Service is not one of the powers which hold heaven and earth together, and it does not lead to sacrifice."[197] The Greeks saw no freedom in serving others.

One must be willing to be humble in order to join the ranks of the followers to Jesus. The servant model is provided for all. The twelve and "his own" disciples do not fit the model. They were sent out to perform specific functions: "to preach and to have authority to drive out demons."[198] Mark records that they preached a sermon of repentence, cast out demons, and anointed the sick.[199] Yet their primary role does not seem to be found in the area of "serving." The word is never used of the twelve nor do the twelve perform servile functions. Not one of the twelve is ever singled out for his serviceability to the community. They do not follow the path outlined by Jesus of suffering and denial of self. To whom does Mark point as the model of servanthood? Mark 15:41 provides one answer. "Some women were watching from a distance. . . . In Galilee these women had followed him (ἠκολούθουν) and served him (διηκόνουν) and many others (ἄλλαι) came up with him to Jerusalem."

The key words in this pericope are "followed him" and "served him." An anonymous group of women are not only uplifted by Mark, but by other Gospel writers also.

Both Matthew and Luke preserve the traditions about the existence of a group of women who traveled with Jesus, listened to his sermons, and witnessed his activities. "Many women were there, watching from a distance. They had followed Jesus from Galilee to care for his needs."[200] Matthew thinks the women followed Jesus to especially meet his personal needs. Luke suggests that the women served the whole group including the twelve. Their assistance was probably monetary. According to Luke 8:3, they served them "out of their own things."

Matthew and Luke also view the act of service as one aspect of discipleship. "For who is greater, the one who is at the table or the one who serves? Is it not the one who is at the table. But I am among you as one who serves."[201]

Matthew reiterates this same value system. "The greatest among you will be your servant."[202] Thus the synoptics agree on the women and the value of such service-oriented activities.

Servanthood and the role of women is not limited to a single reference in Mark. One of the first miracles performed by Jesus was the healing of Peter's mother-in-law. The text reads: "So he went to her, took her hand and helped her. The fever left her and she began to wait on them" (Mark 1:31). At first glance this miracle story seems to have selfish undertones. The woman is healed so that the disciples and Jesus do not have to perform menial tasks. Howard C. Kee sees another role here.

There is a hint of another king of role in the Markan community. That of διάκονος. It is possible that Peter's mother-in-law, who on recovering from her fever ministered to the needs of Jesus and the disciples (1:31) was merely fulfilling the obligations of village hospitality, but the use of what was to become a technical term in early Christian usage (διακόνει) at least raises the possibility—perhaps reinforced by the appearance of the verb in the imperfect—that she took care of their needs on a regular basis.[203]

This woman performs as a servant. The text reads διακόνει αὐτοῖς. The term αὐτοῖω is plural. Yet in all three Gospels that reproduce this story there are variants that point only to Jesus as the one she served.[204] If the αὐτῷ is a better reading, then the serving could be equated to the following. The ambiguity does not limit the significance of this passage. Whether it was service to Jesus alone or to the others, she is still an example of service to the community. Mark does not elaborate on the content of the service. It is enough to point to the woman who carries out such activities in the presence of Jesus.

The New Testament abounds with examples of servanthood. Paul, in his letters to several churches, points out that he was served.[205] Timothy and Erastus are called servants of Paul.[206] And the word finds its way between προφητεία and διδασκαλία in Romans.[207] Matthew attempts to describe the content of serving as providing shelter, food, and drink to strangers, the sick, and prisoners.[208] "The term thus comes to have the full sense of active Christian love for the neighbor and as such it is a mark of true discipleship of Jesus."[209] Yet Mark takes this active love one step further. Those who qualify as leader-examples of the new regime, are the ones to whom the community should look for guidance since the twelve and their descendents as well as others have not carried out the original plans and activities of Jesus.

Service is also viewed from a cosmic perspective. Positive help comes from those who reside outside the mundane world. According to Mark, the angels are the first to serve Jesus. "He was with wild animals, and angels attended him."[210] Who are these angles? Chapter 1 of Mark seems to apply the name of "angel" or "messenger" to John the Baptist.[211] All of the other references to angels in Mark's Gospel point to a cosmic origin. They are from heaven.[212] Their duties are to serve Jesus. They are by his side even until the end of time "when he comes in his Father's glory with the holy angels" (Mark 8:38). The angels do not have foreknowledge,[213] but they do assist Jesus in the gathering of the elect.[214]

It would be presumptuous to say that Mark is equating woman with angels. What Mark is saying is that the role Jesus prescribed for his followers is service. Woman is found performing such functions within the Gospel. Therefore, woman and her function as servant is analogous to the function of the angels. The philological similarities are there. Both the terrestrial beings and woman can be compared in their roles and relationships to Jesus. Woman stands as a role determiner for the community as she stands beside Jesus even until the end of his earthly life following and providing assistance.

Following (ἀκολουθέω) is another criteria for one who would be a model or role determiner for the community. According to Mark, Jesus extended a personal invitation to Simon, Andrew, and Levi to follow him.[215] Many others followed Jesus, including a huge crowd,[216] disciples,[217] Bartimaeus,[218] and even tax collectors and sinners.[219] There are no accounts preserving traditions of personal invitations to a variety of women within Mark's account. It is correct that Jesus in Mark 5 : 24–34 looked for the woman who touched him. But there are no direct words spoken to her in the narrative that include the words "to follow." The story does imply by Jesus' actions that He gave her an invitation to become a follower.

Mark reports that Peter complained that they had left everything to follow Jesus.[220] This negative valuation of leaving material goods is viewed again by Mark when the author relates an incident with a potential disciple. The mandate for discipleship was, "Give to the poor and come, follow me" (Mark 10 : 21). A prerequisite for any leader within the community was a de-emphasis on materialism and love for those who were without material support.[221] Some who followed feared.[222] Yet in the end it is only the women followers who are present at Jesus' death and apparent resurrection. They remained until the last breath. Peter attempted to maintain his position near Jesus as he followed from a distance,[223] but he too left in the final scene when Jesus was murdered.

Thus far, women meet two criteria for leadership within the new regime: they served Jesus and they followed him until the end. Jesus' additional requirement, according to Mark, was to suffer. Each community member must "deny self and take up his own cross and follow me" (Mark 9 : 35). Jesus' own programmed role was "to suffer many things" and then to die after his rejection (Mark 9 : 31–32). Woman is again linked in this activity. The woman with the flow the blood in 5 : 24–34 is characterized as "suffering" under the hands of many physicians (Mark 5 : 26). In no instance do the twelve suffer. πάσχω and πολλά[224] are only used of Jesus and woman. Mark recognizes the suffering of this woman in society as similar to that which Jesus experienced before his death. Another philological parallelism is αἷμα (Mark 5 : 25), which is only used of Jesus' own blood, the blood of the new covenant, and the woman with the flow of blood.[225] Other words only used of Jesus and this woman are σῶμα,[226] μάστιξ, and μαστιγόω.[227] Mark recognizes that the masses are also beaten like Jesus and the woman.[228] Blood, body, suffering, and scourging, are too obvious to overlook when they are employed in the context of only Jesus and woman. Mark compares Jesus with woman and clearly points out through the language that the woman has suffered as Jesus, but she has survived. Therefore, she qualifies as model and leader of the emerging community. The woman with the flow of blood serves as a symbol for the suffering Jesus and all suffering peoples. Woman, above all, understands what it means to suffer and thus can identify best with Jesus who suffered to the point of death.

Another prerequisite for leadership is found in the verb "to deny" (ἀρνέσμαι). "If anyone would come after me, that person must deny himself and take up his cross and follow me" (Mark 8 : 34). A potential follower of Jesus found the requirements for discipleship too steep. That person could not give everything to the poor (Mark 10 : 17–22). Peter complained of his monetary loss and categorically denied his allegiance to Jesus at the most crucial moment in his life.[229] In Mark, woman never denies Jesus; instead, she sets an example of personal denial for the worshiping community.

It is not the rich who are praised by Mark for their large donations to the temple treasury. It is the poor, and specifically a widow, who Jesus points to as a sacrificial model. For the benefit of his disciples, the Marcan Jesus says: "I tell you the truth, this poor widow has put more into the treasury than all the others. They all gave out of their wealth; but she, out of her poverty, put in everthing—all she had to live on."[230]

The woman gave all of her earthly possessions. Mark does not use βίος again.[231] Kee believes that this de-emphasis on materialism is an antidote to a tendency in Mark's own community to prefer honor and rank over the individuality of the person. The parable of the widow's mite "is simply a warning about the hypocritical disparity between the pious ostentation of the scribes and their inward secret avarice and inhumanity."[232]

This parable may be directed toward the scribes, but the context includes the disciples who are listening and therefore learning. The saying is directed to anyone within the community who values money over life. The widow, who is one of those poor who should have been supported by a potential disciple, ironically is the one who knows how to give best.[233] She is an example of one, like Jesus, who gives up all because of her beliefs. She is following the maxim set by Jesus. "Deny yourself."[234] Her endeavor exhibits complete and total generosity.

Serving means denying, and for Mark denial comes in the areas of money and one's own life. Chapter 14 situates Jesus at Simon's house, a leper.[235] A nameless woman, like the anonymous woman who came out of the crowd to touch Jesus, now anoints his body with an expensive perfume. Who was this woman? According to the Gospel of John, she was the sister of Martha, called Mary.[236] Luke calls her a sinner.[237] Those attending a dinner at Simon's house treated her indignantly.[238] Matthew says it is the disciples who criticized her;[239] John says it was Judas,[240] and Luke claims it was a Pharisee, the owner of the house.[241] This attitude reminds one of the disciples when they attempted to keep the children[242] away from Jesus, and Peter when he contradicted Jesus' prediction of the passion.[243] According to Mark, Jesus recognizes the woman's sacrifice and praises her. "She had done a beautiful thing to me. . . . She did what she could" (Mark 14:6, 8). These phrases parallel a similar incident that centered upon the widow's sacrifice.[244] The woman chose to give of herself to Jesus, and thus to the Christian community. She supported Jesus by her show of affection, her willingness to spend her money on the oil for Jesus, and her place of service before him. The Marcan Jesus interprets her action in a serving capacity. It is she who has prepared his body for burial.

This caretaker service of preparation of the body for burial, according to Mark, was performed by the disciples of the teacher. At the death of John the Baptist, ". . . John's disciples came and took his body and laid it in a tomb" (Mark 6:20). The twelve were not present at Jesus' death or burial. Those who did remain, were the women who had followed him since the early days of Galilee.[245] Tradition ascribes the handling of the body of Jesus to an unknown, Joseph of Arimathea, apparently a believer and perhaps a disciple, and also to the women.[246] Neither participant is singled out as one who had special authority or power in the early regime. According to Austin M. Farrer, the woman who anointed Jesus is very similar to the nameless woman of 5:24–34. "There does indeed appear to be some sort of echo of the woman who touched Christ (v. 25–34) in the woman who anointed Christ. Both women have the boldness to touch Christ's sacred person without asking leave, the one with the hand, the other with her unguent. Both women are defended or encouraged by Christ in respect of what they have done."[247]

A woman therefore qualifies as an authentic role determiner for the community. She stands as a bulwark of faith, example of faith healer, proclaimer of truth, and genuine servant, as she lives out the roles of following, suffering, and denying. Where the twelve fail, the women succeed.

Woman: Voice of God to the Community

A CONSISTENT VEHICLE

The woman of 5:24–34 is highlighted by Mark for her consistency

and continuity. The hemorrhaging woman had an illness that lasted
twelve years (Mark 5 : 24). The years did not stop her quest for health.
She exhibited the courage to pursue medical and even supernatural
help. She did not give up. Her solid constitution is emphasized by
Mark indirectly as the author describes all of her ordeals. She suffered
monetary and physical losses (Mark 5 : 26). Even though her condition deteriorated, her search did not. Her persistence is equaled only
to that of the Syro-phoenician woman.[248] There are many similarities
between the events surrounding these two traditions about women.[249]
Both women were introduced to Jesus through healing.[250] Both fall
before Jesus.[251] Jesus holds a conversation with both women, which
was atypical for a Jew.[252] Both women exhibit an enterprising quick-
wittedness in their understanding of truth.[253] Jesus assists both of
them and thus meets their needs.[254] Both would be considered ritually
unclean by Jewish cultic standards.[255] The nameless women in Mark
5 : 24–34 has no home to identify her nationality. Her stigma was
centered in a biologic dysfunction. The Syro-Phoenician woman was
considered to be a "pagan," an outsider, and thus unclean.[256] T. A.
Burkill recognizes Mark's deliberate itinerary of Jesus to non-Jewish
territory as an abrogation of the purity laws.

> The introduction of the northerly journey at Mark 7 : 24 is probably moti-
> vated by a desire on the evangelist's part to provide an illustration of
> Jesus' freedom from the regulations regarding ceremonial cleanness. Being
> unhampered by the ancient laws of external purity, the Lord can move
> into foreign territory, enter a house there and communicate saving grace
> to a pagan, thereby anticipating the church's mission to the Gentile
> world.[257]

Burkill's observations are astute. His perspective is somewhat different from that evidenced by this research. The Gentile mission is not
anticipated; it has happened and is happening. This story, like the
miracle story of the woman with the flow of blood, is a remnant of a
dissension-tradition that arose as Christianity was forced away from
its Judaic roots. It is true that Mark emphasizes her race. She is a
non-Jew. Yet the author purposefully chooses to preserve a tradition
about a woman. Why did the author choose not to catalog a story
about a Gentile man? The answer is obvious. The woman was important, and especially a woman who was Gentile. Like the woman of
5 : 24–34, Mark labels this woman as example to the community. Her
persistence and understanding of the divine intentions of Jesus[258]
qualify her to be an example in the community. Although Jesus
negated her first request, she did not let that stop her.[259] She had the

courage to illicit from Jesus the healing power that she believed was within him.

Consistency and continuity are again exemplified in the women who did not run away when Jesus was arrested. They did not deny nor betray him. They remained loyal followers.[260] Woman is reliable. She will take an active part in the life of the church from its inception and into the future, says Mark.[261]

Mark points out that woman can also physically outlive men. Consider the controversy story about the woman who had seven hundreds (Mark 12:18–27). The point of this story seems to be that in the Resurrection there will be no need for sex differentiation. E. and F. Stagg believe that Mark is referring to deathlessness. Since all will live eternally, there is no need for reproduction, and thus different sexes.[262] Kee views the story as pointing to a life commitment that is seen to take a negative view of marriage within the community.[263] Paul K. Jewett differs with the traditional view of an androgynous heaven.

> There is no good reason to argue, however, that it should be the other way around: marriage should be in terms of male/female distinction; the latter being the more fundamental reality. If this is so, then it does not follow that a life without marriage and procreation is a life that knows no fellowship of male and female. In this regard it must be remembered that Jesus did not say that in heaven there will be no men and women, but only no marriage and giving in marriage."[264]

Some scholars think that Mark is militating against a Jewish view of a "male" only heaven. Augustine had similar ideas on the subject. "The Lord denied that there would be in the resurrection, not women but marriages; and he uttered this denial in circumstances in which the question mooted would have been more easily and speedily solved by denying that the female sex should exist, if this had in truth been fore known by him."[265]

Some manuscripts add to 12:23 the phrase, "When men rise from the dead,"[266] which does point to the possibility of a belief in a unisex heaven.

Women will also rise. He is the god of the living.[267] The importance of this story to the existing community was that woman will survive. She can live longer than seven husbands and thus she exhibits a potential endurance and strength of body and character. There is no comparable story emphasizing the endurance or strength of man. Woman's identity is not limited to her potential as a marriage partner; nor is her function as human being obsolete when she can no longer function as such.

An Authentic Vehicle

As the worshipers of Apollo looked to the Oracle at Delphi,[268] so it is to woman that Mark looks for an authentic voice from the divine. "Then the woman, knowing what happened to her, came and fell at his feet and, trembling with fear, told him the whole truth (Mark 5:33).

There is a mutual happening between the woman with the flow of blood and Jesus. She is individually recognized before the crowd and the witnessing community. Her response is fear and trembling. This anxious reaction is interpreted in a variety of ways. It could be rooted in her sinful condition. H. B. Swete and A. M. Hunter think that she may be presumed to be confessing her sinful activities and condition to Jesus.[269] Some think it to be a natural reaction to the events that have just occurred, namely, her healing.

According to Jewish law, no woman (by herself) was called as a witness. Generally, her judgment was thought to be precarious.[270] Here the woman is brought for the purpose of telling the truth, whatever it might be, before the entire crowd. In the Greco-Roman world, the emotions and bodily reactions of fear and trembling were usually interpreted as signs of the presence of God. The Oracle at Delphi would twist and turn to the point of unconsciousness and sometimes even death.[271]

According to H. Balz, fear ". . . is for Mark a decisive reaction to the deeds and destiny of Jesus understood as the intervention of divine activity."[272] This fear can lead to δοξάζειν of God (Mark 2:12). The noun φόβος is rarely used by Mark.[273] The author prefers to use a verb rather than a noun in order to express an active idea of fear. Fear does not settle down upon someone; it is a direct response to an event or situation. φοβέομαι is consistently used in the context of response to Jesus' activities or an uncontrollable situation like fearing a riotous crowd.[274] φοβέομαι is also used throughout the New Testament as a response to the Almighty who comes in contact with the mundane world.[275] The writer of the Book of Revelation singles out those who fear God.

> Praise our God
> all you his servants,
> you who fear him
> both great and small (Revelation 19:5).

Fear is one proper response to God. In Mark, fear comes automatically in response to divine activity. It is not commanded, but is demonstrated in the lives of the Marcan characters. "Expressions of fear and astonishment serve to emphasize the revelatory content and christological significance of many incidents in the Synoptic gospels .... The term also serves, as customarily in ancient miracle stories, to indicate the accreditation of the miracle by the spectators."[276]

What is Mark saying about the woman with the flow of blood? It appears that she, like the sacred twelve, also exhibited a proper response to Jesus.[277] The author says most definitely that a woman can experience and intelligibly discern the presence of God. Therefore, she is not to be restricted in her activities before God. If a woman can kneel in the presence of Jesus, she can also participate in religious activities, suggests Mark. If a woman can speak to Jesus before all the worshiping and witnessing crowd, then it is a fair inference that Mark would not preclude her role as communicator in the community. In any case, the radically different view of a woman's religious prerogative from that held in traditional Jewish circles, appears to legitimate a woman as a voice of God to the community.

This is not the only example of a woman who has direct contact with the divine. Mark even records that she was given commands to carry out. The twelve were chosen in order "to preach and have authority to drive out demons" (Mark 3:15, 6:7). Jesus commanded them to go. So also is a woman commanded to go. The woman in 5:24–34 is commanded to "go in peace." This phrase is spoken to no one else in the Marcan dialogue. This was a familiar Old Testament and New Testament phrase.[278] Yet it is odd that it is placed at the beginning of one miracle about a woman and at the end of another. The verb "to go" is active. The phrase could be translated, "Depart unto a peaceful existence," or "Depart in order to bring peace."[279]

Again it is woman who received that last divine communication. Standing at the threshold of the empty tomb are the women. Mark places them at the most important junctures of the traditions. They are told by an anonymous person: "He is risen. He is not here. See the place where they laid him. But go, tell his disciples and Peter" (Mark 3:21). Ironically, it is now woman who is chosen to bring the earth-changing message to the disciples and Peter. By abondoning Jesus and denying their allegiance, the inner circle forfeited their privileged place of being the first to hear about the resurrected Christ. Woman becomes a voice of God to the community.

The response of the women to the situation is the proper response to the divine they feared.[280] They recognized the presence of God. Their message is to "his disciples" and Peter.[281] The αὐτοῦ is masculine and it is difficult to translate. Does Mark mean Jesus' disciples or Peter's disciples? In any case, the spotlight has fallen from Peter, the leader of

the twelve, and now it is a group of women who stand as intermediaries between the divine and the emerging community.

The stance of woman is not an unusual one, according to Mark.
The Syro-Phoenician mother correctly terms Jesus "Lord." "St. Mark
never used κυρίος in narrative and never employs the vocative except
here in the woman's reply. . . ."[282]

This revelatory statement can be paralleled with Peter's recognition
of Christ.[283] Peter knew the proper words to say, but the content of his
understanding of those words was in gross error. It is to Peter, after
his apparent magnificent revelatory statement, that Jesus says, "Out
of my sight, Satan" (Mark 8:33). To the Syro-Phoenician woman no
such harsh words are spoken. She perceived the content and person of
Jesus. Her display of humility demonstrated that recognition.[284] What
the twelve and especially Peter said, with their lips, did not always
translate into their lives.

> It would seem, therefore, to be part of the evangelist's doctrinal intent to
> suggest that the Syrophoenician woman, in addressing Jesus as Lord is a
> presage of things to come. Even during the earthly ministry, before the
> Messiah's final rejection by his own people, a representative of the re-
> ligiously unprivileged world can, in a moment of inspiration, recognize
> Jesus as the Lord of the Christian cultus who offers himself as the bread of
> life for the salvation of humanity.[285]

Mark categorically denies that leadership and the voice of God
should come from the traditional hierarchy centered in the twelve and
especially in Peter. The voice of God should come from those who
recognize the divine and seek to implement the divine's policies in
their lives. The women who recognized and followed Jesus until the
end were "preparing the way of the Lord" (Mark 1:2–3).

As Mark intimates that Jesus commanded the woman with the flow
of blood to go, and the women at the empty tomb to go, so Mark says
that women are inextricably bound in the dissemination of the Gospel. F. W. Danker correctly recognizes that the "theme of 1:1 has
come full circle" in chapter 16.[286] "The beginning of the gospel of
Jesus Christ. . . ." (Mark 1:1) finds its actual beginning in the narrative with the women of chapters 15 and 16. The content of this Gospel
will also recognize woman says, Mark. "I tell you the truth, wherever
the gospel is preached throughout the world, what she has done will
also be told in memory of her (Mark 14:9).

Much debate surrounds the last phrase of the Gospel. "And they
said nothing to anyone, for they feared."[287] Woman says very little
verbally within the Gospel itself. Her life is what speaks for her. This
phrase is a mystery. Perhaps Mark is again using irony. Ironically, in

the early days of the primitive church the women said nothing. Now in the later days it is to them that the church looks for guidance. Woman never acts against the divine will in the rest of the Gospel. It is illogical to think that this phrase suggests that the women did not carry out their appointed task. Again Mark could be negating the spoken word. For Mark, preaching was important, but actions always seemed to be the desired objective for any disciple. Woman does act and live according to the divine plan.

In summary, Mark intimates that it is the woman who legitimately perceives, recognizes, and intuitively understands, the voice of God. She is more capable, honest, and exhibits the kind of faithful life needed by the emerging communities. Woman is, and should be, God's representative to the people. Therefore, "Go in peace."

Notes

Preface

1. Anne M. Bennett, "Overcoming the Biblical and Traditional Subordination of Women," *Radical Religion* 1 (1974): 28, Irene Brennan, "Women in the Gospels," *New Blackfriars* 52 (1971): 291–99; Raymond E. Brown, "Roles of Women in the Fourth Gospel," *Theological Studies* 36 (1975): 688–99; Elizabeth Clark and Herbert W. Richardson, *Women and Religion: A Feminist Sourcebook of Christian Thought* (New York: Harper, 1977); Elizabeth S. Fiorenza, "Women in the Pre-Pauline and Pauline Churches," *Union Seminary Quarterly Review* 33 (1978): 153–66 and "The Study of Women in Early Christianity," *Proceedings of the College Theology Society's 1977 Annual Meeting*; J. Massyngberde Ford, "Social Consciousness in the New Testament: Jesus and Paul, a Contrast," *New Blackfriars* 57 (1976): 244–54; Peter Ketter, *Christ and Womankind*, trans. Isabel McHugh (Westminster, Md.: Newman Press, 1952); W. A. Meeks, "The Image of the Androgyne: Some Uses of a Symbol in Earliest Christianity," *History of Religion* 13 (1974): 169–74; Constance F. Parvey, "The Theology and Leadership of Women in the New Testament," in *Religion and Sexism*, ed. R. R. Ruether (New York: Simon & Schuster, 1974); Letha Scanzoni and Nancy Hardesty, *All We're Meant to Be: A Biblical Approach to Women's Liberation* (Waco, Tex.: Word, Inc., 1974); Leonard Swidler, "Greco-Roman Feminism and the Reception of the Gospel," in *Traditio-Krisis-Renovatio aus theologischer Sicht*, Festschrift Winfried Zeller sum 65, eds. Brend Jaspert und Rudolph Mohr (Marburg, W. Germany: N. G. Elwert, 1976) and "Jesus and His Encounter with Women," *African Ecclesiastical Review* 13 (1971): 290–300, and "Jesus Was a Feminist," *Southeast Asian Journal of Theology* 13 (1971): 102–10; Evelyn and Frank Stagg, *Women in the World of Jesus* (Philadelphia: Westminister Press, 1978); and Phyllis Trible, "Depatriarchalizing in Biblical Interpretation," *Journal of the American Academy of Religion* 41 (1973): 30–47.

2. Martin Dibelius, *From Tradition to Gospel* (New York: Scribner, 1965); Rudolph Bultmann, *The History of the Synoptic Tradition*, trans. John Marsh (Oxford: Basil Blackwell, 1963).

3. For studies on the synoptic problem and the dating of Mark, see Werner G. Kümmel, *Introduction to the New Testament*, trans. Howard C. Kee (New York: Abington Press, 1973), pp. 35–97. He says, "Most scholars assign a date in the years 64–70, since the destruction of Jerusalem in the year 70 is mentioned not ambiguously, ..." p. 98. See also Willie Marxsen, *Mark the Evangelist*, trans. James Boyce (Nashville, Tenn.: Abington, 1969).

4. Ibid.

5. John Gager, *Kingdom and Community: The Social World of Early Christianity* (Englewood Cliffs, N. J.: Prentice-Hall, 1975), pp. 11 ff.

6. *The New International Version: Interlinear Greek-English New Testament*, ed. Alfred Marshall (Grand Rapids, Mich.: Zondervan Publishing House, 1976); and *The Jerusalem Bible*, ed. Alexander Jones (New York: Doubleday, 1966).

Chapter 1. Survey

1. Philip Schaff and Henry Wace, *A Select Library of Nicene and Post Nicene Fathers of the Christian Church*, second series, 14 vols. *The Seven Ecumenical Councils* (Grand Rapids, Mich.: Eerdmans, 1956, 1979), 14:600. For the text see William Beveridge. Συνοδικόν *sive Padectae Canonum SS. Apostolorum, et Conciliorum ab Ecclesia Graeca Receptorum*, 2 vols. (Oxonii: E. Theatro Sheldoniano, 1877).

2. Wace, *The Seven Ecumenical Councils*, p. 591.

3. Ibid., p. 600.

4. *A General Biographical Dictionary*, 1851 ed., s.v. "Balsamon."

5. Schaff and Wace, *Nicene and Post Nicene Fathers*, 14:600. The text is unclear as to who abstracted this statement. It could be a translation of W. Beveridge's Συνοδικού, or it could be by John Johnson in *The Clergyman's Vade-mecum* (London: n.p., 1714).

6. Leviticus 15:9.

7. Marie Liguori Ewald, ed. and trans. *The Homilies of St. Jerome*, 2 vols. (Washington D.C.: Catholic University Press, 1966), 2:148. For the text see D. Germanus Morin, ed., *S. Hieronymi Presbyteri: Tractatus sive Homiliae in Psalmos* (St. Jerome: Homilies of St. Jerome), in *Marci Evangelium Aliaque varia Argumenta* (Turnholti: Typographi Brepols Editores Pontificii, 1958), p. 470.

8. Ewald, *Homilies of St. Jerome*, 2:148.

9. Schaff and Wac, *Nicene and Post Nicene Fathers, St. Augustine. Sermons on Selected Lessons of the New Testament*, 6:344. For the text see *Sancti Aureluii Augustini Sermones. De Vetere Testamento* (sermons of St. Augustine), ed. Cyrillus Lambot (Turnholti: Typographi Brepolis Editores Pontificii, 1961, 1979), p. 363.

10. Ibid., *St. Ambrose. Selected Works and Letters Concerning Repentance*, 10:334. For the text see *De Poenitentia* (concerning repentence) 2.7.31, which is found in *Sancti Ambrosii Mediolanesis Episcopi*, ed. J. P. Migne (Paris: Excudebat Vrayet, 1845), 16:476.

11. Wace, *St. Ambrose*, p. 334.

12. Allan Menzies, ed. *The Ante-Nicene Fathers: Origen's Commentary on Matthew*. (New York: Scribner, 1925, 1978), 10:426. For the text see *Origenes Werke: Origenes Matthäuserlärung* 10.19, found in *Die Griechisch Erhaltenen Tomoi*, 26 vols., ed. E. Klostermann (Leipzig, Germany: J. C. Hinrichs Verlag, 1935), 1:24.

13. Menzies, *Origen's Commentary on Matthew*, p. 426.

14. Schaff and Wace, *Nicene and Post Nicene Fathers, Saint Chrysostom: Homilies on the Gospel of Matthew*, 10:323. For the text see *Obras de San Juan Crisostomo: Homiliás sobre el Evangelio de San Mateo (46–90)* (St. Chrysostom's homilies), ed. Daniel Ruiz Bueno (Madrid: Biblioteca De Autores Cristianos, 1952, 1978), pp. 110–13.

15. Ibid., 10:205.

16. Ibid., 10:206.

17. Ibid., 10:207.

18. Ibid., 10:205.

19. Schaff and Wace, *Nicene and Post Nicene Fathers, Saint Athanasius. Letter 60: To Adelphus Bishop and Confessor against the Arians*, 4:575–76. For the text see *Patrologae Cursus Completus: Series Graeca, S. Athanasius Alexandrinus Archiepiscopus*, ed. J. P. Migne (Paris: Geuthner, 1957), 25:221–240, 537–594.

20. Ibid., *Hymns and Homilies of Ephraim the Syrian and from the Demonstrations of Aphrahat the Persian Sage*, 13:310. For the text see *S. Ephroem syri Hymni et sermones* (ephraim the syrian hymns and sermons), 4 vols. ed. J. Lamy (Malines, Belgium: n.p., 1882–1902).

21. Ibid.

22. J. E. Oulton and H. J. Lawlor, trans. *The Loeb Classical Library. Eusebius: The Ecclesiastical History*, 2 vols. (New York: Putnam, 1932), 2:175–76.

23. Schaff and Wace, *Nicene and post Nicene Fathers*, Saint Athanasius. The Life of Saint Anthony, 4:2. For the text see *Patrologiae Cursus Completus. Series Graeca. Vita S. Antoni*, ed. J. P. Migne (Paris: P. Geuthner, 1987), 26:835–976.

24. Ibid.

25. Alexander Roberts and James Donaldson, eds. *The Ante Nicene Fathers. Latin Christianity. Its Founder Tertullian* (Grand Rapids, Mich.: Eerdmans, 1973, 1978), 3:379. For the text see *Corpus Christianorum* (Christianity). *Series Latina* (Latin series). *Quinta Septimi Florentis. Tertulliana Opera* (Tertullian's works). 2 vols. (Turnholti: Typographi Brepols Editores Pontificii, 1954), 1:460–61.

26. Ibid., p. 380.

27. Roberts and Donaldson, *The Ante Nicene Fathers. The Apostolic Fathers. Justin Martyr and Irenaeus*, 1:319. For the text see *Patrologae Cursus Completus. Series Graeca. Sanctus Irenaeus Episcopus Lugdunensis et Martyr*, ed. J. P. Migne (Paris: P. Geuthner, 1857), 7:243–46.

28. Ibid.

29. Henry B. Swete, *The Gospel According to Mark* (London: Macmillan & Co., 1908), p. CXV.

30. Venerbailis Opera Bedae, *Pars II. Opera Exegetica. In Lucae Evangelium Expositio*, trans. D. Hurst (Turnholti: Typographi Brepols Editores Pontificii, 1960), pp. 469–49.

31. Thomas Aquinas, *Catena Aurea in Quatuor Evangelia*, 2 vols. 1, *Expositio in Matthaeum et Marcum*, trans. Angelici Guarienti (Rome: Marietti, 1953), 1:469–71.

32. *Euthymii Zigabeni Commentarius in Quatuor Evangelia*, in *Patrologiae Cursus Completus. Series Graeca*, ed. J. P. Migne (Paris: P. Geuthner, 1864), 2:541–46.

33. Ibid., *Theophylact: Bulgariae Archiepoiscopi*, 123:802–4.

34. Swete, *Gospel According to Mark*, p. CXV lists the major commentaries published during the Middle Ages.

35. John Haas, *Annotations on the Gospel According to St. Mark* (New York: The Christian Literature Society, 1895), p. 96. Haas gives a footnote to Luther, but no reference to the original text. For sermons on Mark 5:24–34 see *D. Martin Luthers Werke* ed. Johannes Weimar (Berlin: Bohlaus Nachfolger, 1910), 37:198–99; 17:460–64.

36. John Calvin, *Calvin's Commentaries: A Harmony of the Gospels. Matthew, Mark, and Luke*, eds. David W. Torrance and Thomas F. Torrance, vol. 1, *Matthew and Mark* (Grand Rapids, Mich.: Eerdmans, 1972), 1:270–72.

37. Ibid.

38. Haas, *Annotations According to Mark*, p. 96.

39. H. Van der Loos, *The Miracles of Jesus* (Leiden, Netherlands: E. J. Brill, 1965), pp. 509–18.

40. E. Lohmeyer, *Das Evangelium des Markus* (Göttingen, Germany: Vanderhoeck and Ruprecht, 1937); R. H. Lightfoot, *The Gospel of Mark* (Oxford: Clarendon Press, 1950); Willie Marxsen, *Mark the Evangelist*, trans. James Boyce (Nashville, Tenn.: Abingdon Press, 1969).

41. Gerhard Barth and Heinz Joachim Held, *Tradition and Interpretation in Matthew*, trans. Percy Scott (Philadelphia: Westminster Press, 1963); P. Minear, *The Gospel According to Mark: They Layman's Bible Commentary.* (Atlanta: John Knox Press, 1962); D. E. Nineham, *The Gospel of Mark: The Pelican Gospel Commentaries* (Baltimore: Penguin Books, 1963); L. Sabourin, *The Divine Miracles Discussed and Defended* (Rome: Catholic Book Agency, 1977); and "The Miracles of Jesus, III. Healings, Resuscitations, Nature Miracles," *Biblical Theology Bulletin* 5 (1975): 146–200; Eduard Schweizer, *The Good News According to Mark*, trans. Donald H. Madvig (Atlanta: John Knox Press, 1966); H. J. Holtzmann, *Commentar zum Neuen Testament, Switzerland* vol. 1, *Die Synoptiker: Die Apostelgeschichte* (The Synoptics: The Acts of the Apostles) (Freiburg,

Switzerland: Mohr, 1889); Ralph P. Martin, *Mark: Evangelist and Theologian* (Grand Rapids, Mich.: Zondervan, 1973); Ernst Haenchen, *Der Weg Jesu. Eine Erklärung des Markus. Evangeliums und der kanonischen Paralleln* (Berlin: Alfred Töpelmann, 1966).

42. Vincent Taylor, *The Gospel According to St. Mark.* London: Macmillan & Co., 1952), pp. 289–93; John M. Hull, *Hellenistic Magic and the Synoptic Tradition: Studies in Biblical Theology,* second series (London: S.C.M. Press, 1974); Hugh Anderson, *The Gospel of Mark: The New Century Bible* (Greenwood, S.C.: Attic Press, 1976).

43. Matthew Henry, *Matthew Henry's Commentary on the Whole Bible,* vol. 5, *Matthew to John* (Old Tappan, N.J.: Fleming H. Revell Co., 1974), p. 480.

44. E. R. Micklem, *Miracles and the New Psychology* (London: n.p., 1922), p. 44.

45. William L. Lane, *The Gospel According to Mark: The New International Commentary on the New Testament* (Grand Rapids, Mich.: Eerdmans, 1974), p. 193.

46. Theodore J. Weeden, *Mark: Traditions in Conflict* (Philadelphia: Fortesss Press, 1971); Aloysius M. Ambrozic, *The Hidden Kingdom: A Redaction-Critical Study of the References to the Kingdom of God in Mark's Gospel* (Washington, D.C.: Catholic Biblical Association of America, 1972); E. Klostermann, *Das Markusevangelium: Handbuch zum Neuen Testament* (Tübingen, W. Germany: Mohr, 1950).

47. John Bowman, *The Gospel of Mark: The New Christian Jewish Passover Haggadah* (Leiden, Netherlands: E. J. Brill, 1965), p. 90.

48. Ibid.; See also E. P. Gould, *A Critical and Exegetical Commentary on the Gospel to St. Mark* (New York: Scribner, 1896), p. 97; William Barclay, *The Gospel of Mark* (Philadelphia: Westminster Press, 1975), p. 129.

49. Lyman Abbott, *The New Testament with Notes and Comments: Matthew and Mark* (New York: A. S. Carnes and Co., 1865), p. 356.

50. Matthew B. Riddle, *The Gospel According to Mark* (New York: Scribner, 1881), pp. 63–64.

51. D. M. Slusser and G. H. Slusser, *The Jesus of Mark's Gospel* (Philadelphia: Westminster Press, 1967), p. 87.

52. Allan Menzies, *The Earliest Gospel: A Historical Study of the Gospel According to Mark* (London: Macmillan & Co., 1901), p. 15.

53. *Eusebius,* Loeb Classical Library, 1 : 39. See also Kurt Aland, *Synopsis Quattuor Evangeliorum* (Stuttgart, W. Germany: Württembergische Bibelanstalt, 1964), pp. 542–43.

54. Wilhelm Wrede, *The Messianic Secret,* trans. J. C. G. Greig (Greenwood, S.C.: Attic Press, 1971).

55. Weeden, *Traditions in Conflict,* p. 138.

56. Ibid.

57. See H. J. Ebeling, *Das Messiasgeheimnis und die Bötschaft des Markusevangelium* (Berlin: n.p., 1939); J. Rhode, *Rediscovering the Teaching of the Evangelists,* trans. D. M. Barton (London: S.C.M. Press, 1968).

58. H. J. Holtzmann, *Die Synoptischen Evangelien. Ihr Ursprung and und ihr geschichlicher Charakter* (Leipzig, Germany: n.p., 1863), pp. 156–59.

59. Lohmeyer, *Das Evangelium des Markus,* p. 101.

60. R. H. Lightfoot, *Locality and Doctrine in the Gospels* (London: Clarendon Press, 1938); E. Lohmeyer, *Galiläa und Jerusalem* (Göttingen, Germany: Vanenhoeck and Ruprecht, 1936).

61. Marxsen, *Mark the Evangelist,* p. 216.

62. Etienne Trocmé; *La Formation de l'evangile selon Marc* (Paris: Presses Universitaries de France, 1963), p. 168.

63. Ibid., p. 168. Translated by T. A. Burkill in *New Light on the Earliest Gospel: Seven Marcan Studies.* (Ithaca and London: Cornell University Press, 1972), p. 187.

64. Philipp Vielhauer, "Erwagungen zur Christologie des Markusevangeliums,"

Zeit und Geschichte: Bultmann Festschrift, ed. Erich Dinkler (Tübingen, W. Germany: Mohr, 1964), 155–69.

65. Martin, *Mark the Evangelist*. P. 104 gives a summary of Vielhauer's arguments.

66. Howard C. Kee, *Community of the New Age: Studies in Marks Gospel* (Philadelphia: Westminster Press, 1977), p. 76.

67. Ibid., p. 75.

68. Ibid.

69. Weeden, *Traditions in Conflict*, p. 160. See also J. B. Tyson, "The Blindness of the Disciples in Mark," *Journal of Biblical Literature* 80 (1961): 261–68.

70. Weeden, *Traditions in Conflict*, p. 160.

71. Irene Brennan, "Women in the Gospels," *New Blackfriars* 52 (1971): 291–99; Raymond E. Brown, "Roles of Women in the Fourth Gospel," *Theological Studies* 36 (1975): 688–99; D. Catchpole, "The Fearful Silence of the Women at the Tomb: A Study in Marcan Theology," *Journal of Theology for Southern Africa* 18 (1977): 3–10; Jean Danielou, *Ministry of Women in the Early Church* (London: Faith Press, 1961); Peter Ketter, *Christ and Womenkind*, trans. Isabel McHugh (Westminster, Md.: Newman Press, 1952); Johannes Leipoldt, *Die Frau in der Antiken Welt und im Urchristentum* (Leipzig, E. Germany: Koehler und Amelung, 1955); L. Swidler, "Jesus and His Encounter With Women," *African Ecclesiastical Review* 13 (1971): 290–300; and "Jesus was a Feminist," *South East Asia Journal of Theology* 13 (1971): 102–10.

72. Martin Dibelius, *From Tradition to Gospel* (New York: Scribner, 1965), p. 4.

73. Ibid., pp. 7–8.

74. Ibid., p. 3.

75. K. L. Schmidt, *Der Rahmen der Geshichte Jesu* (Berlin: Trowitzsch and Sohn, 1919).

76. Ibid. For his remarks on Mark 5:24–34 see pp. 144–52.

77. Dibelius, *From Tradition to Gospel*, p. 71.

78. Ibid., p. 72.

79. Ibid., pp. 82–85.

80. Rudolph Bultmann, *The History of the Synoptic Tradition*, trans. John Marsh (Oxford: Basil Blackwell, 1963), p. 214.

81. Ibid.

82. Kee, *Aretalogies, Hellenistic Lives, and the Sources of Mark. Colloquy 12*, ed. W. Wuellner (Berkeley, Calif.: Center for Hermeneutical Studies in Hellenistic and Modern Culture, 1975), p. 1.

83. H. Riesenfeld, *The Gospel Tradition*, trans. E. M. Rowley and R. A. Kraft (Philadelphia: Fortress Press, 1970).

84. R. A. Harrisville, *The Miracle of Mark: A Study in the Gospel* (Minneapolis, Minn.: Augsburg Publishing House, 1967).

85. P. Carrington, *The Primitive Christian Calendar: A Study in the Making of the Marcan Gospel* (Cambridge: Cambridge University Press, 1952).

86. John Bowman, *The Gospel of Mark: The New Christian Jewish Passover Haggadah* (Leiden, Netherlands: E. J. Brill, 1965).

87. Kee, *Aretalogies*, p. 11.

88. Harrisville, *Miracle of Mark*, pp. 24–72.

89. Carrington, *Primitive Christian Calendar*, p. 119.

90. See also Bowman, *Gospel of Mark* for another Jewish *Sitz im Leben* for Mark's work.

91. P. J. Achtemeier, "The Origin and Function of the Pre-Markan Miracle Catenae," *Journal of Biblical Literature* 91 (1972): 189–221; and "Toward the Isolation of the Pre-Markan Miracle Catenae," *Journal of Biblical Literature* 89 (1970): 265–91.

92. Achtemeier, "The Origin and Function of the Pre-Markan Miracle Catenae," pp. 198–221.

93. Achtemeier, "Origin and Function of Catanae," p. 291.

94. Ibid., p. 198.

95. Jean-Thierry Maertens, "La structure des reċits de miracles dans les synoptiques," *Sciences Religieuses* 6 (1977): 253–66.

96. Ibid., as digested in *Theology Digest* 26 (1978): 159.

97. Vernon K. Robbins, "The Woman Who Touched Jesus' Garment: Social-Rhetorical Analysis of the Synoptic Accounts," forthcoming in *New Testament Studies*.

98. David Rhoades and Donald Michie, *Mark as Story: An Introduction to the Narrative of the Gospel* (Philadelphia: Fortress Press, 1982).

99. Elizabeth Malbon Struthers, "Fallible Followers: Women and Men in the Gospel or Mark," *Semeia* 28 (1983): 29–48.

100. Gerd Theissen, *The Miracle Stories of the Early Christian Tradition* (Edinburgh: T. and T. Clark, 1983), p. 133, as summarized by Robbins, "The Woman Who Touched Jesus' Garment," p. 14.

101. John J. Pilch, "Healing in Mark: A Social Science Analysis," *Biblical Theology Bulletin* 15 (1985): 142–50.

102. Ibid., p. 146.

103. J. Duncan Derrett, "Mark's Technique: The Haemorrhaging Woman and Jarius' Daughter," *Biblica* 63 (1982): 474–505.

104. Marla J. Selvidge, "Mark 5 : 24–34 and Leviticus 15: A Reaction to Restrictive Purity Regulations," *Journal of Biblical Literature* 103 (1984): 619–23; and *Daughters of Jerusalem* (Scottsdale, Pa.: Herald Press: 1986).

105. Winsom Munro, "Woman Disciples in Mark," *Catholic Biblical Quarterly* 44 (1982): 225–41.

106. Leonard Swidler, "Jesus Was a Feminist," *Southeast Asia Journal of Theology* 13 (1971) 102–110; and *Biblical Affirmations of Women* (Philadelphia: Westminster Press, 1979).

107. Constance F. Parvey, "The Theology and Leadership of Women in the New Testament," in *Religion and Sexism: Images of Women in Jewish and Christian Traditions*, ed. Rosemary Radford Ruether (New York: Simon & Schuster, 1974), pp. 117–50.

108. Irene Brennan, "Women in the Gospels," *New Blackfriars* 52 (1971), pp. 291–95. See also Janice Nunnally-Cox, *Foremothers: Women of the Bible* (New York: Seabury Press, 1981); Alicia C. Faxon, *Women and Jesus* (Philadelphia: United Church Press, 1973); Peter Ketter, *Christ and Womankind*, trans. Isabel McHugh (Westminster, Md.: Newman Press, 1952); Ben Witherington III, *Jesus and the Ministry of Women: A Study of Jesus' Attitude to Women and Their Roles as Reflected in His Early Life* (Cambridge: Cambridge University Press, 1984).

109. Alice Buchanan Lane, "The Significance of the Thirteen Women in the Gospel of Mark," *Unitarian Universalist Christian* 38 (1983): 18–27.

Chapter 2. The Audience of Mark

1. S. J. Chase, *The Social Origins of Christianity* (Chicago: University of Chicago Press, 1923); J. Z. Smith, "The Social Description of Early Christianity," *Religious Studies Review* 1 (1975): 19–25; J. Gager, *Kingdom and Community: The Social World of Early Christianity* (Englewood Cliffs, N.J.: Prentice-Hall, 1975); E. Troeltsch, *The Social Teaching of the Christian Churches*, 2 vols. trans. Olive Wynon (London: Allen & Unwin, 1931); C. J. Cadoux, *The Early Church and the World* (Edinburgh: Clark, 1925); A.

Deissman, *Light from the Ancient East* (New York: Hodder and Stoughton, 1909); F. C. Grant, *The Economic Background of the Gospels* (New York: Russell, 1973); W. Stark, *The Sociology of Religion*, vol. 2, *Sectarian Religion* (New York: Fordham University Press, 1967).

2. Robin Scroggs, "Earliest Christian Communities as Sectarian Movement," in *Christianity, Judaism, and Other Greco-Roman Cults*, vol. 2, ed. Jacob Neusner (Leiden, Netherlands: E. J. Brill, 1975), pp. 1–23.

3. Ibid., p. 8.

4. Ibid.

5. Gerd Theissen, *Sociology of Early Palestinian Christianity*, trans. John Bowden (Philadelphia: Fortress Press, 1978), p. 75. Instead of the term *Renewal movement* this paper will employ the word *Dissenter* or *Dissenting Movement*.

6. Scroggs, "Earliest Christian Communities," p. 21.

7. W. R. Farmer, *The Synoptic Problem* (New York: Macmillan, 1964); F. Grant, *The Earliest Gospel* (New York: Abington, 1943); P. Parker, *The Gospel Before Mark* (Chicago: University of Chicago Press, 1953).

8. Étienne Trócmé, *La Formation de l'évangile selon Marc* (Paris: Presses Universitaries de France, 1963; S. Sandmel, "Prolegomena to a Commentary on Mark," *Journal of Biblical Literature* 31 (Winter, 1963): 294–300; T. J. Weeden, "The Heresy that Necessitated Mark's Gospel," *Zeitschrift für die Neutestamentliche Wissenchaft* 59 (1968): 145–58; Michael J. Cook, *Mark's Treatment of the Jewish Leaders*, *Novum Testamentum Supplement 5* (Leiden, Netherlands: E. J. Brill, 1978).

9. Mark 6:17–29.

10. Mark 12:13–17.

11. Mark 8:2ff.

12. See also Mark 11:32, 12:12.

13. Mark 2:4, 13; 3:9, 20; 3:32; 5:21, 24, 27, 30; 6:34.

14. Mark 3:9; 4:1; 5:24, 31.

15. Mark 11:15–17.

16. Mark 2:23.

17. Mark 2:6.

18. Mark 12:27.

19. Irene Brennan, "Women in the Gospels," *New Blackfriars* 52 (1971): 294. She bases her opinion on *Aboth* 1.5 (12a, b) in *The Babylonian Talmud*, vol. 28, *Horayoth*, ed. and trans. Israel W. Slocki (New York: Rebecca Bennet Publishing House, 1959), p. 270.

20. See Leviticus, chapters 11, 13, and 15.

21. Mark 5:24–34; 7:24–30

22. Mark 1:31; 5:24–34; 14:2ff.

23. Mark 5:31ff.

24. Mark 14:3.

25. See chapter 3.

26. Mark 6:1–6.

27. Mark 3:22; 9:19.

28. Genesis 9:1.

29. See also Mark 1:43; 6:7.

30. Mark 10:52.

31. Mark 3:1–3

32. Mark 5:1ff.

33. Mark 5:24–34.

34. Mark 5:35ff.

35. Mark 7 : 25 ff.

36. Mark 14 : 3–8; 7 : 1 ff.

37. ἐκβάλλω is also used in Mark 3 : 15–16.

38. Mark 3 : 7; 5 : 24; 8 : 34.

39. See Mark 15 : 40–41. The part the women played within the developing community will be detailed in chapter 5.

40. Mark 14 : 1–8.

41. Mark 10 : 52.

42. Mark 2 : 15.

43. Mark 12 : 6.

44. Possibly Mark 7 : 6 also if another manuscripts reading is chosen.

45. Mark 10 : 21.

46. Some manuscripts gave, "The Lord our God is one God."

47. See also Mark 2 : 14.

48. Mark 3 : 13–19.

49. Mark 14 : 50.

50. Mark 4 : 40.

51. Mark 9 : 24.

52. Mark 10 : 28–31.

53. Mark 13 : 13.

54. Confer: Paul D. Hanson, *The Dawn of Apocalyptic* (Philadelphia: Fortress Press, 1975); M. S. Enslein, "A New Apocalyptic," *Religion in Life* 44 (1975): 105–10; Lars Hartman, *Prophecy Interpreted: The Formation of Some Jewish Apocalyptic Texts and of the Eschatological Discourse of Mark 13* (Lund, Sweden: Gleerup, 1966); W. R. Millar, *Isaiah 24–27 and the Origin of Apocalyptic* (Missoula, Mont.: Scholars Press, 1976); W. Schmithals, *The Apocalyptic Movement: Introduction and Interpretation*, trans. J. E. Steely (Nashville, Tenn.: Abingdon Press, 1975).

55. Scroggs, "Earliest Christian Communities," p. 20.

56. Morna D. Hooker, *The Son of Man in Mark* (London: S.P.C.K., 1967); Norman Perrin, *A Modern Pilgrimage in New Testament Christology* (Philadelphia: Fortress Press, 1974); Heinz E. Todt, *The Son of Man in Synoptic Tradition*, trans. Dorothea M. Barton (Philadelphia: Westminster Press, 1965).

57. Mark 13 : 36 is my own translation. See also Mark 8 : 38 and 14 : 62.

58. For opposing views that see the twelve in a positive manner see K. Kertelge, "Die Funktion der Zwölf im Markusevangelium," *Trier Theologische Zeitschrift* 78 (1969): 193–206; R. P. Meye, *Jesus and the Twelve: Discipleship and Revelation in Mark's Gospel* (Grand Rapids, Mich.: Eerdmans, 1968); Camille Focant, "L 'incompréhension des disciples dans le deuxieme evangile," *Revue Biblique* 82 (1975): 161–85; E. Best, "The Role of the Disciples in Mark," *New Testament Studies* 23 (1977): 377–40.

59. Trocmé, *The Formation of the Gospel According to Mark*, trans. Pamela Gaughan (Philadelphia: Westminster Press, 1975), p. 196.

60. T. A. Burkill, *New Light on the Earliest Gospel: Seven Markan Studies* (Ithaca and London: Cornell University Press, 1972), pp. 180–98. According to A. Oppenheimer in *The 'Am Ha-Aretz: A Study in the Social History of the Jewish People in the Hellenistic-Roman Period*, trans. I. H. Levine, vol. 8 of *Arbeiten zur Literatur und Geschichte des hellenistischen Judentums* (Study of the literature and history of the Hellenistic Jews) (Leiden, Netherlands: E. J. Brill, 1977) historically this is just what happened. Galilee became a center for Christianity.

61. Trocmé, *Formation of the Gospel*, p. 214.

62. Ibid., pp. 183–214.

63. Ibid., p. 186.

64. Ibid., p. 187.
65. Ibid., p. 179.
66. Ibid., p. 187.
67. T. J. Weeden, *Traditions in Conflict* (Philadelphia: Fortress Press, 1971), pp. 26–38.
68. See footnote number 8. Wilhelm Wrede, *The Messianic Secret*, trans. J. C. G. Greig (Greenwood, S.C.: Attic Press, 1971); J. B. Tyson, "The Blindness of the Disciples in Mark," *Journal of Biblical Literature* 80 (1961): 261–68; Johannes Schreiber, "Die Christologie des Markusevangeliums," *Zeitschrift für Theologie und Kirche* 58 (1961): 175–83; J. Coults, "The Authority of Jesus and of the Twelve in St. Mark's Gospel," *Journal of Theological Studies* 8 (1957): 111–18; G. Schmahl, "Die Zwölf im Markusevangelium," *Trierer Theologische Studien* 30 (1974): 20.
69. Weeden, *Traditions in Conflict*, p. 26.
70. David J. Hawkin, "The Incomprehension of the Disciples in the Marcan Redaction," *Journal of Biblical Literature* 91 (1972): 500.
71. Weeden, *Traditions in Conflict*, p. 24.
72. Ibid., p. 69.
73. Ibid., p. 52 and Mark 8 : 34–35; 10 : 28–30; 43–44; 13 : 9–13.
74. H. D. Betz, "Jesus as Divine Man," in *Jesus and the Historican*, ed. F. F. Trotter (Philadelphia: Westminster Press, 1969) pp. 114–33; D. L. Tiede, *The Charismatic Fugure as Miracle Worker*. SBL Dissertation Series I (Missoula, Mont.: Scholars Press, 1972); C. H. Holloday, *Theios Aner in Hellenistic Judaism: A Critique of the Use of this Category in New Testament Christology*. SBL Dissertation Series 40 (Missoula, Mont.: Scholars Press, 1977).
75. W. L. Lane, "The Gospel of Mark in Current Study," *Southwestern Journal of Theology* 21 (1978) : 14.
76. See the following for reviews of Weeden, *Traditions in Conflict*: S. Brown, *Theological Studies* 33 (1972) : 754–756; E. Schweizer, "Neuere Markus-Forschung in U.S.A.," *Evangelishe Theologie* 33 (1973) : 533–37, A. J. Hultgren, *Lutheran World* 20 (1973):71–74; Q. Quesnell, *Catholic Biblical Quarterly* 35 (1973) : 124–25.
77. Weeden, *Traditions in Conflict*, p. 48.
78. Mark 3 : 16.
79. Mark 2 : 15.
80. Mark 6 : 7–11.
81. Mark 9 : 35.
82. Mark 10 : 32ff.
83. Mark 11 : 11; 14 : 1.
84. Mark 14 : 10, 43.
85. Mark 14 : 43. See also E. Best, "The Twelve in Mark," *Zeitschrift für die Neutestamentliche Wissenschaft* 69 (1978) : 11–35.
86. Mark 2 : 16.
87. Mark 6 : 4.
88. Mark 6 : 12.
89. Mark 2 : 23.
90. Hawkin, "Incomprehension of the Disciples," *Journal of Biblical Literature* 91 (1972) : 493.
91. Mark 10 : 35–41.
92. Mark 9 : 41 ff.
93. Mark 9 : 38.
94. Mark 9 : 39.
95. Mark 6 : 1; 8 : 34.

96. Mark 8 : 4. See also Mark 6 : 50–52.

97. Mark 4 : 4.

98. Mark 5 : 31; 8 : 33.

99. Mark 9 : 18–31.

100. Mark 14 : 10.

101. Mark 8 : 29.

102. For a discussion of the role of Peter in the Gospel see E. Best, "Peter in the Gospel According to Mark," *Journal of Biblical Literature* 40 (1978) : 547–58 for a mediating position; R. E. Brown, *Peter in the New Testament* (Augsburg, W. Germany: Paulist Press, 1973), pp. 64–69; O. Cullman, *Peter, Disciple, Apostle, Martyr* (London: SCM Press, 1953); E. Dinkler, "Peter's Confession and the Satan Saying: The Problem of Jesus' Messiahship," *The Future of Our Religious Past*, ed. J. M. Robinson (London: SCM Press, 1971): 169–202; R. Pesch, "Peter in the Church of the New Testament," *Concilium* 4 (1971): 21–35.

103. Weeden, *Traditions in Conflict*, pp. 50–51.

104. V. Taylor, *The Gospel According to Mark* (London: Macmillan & Co., 1966), p. 65.

105. Frederick C. Grant, *The Earliest Gospel* (New York: Abington Press, 1966), p. 65.

106. C. C. Torrey, *Our Translated Gospels* (London: Hodder, n.d.), pp. 1–54.

107. E. Nestle, *Introduction to the Textual Criticism of the Greek New Testament* (London: Williams and Norgate, 1901), p. 93.

108. J. Wellhausen, *Einleitung in die drei ersten Evangelien* (Berlin: Remier, 1911), pp. 10 ff.

109. Deissmann, *Light from the Ancient East*, pp. 1–53.

110. Taylor, *Gospel of Mark*, p. 55.

111. Allan Menzies, *The Earliest Gospel: A Historical Study of the Gospel According to Mark* (London: Macmillan & Co., 1901), p. 15; Mark 3 : 17 Boanerges; 5 : 41 Talitha Cum; 7 : 2 Korban; 7 : 33 Effatha, and 15 : 22 Golgotha.

112. Taylor, *Gospel of Mark*, p. 56. See also A. Wikenhauser, *New Testament Introduction*, trans. J. Cunningham (W. Germany: Herder and Druck, 1958), pp. 165–66.

113. H. C. Kee, *Community of the New Age: Studies in Mark's Gospel* (Philadelphia: Westminster Press, 1977) sees Mark's community as apocalyptic and Essene in nature. He places the Gospel in the midst of rural Syria among a Jewish sectarian group.

114. See Eusebius, *Ecclesiastical History*, Loeb Classical Library, 2 : 43.

115. Chrysostom, *Homilies of the Gospel of Matthew, Homily I*, in *Obras de San Juan Crisostomo: Homilias sobre el Evangelio de San Mateo* (Homilies of St Chrysostom: Homilies of St Matthew) (1–45), ed. Daniel Ruiz (Madrid: Biblioteca de Autores Cristianos, 1952), p. 1.

116. C. E. B. Cranfield, *The Gospel According to Mark* (Cambridge: University Press, 1959), p. 8.

117. Taylor, *Gospel of Mark*, p. 45; J. A. W. Haas, *Annotations on the Gospel According to Mark* (New York: Christian Literature Society, 1895), p. xxv.

118. Mark 7 : 3–4.

119. Mark 14 : 12; 15 : 42. See also J. A. Fitzmyer, ed. et al., *The Jerome Biblical Commentary* (Englewood Cliffs, N.J.: Prentice-Hall, 1968), 2 : 22; Menzies, *Earliest Gospel*, p. 15; E. P. Gould, *A Critical and Exegetical Commentary on the Gospel According to St. Mark* (New York: Scribner, 1896), p. xviii.

120. Fitzmyer, *Jerome Biblical Commentary*, p. 22.

121. Mark 12 : 42. See also A. E. J. Rawlinson, *St. Mark* (London: Methuen, 1925), p. xxx.

122. Mark 1 : 5, 9 : 11 : 1.

123. Wikenhauser, *Introduction to the New Testament*, p. 166; W. G. Kummel, *Introduction to the New Testament*, trans. H. C. Kee (New York: Abington Press, 1973), pp. 97–98. Here are a few of the Latinisms: Mark 4 : 21 μόδιος, 5 : 9, 15 λεγιών, 6 : 27 σπεκουλάτωρ, 6 : 37 δηοάριον, 7 : 4 ξέστης, 12 : 14 κῆσον; 15 : 15 φραγελλοῦν, and 15 : 39, 44 ff. κεντυριών.

124. Mark 8 : 34–38, 10 : 38–39; 13 : 9–13. See also Fitzmyer, *Jerome Biblical Commentar*, p. 22.

125. Haas, *Annotations on the Gospel*, p. xxv.

126. Mark 7 : 27, 8 : 1–9; 10 : 12; 11 : 17; 13 : 10.

127. W. Storch, "Zur Perikope von der Syrophönizierin: Mk. 7 : 28 und Re 1.7," *Biblische Zeitschrift* 14 (1970): 256–57; A Dermience, "Tradition et redaction dans le péricope de la Syrophénicienne. Marc 7, 24–30," *Revue Theólogique de Louvain* 8 (1977) : 15–29.

128. Mark 15 : 39.

129. Mark 5 : 1–17.

130. Mark 1 : 39.

131. Mark 3 : 8.

132. F. W. Danker, "Mark 8 : 3," *Journal of Biblical Literature*, 83 (1963) : 215–16.

133. Mark 6 : 37–44.

134. Mark 8 : 1–21; 7 : 24.

135. C. Roth, "The Cleansing of the Temple and Zechariah 14 : 21," *Novum Testamentum* 4 (1960) : 174–81.

136. R. Scroggs, "The Exaltation of the Spirit by Some Early Christians," *Journal of Biblical Literature* 84 (1965) : 359–73.

137. Mark, chap. 13.

138. Stark, *Sociology of Religion*, p. 129.

Chapter 3. Judaic Heritage of Mark

1. *Soranus' Gynecology*, trans. Owsei Temkin, p. 166. For text see *Sorani Gynaeciorum*, ed. Ioannes Ilberg (Lipsiae et Berolini: B. G. Teubneri, 1927), 13–17.

2. Plutarch, *Moralia*, Loeb Classical Library, 6 : 345–49.

3. Hippocrates, *Aphorisms*, Loeb Classical Library, p. 173.

4. Hippocrates, *Air, Waters, Places*, Loeb Classical Library, p. 79.

5. Diodus Siculus, *Historicus* 5 : 41–42. For the text see *Diodori: Bibliotheca Historica*, eds. I. Bekker and L. Dindorf, F. Vogel (Stuttgart, W. Germany: B. G. Teubner, 1964), pp. 62–63.

6. Aristotle, *Generation of Animals*, Loeb Classical Library, p. 180.

7. Ibid.

8. Ibid., p. 274.

9. Aelian, *On the Characteristics of Animals*, Loeb Classical Library, 2 : 6–11.

10. Demosthenes, *Epistulae Prooemia* 54.12. For the text see *Demosthenes Prooemia*, ed. F. Blass (Leipzig, E. Germany: n.p., 1888–92).

11. Pliny the Elder, *Natural History*, Loeb Classical Library, 5 : 185.

12. Leviticus 15 : 2.

13. See for example Sirach 21 : 13; Proverbs 10 : 11; Jeremiah 17 : 13; 28(51) : 36.

14. *Encyclopedia Judaica*, 1971 ed., "Daughter."

15. Leviticus 12 : 2; 15 : 18, 19; 18 : 8, 11, 14, 15, 16, 17, 18, 22, 23; 19 : 20–22; 20 : 10, 11, 14, 16, 18, 21, 21 : 7, 13, 14.

16. Caroline M. Breyfogle, "The Religious Status of Women in the Old Testament," *Biblical World* 35 (1910):411.

17. W. A. Meeks, "The Image of Androgyne: Some Uses of a Symbol in Earliest Christianity," *History of Religions* 13 (Fall, 1974):178.

18. N. H. Snaith, ed., *Leviticus and Numbers, The Century Bible* (London: Thomas Nelson, 1967), p. 135.

19. Mark 5:27, 28, 30, 31; Leviticus 5:2, 3; 6:18, 27; 7:9; 7:11; 11:8, 24, 26, 27, 31, 36, 39; 12:4; 15:5, 7, 10, 11, 12, 19, 21, 22, 23, 27; 22:4, 5, 6.

20. Leviticus 5:2, 3; 7:9, 11; 11:8, etc.

21. Leviticus 6:18(11).

22. Leviticus 12:4; 15:5, 7, 10, 11, 12, 19, 21, 22, 23, 27.

23. Women may be indirectly classified under the laws pertaining to lepers in Leviticus 13:59ff.

24. Leviticus 21:10.

25. Leviticus 16:4, 26, 28.

26. Leviticus 17:15, 16.

27. Leviticus, chap. 15.

28. Mark 5:27.

29. Leviticus 5:1; 10:20; 24:14.

30. Mark 5:29, 30, 31, 32, 33, 34.

31. Leviticus 21:1.

32. Leviticus 21:1 ἱερεῦσιν τοῖς υίοῖς 'Ααρων; 19:1 τῇ συναγωγῇ τῶν υίῶν Ισραηλ; 21:16 πρός μωυσῆν; 9:3 τη γερουσία Ισραηλ; 10:8 τῷ 'Ααρων; 16:26 τῷ 'Ααρων του ἀδελφόυ σου; 17:1 προς 'Αάρον καὶ πρὸς τοὺς υίοίς αὐτοῦ. Woman could be indirectly included in συναγωγη (19:1).

33. Mark 5:29.

34. Leviticus 4:14, 23, 28; 5:3, 4, 17.

35. Leviticus 14:9, 11, 13, 16, 21, 27; 15:2, 3, (four times), 19; 16:24, 26, 28; 17:16; 22:6.

36. Mark 5:29 ἰάομαι; Mark 5:29 σώζω.

37. Leviticus 14:3.

38. Leviticus 14:48.

39. Mark 5:30.

40. Mark 5:28-30.

41. Leviticus 9:22.

42. Leviticus 5:42.

43. Leviticus 15:15, 30; 2:7, 8, 11; 4:20; 5:10; 7:7, 16, 22; 14:19, etc.

44. Mark 5:33.

45. Leviticus 19:14, 32; 25:17, 36, 43; 19:30; 26:2.

46. Leviticus 19:3.

47. Mark 5:34.

48. Leviticus 26:26.

49. Mark 5:34.

50. Leviticus 13:10, 15, 16.

51. Snaith, *Leviticus*, pp. 18-23; M. Noth, *Leviticus. A Commentary* (Philadelphia: Westminster Press, 1977), pp. 10-15.

52. Snaith, *Leviticus*, p. 19.

53. Leviticus 15:21.

54. Leviticus chap. 11.

55. Leviticus chap. 13.

56. Leviticus chap. 15.

57. Leviticus 12:1-8.

58. Leviticus chaps. 17–26.
59. Leviticus 20:8.
60. Leviticus chap. 18.
61. Leviticus 19:9 ff.
62. Leviticus 19:29.
63. Leviticus 19:11–18.
64. Leviticus 19:26, 27.
65. *Encyclopedia Judaica*, 1971 ed., s.v. "Purity."
66. *Theological Dictionary of the New Testament*, 1965 ed., s.v. κάθαρος, by Friedrick Hauck.
67. Leonard Swidler, *Woman in Judaism: The Status of Women in Formative Judaism* (Metuchen, N.J.: Scarecrow Press, 1976), p. 130.
68. Clarence J. Vos, *Woman in Old Testament Worship* (Delft, Netherlands: Verenigde Drukkerijen Jedels and Brinkman, 1978), pp. 72–77.
69. Leviticus 15:13; Snaith, *Leviticus*, p. 108.
70. Letha Scanzoni and Nancy Hardesty, *All We're Meant to Be: A Biblical Approach to Women's Liberation* (Waco, Tex.: Word, 1974), p. 130.
71. Leviticus 15:21, 22, 27; 15:5, 6, 7, 8, 10, 11, 13.
72. Hippocrates, *Heracleitus on the Universe*, Leob Classical Library, p. 174; Plutarch *Moralia*, Loeb Classical Library, 6: 439–523; *Soranus' Gynecology*, trans. Owsei Temkin, p. 166.
73. Leviticus 15:1, 4.
74. Exodus 19:14–15.
75. Exodus 19:11–12.
76. Ezra 9:11–12.
77. Ibid.
78. Leviticus 15:19.
79. Ezra 9:12.
80. Lamentations 1:8–9.
81. Lamentations 1:17.
82. Ibid.
83. Lamentations 1:9.
84. 2 Chronicles 29:5.
85. Ibid.
86. Ibid.
87. I Samuel 21:5, 7 (6–7).
88. Ezekiel 18:5–6.
89. Theodore H. Gaster, *The Dead Sea Scriptures* (New York: Anchor Press, 1976), p. 3.
90. Damascus Document 6. 17–18 (hereafter CD); Eduard Löhse, *Die Texte Aus Qumran: Hebräisch und Deutsch* (Germany: Satz and Druck, 1981), p. 79.
91. CD 7. 19–22; Löhse, *Texte aus Qumran*, p. 79.
92. CD 3.17; Löhse, *Texte aus Qumran*, p. 70.
93. CD 5. 6–7; Löhse, *Texte aus Qumran*, pp. 75–76. See also CD 4.12–5.17.
94. Gaster, *Dead Sea Scrolls*, p. 441.
95. CD 10. 10–13; Löhse, *Texte aus Qumran*, p. 87.
96. CD 11.18 to 12.2; Lohse, *Texte aus Qumran*, pp. 88–91.
97. CD 12. 1–2; Löhse, *Texte aus Qumran*, pp. 90–91.
98. Gaster, *Dead Sea Scrolls*, pp. 497–98.
99. Ibid.
100. Ibid., p. 487.
101. CD 4.12–5.17; Löhse, *Texte aus Qumran*, pp. 72–77.

102. Edmond Sutcliff, *The Monks of Qumran* (Westminster, Md.: Newman Press, 1960), pp. 97–98.

103. Gaster, *Dead Sea Scrolls*, p. 439.

104. Jacob Neusner, *The Idea of Purity in Ancient Judaism* (Leiden, Netherlands: E. J. Brill, 1973), p. 58.

105. R. H. Charles, ed., *The Apocrypha and Pseudepigrapha of the Old Testament in English*, 2 vols. (Oxford: Clarendon Press, 1963), 2 : 1.

106. Neusner, *Idea of Purity*, p. 58.

107. Jubilees 3 : 4–14; Charles, *Apocrypha and Pseudepigrapha*, 2 : 1.

108. Neusner, *Idea of Purity*, pp. 35–38.

109. Epistle of Jeremiah 5 : 29; Charles, *Apocrypha and Pseudepigrapha*, 1 : 602–4.

110. Ibid.

111. Charles, *Apocrypha and Pseudepigrapha*, 2 : 625.

112. Psalms of Solomon 8 : 13; Charles, *Apocrypha and Pseudepigrapha*, 2 : 640; for the text see Albert-Marie Denis, *Introduction aux Pseudépigraphes d'Ancien Testament* (Leiden, Netherlands: n.p., 1970), pp. 60–69; Neusner, *Idea of Purity*, p. 35.

113. Charles, *Apocrypha and Pseudepigrapha*, 2 : 407.

114. The Assumption of Moses 7 : 9–10; Charles, *Apocrypha and Pseudepigrapha*, 2 : 420.

115. Charles, *Apocrypha and Pseudepigrapha*, 2 : 282; Denis, *Introduction aux Pseudépigraphes*, pp. 49–59.

116. Neusner, *Idea of Purity*, p. 36.

117. Charles, *Apocrypha and Pseudepigrapha*, 2 : 326.

118. R. H. Charles, trans., *The Book of Enoch* (London: S.P.C.K., 1974), p. 35.

119. Ibid., *Enoch* 7. 1–2.

120. Enoch 10.20; Charles, *Enoch*, p. 38.

121. Enoch 10.22; Charles, *Enoch*, p. 39.

122. Swidler, *Woman in Judaism*, p. 132; Saul Berman, "The Status of Women in Halachic Judaism," *Tradition* 14 (Fall 1973): 5–27; Joachim Jeremias, *Jerusalem in the Time of Jesus* (Philadelphia: Fortress Press, 1969), p. 373–75; Kalman Kahane, *Daughter of Israel* (Jerusalem: Feldeim, 1973); Jacob Neusner, "From Scripture of Mishnah: The Origins of Tractate Niddah," *Journal of Jewish Studies* 39 (1978): 137–48; Rudolph Otto, *The Idea of the Holy* (New York: Oxford University Press, 1923).

123. Riv-Ellen Prell-Foldes, "Coming of Age of Kelton: The Constraints on Gender Symbolism in Jewish Ritual," in *Women in Ritual and Symbolic Roles*, eds. Judith Hock-Smith and Anita Spring (New York: Plenum, 1978), pp. 75–99; Gail B. Shulman, "View from the Back of the Synagogue: Women in Judaism," in *Sexist Religion and Women in the Church: No More Silence*, ed. Alice L. Hageman (New York: Association Press, 1974), pp. 143–66.

124. Swidler, *Women in Judaism*, p. 132.

125. Peshahim 2. 3a; *The Babylonian Talmud: Seder Mo'ed.*, trans. H. Freidman, p. 571.

126. Swidler, *Women in Judaism*, pp. 137–38.

127. Niddah 2. 13a–21a; *The Babylonian Talmud*, 1: 84–138.

128. *Encyclopedia Judaica*, 1971 ed., s.v., "Niddah."

129. Ibid.

130. Josephus, *The Jewish War*, Loeb Classical Library, pp. 269–70.

131. Ibid., p. 499.

132. Josephus, *Jewish Antiquities*, Loeb Classical Library, p. 447.

133. Ibid., p. 445.

134. Josephus, *Against Apion*, Loeb Classical Library, p. 375.

135. Philo, *The Unchangeableness of God*, Loeb Classical Library, p. 15.

136. Philo, *Special Laws*, Loeb Classical Library, pp. 32–33.

137. Elizabeth Mary McDonald, *The Position of Women as Reflected in Semitic Codes of Law* (Toronto: University of Toronto Press, 1931); Clarence J. Vos, *Woman in Old Testament Worship* (Delft, Netherlands: Verenigde Drukkerijen Judels and Brinkman, 1978); Ismar J. Peritz, "Woman in the Ancient Hebrew Cult," *Journal of Biblical Literature* 17 (1898): 111–48 all agree that woman was not discriminated against in cultic activities.

138. G. Beer, *Die soziale und religöse Stellung der Frau im israelitischen Altertums* (Tübingen, Germany: Mohr, 1919) and E. B. Cross, *The Hebrew Family* (Chicago: n.p., 1927) disagree. Woman was systematically discriminated against and withheld from cultic responsibilities.

139. Vos, *Woman in Old Testament Worship*, p. 207.

140. Leviticus 12 : 1–5.

141. Jewett, *Man as Male and Female*, p. 90.

142. Genesis 17 : 1–27.

143. Jewett, *Man as Male and Female*, p. 90.

144. J. B. Segal, "Popular Religion in Ancient Israel," *Journal of Jewish Studies* 27 (1976): 5.

145. Vos, *Woman in Old Testament Worship*, pp. 60–61 has an extensive analysis of the Greek.

146. G. B. Gray, *Sacrifice in the Old Testament* (New York: KTAV, 1971), pp. 188–92.

147. Leviticus 21 : 7, 13–14.

148. Deuteronomy 22 : 14.

149. Exodus 20 : 17; Deuteronomy 5 : 21.

150. Breyfogle, "The Social Status of Woman," p. 110; Cross, *Hebrew Family*, p. 43; A. Bertholet, *A History of Hebrew Civilization* (London: n.p., 1926), pp. 149, 154, 156.

151. Exodus 22 : 15–16; Deuteronomy 22 : 29.

152. Breyfogle, "The Social Status of Woman," pp. 108–13; MacDonald, *The Position of Women in the Codes*, p. 51.

153. Leviticus 21 : 9.

154. Barrois, "Woman and the Priestly Office," p. 185.

155. Ibid., p. 180.

156. Leviticus 10 : 1–3; 15 : 31.

157. MacDonald, *The Position of Women in the Codes*, p. 67 says: "Woman could not be sacrificing priests, and as the priesthood tended to become more complex (e.g., with P) such a possibility would become less likely. Even if a woman's ritual uncleanness had not excluded her from the office she was by nature unfitted for the sacrificing priesthood. The slaughtering of animals is contrary to their nature. . . ."

158. Exodus 23 : 17; 34 : 23; Deuteronomy 16 : 16.

159. MacDonald, *Position of Women in the Codes*, p. 66.

160. Judges 21 : 21; I Samuel 1 : 3ff; 2 : 19; 2 Samuel 6 : 19; Ezekiel 3 : 1; Nehemiah 8 : 2, 3; 12 : 43.

161. Beer, *Die soziale und religöse Stellung der Frau*, p. 8. For an opposing view see L. Freund, "Aum semitischen Ehegüterrecht bei Auflösung der Ehe," *Wiener Zeitschrift für Kunde des Morganlandes* 30 (1917–18): 163–76.

162. Leviticus 21 : 1–7.

163. Phyllis Bird, "Images of Women in the Old Testament," in *Religion and Sexism*, ed. Rosemary Radford Ruether (New York: Simon & Schuster, 1974), p. 55.

164. Eliezer L. Sukenik, *Ancient Synagogues in Palestine and Greece* (London: Oxford University Press, 1934), p. 47. See also Jewett, *Man as Male and Female*, pp. 90–91;

Swidler, *Women in Judaism*, pp. 88–90; Jewett, *Man as Male and Female*, p. 91; Joachim Jeremias, *Jerusalem in the Time of Jesus: An Investigation into Economic and Social Conditions During the New Testament Period*, trans. F. H. and C. H. Cave (Philadelphia: Fortress Press, 1969), p. 374.

165. Bernadette J. Brooten, *Women Leaders in the Ancient Synagogue*. Brown Judaic Studies 36. (Chicago: Scholars Press, 1982), pp. 1–131.

166. *Encyclopedia Judaica*, 1971 ed., s.v. "Minyan." See also Jewett, *Man as Male and Female*, p. 91; Raphael Loewe, *The Position of Women in Judaism* (London: S.P.C.K., 1966), p. 45.

167. Swidler, *Women in Judaism*, p. 123.

168. Irene Bernnan, "Women in the Gospels," *New Blackfriars* 52 (1971): 294. Brennan bases her comments upon the *Mishnah, Aboth* 1.5, 1a, b. For the text see *The Babylonian Talmud*, ed. I. Epstein, vol. 28, *Horayoth* (New York: Rebecca Bennet Publishing Co., 1959), 28:4. See also G. F. Moore, *Judaism in the First Centuries of the Christian Era*. (Cambridge: Harvard University Press, 1927), 2:27.

169. Brennan, "Women in the Gospels," p. 294.

170. W. A. Meeks, "The Image of the Androgyne: Some Uses of a Symbol in Earliest Christianity," *History of Religions* 13 (Fall 1974): 175.

171. Harry J. Leon, *The Jews of Ancient Rome* (Philadelphia: Jewish Publication Society, 1960), p. 188; see Inscriptions, numbers 523, 496, and 166.

172. Josephus, *Against Apion*, Loeb Classical Library, pp. 333–35.

173. Josephus, *Antiquities*, Loeb Classical Library, p. 418.

174. Josephus, *Jewish Wars*, Loeb Classical Library, 3:261.

175. Ibid.

176. Barrois, "Women in the Priestly Office," p. 198.

177. C. G. Montefiore and H. Loewe, eds., *A Rabbinic Anthology* (Philadelphia: Jewish Publication Society, 1960), pp. xviii–xix; Loewe, *Position of Women*, pp. 22 ff.

178. Loewe, *Position of Women*, p. 22.

179. Swidler, *Women in Judaism*, p. 94.

180. M. Kiddusin 4.13. For the text see *The Mishnah*, trans. Herbert Danby (London: Oxford University Press, 1933), p. 329.

181. Evelyn and Frank Stagg, *Woman in the World of Jesus* (Philadelphia: Westminster Press, 1978), p. 31.

182. Boaz Cohen, *Jewish and Roman Law*, 2 vols. (New York: Jewish Theological Seminary of America, 1966), 1:128–29.

183. Midrash Pirke Rel 14. 7d.7.

184. Leviticus 6:11–22.

185. Max Löhr, *Die Stellung des Weibes zu Yahweh-Cult und Religion* (Leipzig, Germany: J. C. Hinrich's, 1908), p. 40. The word "prophetess" in the Greek is προφητις.

186. Numbers chap. 12.

187. Numbers 12:6–10.

188. Exodus 15:20.

189. Judges 4:4.

190. Barrois, "Woman and the Priestly Office," p. 183.

191. Vos, *Woman in Old Testament Worship*, p. 183.

192. 2 Kings 22:14–20; 2 Chronicles 34:22–28.

193. Isaiah 8:3.

194. Vos, *Woman in Old Testament Worship*, p. 183.

195. A. Jepsen, "Die Nebiah in Jes. 8:3," *Zeitschrift für die Alttestamentliche Wissenschaft* 72 (1960): 267 ff.

196. Barrois, "Women and the Priestly Office," p. 184.

197. See also The Witch of Endor in I Samuel 27 : 8 ff and Noadiah in Nehemiah 6 : 14. Both were prophetesses.

198. Joel 2 : 28–32.

199. Breyfogle, "The Religious Status of Women," p. 414.

200. Barrois, "Woman and the Priestly Office," p. 184.

201. Genesis 38 : 21–22; Deuteronomy 23 : 18; Hosea 4 : 14.

202. De Vaux, *Ancient Israel*, p. 383.

203. Brevard S. Childs, *The Book of Exodus: A Critical, Theological Commentary* (Philadelphia: Westminster Press, 1974), p. 636.

204. Breyfogle, "Religious Status of Woman," p. 405.

205. I Samuel 31 : 10.

206. I Kings 11 : 5, 33.

207. 2 Kings 23 : 13.

208. Jeremiah 7 : 18; Ezekiel 8 : 14; Genesis 38 : 21 ff.

209. Breyfogle, "The Religious Status of Woman," pp. 408–9.

210. 2 Samuel 6 : 19; Hosea 4 : 13; Jeremiah 31 : 4, 13; Ezra 10 : 1; Nehemiah 16 : 6–8; 9 : 17; Zechariah 12 : 11 ff.

211. Peritz, "Woman in the Ancient Hebrew Cult," p. 128.

212. Numbers 30 : 3–15.

213. Breyfogle, "The Religious Status of Women," p. 154.

214. Leviticus 12 : 1–2; 3 : 2; 15 : 19–33; Ezekiel 36 : 17.

215. Judges 13 : 15–23.

216. Exodus 35 : 22–29.

217. I Samuel 1 : 10–13; J. Pederson, *Israel* (Cophenhagen: n.p., 1933), 3 : 327.

218. Genesis 25 : 22; I Kings 14 : 1.

219. Vos, *Status of Woman in the Old Testament*, p. 161.

220. Peritz, "Woman in the Ancient Hebrew Cult," p. 126.

221. Meeks, "Image of the Androgyne," p. 179.

222. I Samuel 18 : 6; Exodus 15 : 1 ff; 32 : 19; Judges 5 : 1 ff; Song of Solomon 6 : 13; W. O. E. Oesterley, *The Sacred Dance: A Study in Comparative Folklore* (New York: Macmillan, 1923), pp. 35–42.

223. Breyfogle, "The Religious Status of Women," p. 419.

224. Peritz, "Woman in the Ancient Hebrew Cult," p. 122; Deuteronomy 12 : 12–18; 14 : 26; 15 : 20; 16 : 11–14.

Chapter 4. Greco-Roman Heritage of Mark

1. Constance F. Parvey, "The Theology and Leadership of Women in the New Testament," in *Religion and Sexism* ed. Rosemary Radford Ruether (New York: Simon & Schuster, 1974), p. 117.

2. Mary Douglas, *Purity and Danger* (London: Routledge and Kegan Paul, 1966), p. 27.

3. Sarah B. Pomeroy, *Goddesses, Whores, Wives, and Slaves: Women in Classical Antiquity* (New York: Schocken, 1975), p. 236.

4. L. Swidler, "Greco-Roman Feminism and the Reception of the Gospel," in *Traditio-Krisis-Renovatio aus theologischer Sicht: Festschrift für Winfried Zeller zum 65*, ed. Bernd Jaspert and Rudolph Mohr (Marburg, W. Germany: N. G. Elwert, 1976), p. 49. See also Johannes Leipodlt, *Die Frau in der Antiken Welt und im Urchristentum* (Leipzig, E. Germany: Koehler and Amelung, 1975), p. 53.

5. Plutarch, *Moralia*, Loeb Classical Library, p. 496.
6. Ibid.
7. Columella, *On Agriculture and Trees*, Loeb Classical Library, pp. 38–39.
8. Ibid., pp. 50–51.
9. Aelian, *Nature and Animals*, Loeb Classical Library, p. 53.
10. Pliny, *Natural History*, Loeb Classical Library, 8:63.
11. Ibid.
12. Ibid., 8:80–82.
13. Ibid., 8:84.
14. Ibid., 8:78.
15. Ibid., 8:79–81.
16. Ibid., 8:64.
17. Ibid., 8:57.
18. Ibid., 2:547.
19. Plutarch, *Moralia*, Loeb Classical Library, 6:495–96.
20. Aristotle, *Generation of Animals*, Loeb Classical Library, 6:303–5.
21. Ibid.
22. Ibid.
23. *Soranus Gynecology*, trans. Owsei Temkin (Baltimore: Johns Hopkins University Press, 1956). For the text see Ioannes Ilberg, ed. *Sorani Gynaeciorum* (Leipzig, Germany: B. G. Teubneri, 1927).
Slaves; Hans Licht, *Sexual Life in Ancient Greece* (New York: Barnes & Noble, 1974).
25. W. A. Meeks, "The Image of the Androgyne: Some Uses of a Symbol in Earliest Christianity," *History of Religions* 13 (Fall 1974): 170.
26. Ibid., p. 168.
27. Ibid., p. 169.
28. Ibid. For the text see Wilhelm Dittenberger, *Syllöge inscriptionum graecarum*, 3rd ed. (Leipzig, Germany: S. Hirzel, 1915–24), p. 985.
29. Meeks, "Image of the Androgyne," p. 170; Cf. Hugo Hepding, *Attis, seine Mythen und sein Vorarbeiten* (Gressen: Richer, 1903), pp. 178ff, 187ff.
30. M. Esther Harding, *Woman's Mysteries* (London: Longmans Green and Co., 1935), p. 155.
31. J. P. V. D. Balsdon, *Roman Women: Their History and Habits* (London: Badley Head, 1962), p. 236. Balsdon gives a list of the holidays and festivals on p. 237.
32. W. Warde Fowler, *The Roman Festivals* (London: Macmillan & Co., 1925), pp. 114ff.
33. Balsdon, *Roman Women*, p. 236.
34. Ibid.
35. Pomeroy, *Goddesses, Whores, Wives, Slaves*, p. 213.
36. Balsdon, *Roman Women*, p. 238.
37. Pomeroy, *Goddesses, Whores, Wives, and Slaves*, p. 213.
38. Ibid., pp. 213–14.
39. Balsdon, *Roman Women*, p. 238.
40. Pomeroy, *Goddesses, Whores, Wives, and Slaves*, p. 214.
41. Ibid.
42. Ibid., p. 216.
43. A. D. Nock, "Eunuchs in Ancient Religion," *Archiv für Religionwissenschraft* 23 (1925): 27ff; A. M. Blackman, "On the Position of Women in Ancient Egyptian Hierarchy," *Journal of Egyptian Archaeology* 7 (1921): 8–20.
44. Pomeroy, *Goddesses, Whores, Wives, and Slaves*, p. 219.
45. Ibid.

46. Ibid., pp. 214–16. For the text see P. Oxyrhynchus 2 : 1380.

47. Ibid., p. 223; Michel Malaise, *Les Conditions de pénétration et de diffusion des cultes e'gyptiens en Italie* (Leiden, Netherlands: E. J. Brill, 1972), pp. 127, 136–37.

48. Pomeroy, *Goddesses, Whores, Wives, and Slaves*, p. 223.

49. Ibid., p. 225.

50. Jack T. Sanders, "Dionysius, Cybele, and the 'Madness' of Women," in *Beyond Androcentrism: New Essays on Woman and Religion*, ed. Rita M. Gross (Missoula, Mont.: Scholars Press, 1977), p. 131.

51. Ibid., p. 127.

52. Walter F. Otto, *Dionysius: Myth and Cult* (Bloomington: University of Indiana Press, 1965), p. 142.

53. Sanders, "Dionysius, Cybele, and Women," p. 132.

54. Hepding, *Attis: seine Mythen*, pp. 133–39; Sanders, "Dionysius, Cybele, and Women," p. 132.

55. Carol Ochs, *Behind the Sex of God: Toward a New Consciousness-Transcending Matriarchy and Patriarchy* (Boston: Beacon, 1978), pp. 15–16.

56. Pomeroy, *Goddesses, Whores, Wives, and Slaves*, p. 206.

57. Ibid., p. 206.

58. Balsdon, *Roman Women*, pp. 24344.

59. Pomeroy, *Goddesses, Whores, Wives, and Slaves*, p. 207.

60. Harding, *Woman's Mysteries*, p. 250; see also Cassion Dio 5.9.11 and Seneca *Apocolocymtosis 1*.

61. Balsdon, *Roman Women*, p. 250.

62. Ibid.

63. Ibid., p. 251; Tacitus, *Annuals* 15.23.4; 16.6.3.

64. Swidler, "Greco-Roman Feminism," p. 54.

65. *Oxford Classical Dictionary*, 1970 ed., s.v. "Hercules."

66. Ibid., "Mithras," and A. D. Nock, "The Genius of Mithraism," *The Journal of Roman Studies* 27 (1937): 108–13.

67. *Oxford Classical Dictionary*, 1970 ed., s.v. "Oracles."

68. Ibid., "Delphic Oracle."

Chapter 5. Woman

1. R. Bultmann, *The History of the Symbolic Tradition* trans. John Marsh (Oxford: Basil Blackwell, 1963), p. 221.

2. Martin Dibelius, *From Tradition to Gospel* (New York: Scribner, 1965), p. 71.

3. Bultmann, *History of the Synoptic Tradition*, p. 221.

4. Matthew and Luke appropriated this story that fits into their own theological schemata. For a differing opinion see Harald Riesenfeld, *The Gospel Tradition*, trans. E. M. Rowley and R. A. Kraft (Philadelphia: Fortress Press), 1970, pp. 51–74; Birger Gerhardsson, *Tradition and Transmission in Early Christianity* (Lund, Sweden: Gleerup, 1964). Both of these men think that the beginning of the Gospel was not the church, but Jesus Himself.

5. See Mark, 3, 5, 6, 11, 14 and also Robert H. Stein, "The Proper Methodology for Ascertaining a Markan Redaction History," *Novum Testamentum* 13 (1971): 193–96.

6. Benjamin W. Bacon, *The Beginnings of the Gospel Story* (New Haven: Yale Uni-

versity Press, 1909), p. 60; K. L. Schmidt, *Der Rahmen der Geschichte Jesus* (Berlin: Trowitsch, 1919), p. 148; H. Van der Loos, *The Miracles of Jesus* (Leiden, Netherlands: E. J. Brill, 1965), pp. 509–19; B. Weiss, *Das Evangelium Markus in Kritisch exegetischer Kommentar* (Göttingen, Germany: Vandenhoeck and Ruprecht, 1892), p. 188; A. Meyer, *Die Enstehung des Markusevangeliums* (Tübingen, Germany: Mohr, 1927), p. 40.

7. E. Wendling, *Die Entstehung des Marcusevangeliums* (Tübingen, Germany: Mohr, 1908), pp. 47 ff.

8. Walter E. Bundy, *Jesus and the First Three Gospels* (Cambridge: Harvard University Press, 1955), p. 244 says, "The two stories have little in common"; H. A. Guy, *The Origin of the Gospel of Mark* (London: Hodder and Stoughton, 1954), p. 22.

9. S. E. Johnson, *A Commentary on the Gospel According to St. Mark* (London: Adam and Charles Black, 1960), p. 104. See also Schmidt, *Der Rahmen der Geschichte Jesus*, p. 148; Dibelius, *From Tradition to Gospel*, p. 219; Bultmann, *History of the Synoptic Tradition*, p. 228; Robert H. Lightfoot, *The Gospel of St. Mark* (Oxford: Clarendon Press, 1950), p. 289.

10. Paul J. Achtemeier, "Toward the Isolation of Pre-Markan Miracle Catena," *Journal of Biblical Literature* 89 (1970): 227.

11. Paul J. Achtemeier, *Mark: Proclamation Commentaries* (Philadelphia: Fortress Press, 1975), p. 77.

12. Paul J. Achtemeier, "The Origin and Function of the Pre-Markan Miracle Catena," *Journal of Biblical Literature* 91 (1972): 198–221.

13. Laurence J. McKinley, *Form Criticism of the Synoptic Healing Narratives: A Study in the Theories of Martin Dibelius and Rudolph Bultmann* (Maryland: Woodstock College Press, 1944), pp. 152–53. See also E. Lohmeyer, *Das Evangelium des Markus* (Göttingen, W. Germany: Vanderhoeck and Ruprecht, 1937), p. 101.

14. Van der Loos, *Miracles of Jesus*, p. 249.

15. Alan Richardson, *The Miracle Stories of the Gospels* (London: S.C.M. Press, 1941), p. 62.

16. Van der Loos, *Miracle of Jesus*, p. 233.

17. Ibid., p. 247.

18. Theodore J. Weeden, *Mark: Traditions in Conflict* (Philadelphia: Fortress Press, 1971), p. 59. See also Bultmann, *History of Synoptic Tradition*, p. 219, who sees the deeds of Jesus as proofs of his own divine power.

19. Achtemeier, *Mark*, p. 78.

20. G. W. Allport and L. J. Postman, "The Basic Psychology of Rumor," in *Basic Studies in Social Psychology*, eds. H. Proshansky and B. Seedenberg (New York: Holt, 1965), pp. 47, 49.

21. N. Q. Hamilton, "Resurrection Tradition and the Composition of Mark," *Journal of Biblical Literature* 84 (1965): 415–21; C. E. Faw, "The Outline of Mark," *Journal of Bible and Religion* 25 (1957): 19–23; Willie Marxsen, *Mark, the Evangelist*, trans. Roy A. Harrisville (Nashville, Tenn.: Abingdon, 1969).

22. J. B. Segal, "Popular Religion in Ancient Israel," *Journal of Jewish Studies* 27 (1967): 3.

23. See Chap. 3.

24. Mark 2:13; 3:32, 4:36; 5:21, 7:14, 11:32; 12:12; 15:11. The crowd is capable of both manipulating for their own benefit of being manipulated.

25. William L. Lane, *The Gospel According to Mark* (Grand Rapids, Mich.: Eerdmans, 1974), p. 194. See also *Acts of Pilate*, chap. 7. The text is found in K. Aland, *Synopsis Quattuor Evangeliorum* (Stuttgart, W. Germany: Württembergischen Bibelanstalt, 1964), p. 193.

26. Mark 4:23; 6:11.

27. Mark 9:7.

28. Chap. 3 traces the terms used for diagnosing her physical problem back to Leviticus. The most common Greco-Roman terms for her illness are not employed.

29. *Soranus' Gynecology*, trans. Owsei Temkin (Baltimore: Johns Hopkins University Press, 1956), p. 165. For the text see *Sorani: Gynaeciorum*, Libri I–IV, ed. Ionnaes Ilberg (Lipsiae: B. G. Teubneri, 1927), pp. 13–17.

30. Ibid., p. 166.

31. Matthew 9:20.

32. Luke 8:43.

33. Ancilla to the Pre-Socratic Philosophers. A translation of *Die Fragmente der Vorsokratiker*, vol. I., trans. Kathleen Freeman (Oxford: Basil Blackwell, 1946), p. 28; *Heraclitus, Fragment 58.*

34. Lane, *Mark*, p. 192. See also Hermann L. Strack and Paul Billerbeck, *Kommentar zum Neuen Testament aus Talmud und Midrasch* (Munich: Beck, 1922–28), 1:520; Julius Preuss, *Biblisch-talmundische Medizin* (New York: KTAV, 1971), p. 439.

35. Johan A. Haas, *Annotatios on the Gospel According to St. Mark* (New York: Christian Literature Society, 1895), p. 95; Kiddushin 4.14. See also Alfred Edersheim, *The Life and Times and Jesus the Messiah*, 2 vols. (New York: Longmans, Green, and Co., 1912), 1:620.

36. *Soranus' Gynecology*, p. 167.

37. See John Bowman, *The Gospel of Mark: The New Christian Jewish Passover Haggadah* (Leiden, Netherlands: E. J. Brill, 1965), pp. 145–46.

38. See chap. 3.

39. Paul J. Achtemeier, "Gospel Miracle Tradition and the Divine Man," *Interpretation* 26 (1972): 179. See also Walter A. Jayne, *The Healing Gods of Ancient Civilizations* (New York: New York University Books, 1962), pp. 234–41.

40. See Acts 21:24; James 4:3; Luke 14:28, 15:14.

41. 2 Corinthians 12:15.

42. Mark 12:38–40.

43. Possibly the story of the boy possessed by a deaf and dumb spirit was an "apparent" resurrection, Mark 9:26–27.

44. Mark 1:29–31.

45. Mark 7:24–30.

46. Mark 13:7.

47. Mark 10:2.

48. Matthew 19:9.

49. Luke 18:18.

50. Howard C. Kee, *Community of the New Age: Studies in Mark's Gospel* (Philadelphia: Westminster Press, 1977), p. 142. See also L. W. Batten, "The Social Life of the Hebrews from Josiah to Ezra," *Biblical World* 11 (1898): 404–6 for a Jewish view of divorce. A. L. Descamps, "Les textes evangéliques sur le mariage," *Revue Théologique de Louvain* 9 (1978): 259–86 sees the denunciation of remarriage as a genuine resolution.

51. Mark 6:3. See also Mark 10:12ff. For a discussion of the textual problems involving a corruption in the text see Lane, *Gospel of Mark*, pp. 201–3. He says: "The additional phrase 'the son of Mary' is probably disparaging. It was contrary to Jewish usage to describe a man as the son of his mother," p. 203. For other opinions contrary to those stated in this paper see E. Stauffer, "Jeschu ben Mirjam: Kontroversgeschichtliche Anmerkungen zu Mark 6:3, in *Neo Testamentica et Semitica: Studies in Honor of Matthew Black*, eds. E. Earle Ellis and Max Wilcox (Edinburgh: Clark, 1969), pp. 119–28; A. Feuillet, "Les temoignages de saint Paul, saint Marc et saint

Matthieu relatifs a la Vierge Marie," *Bible et Vie Chretienne* 30 (1959): 45–54. According to Taylor, *Gospel of Mark*, pp. 300–1, "The phrase 'son of Mary' has no parallel in the Gospels and raises difficult historical questions." Matthew 8:55 and Luke 4:22 both agree to the "son of Joseph."

52. See chap. 3.
53. Ibid.
54. Luke 7:21.
55. Hebrew 11:36; Acts 22:24.
56. *Theological Dictionary of the New Testament*, 1967 ed., s.v. μαστίξ.
57. Psalm 91:10.
58. Job 21:9; Alan Richardson, *The Miracle Stories of the Gospels* (London: S.C.M. Press, 1952), p. 62.
59. Jeremiah 6:7.
60. 2 Maccabees 7:37.
61. See chap. 3.
62. This problem would not have been so important to the Greek mind. See chap. 4.
63. Leonard Swidler, *Women in Judaism: The Status of Women in Formative Judaism* (Metuchen; N.J.: The Scarecrow Press, Inc., 1976), p. 135.
64. Mary Douglas, *Purity and Danger* (London: Routledge and Kegan Paul, 1966), p. 153.
65. Mark 7:1–20. See Joachim Gnilka, *Das Evangelium nach Markus* (Ensiedelin: Benzigner, 1978; distributed by Glencoe, Mission Hills, Calif.), pp. 279–89.
66. Mary Douglas, *Purity and Danger* (London: Routledge and Kegan Paul, 1966), p. 53.
67. See chap. 2.
68. Kee, *Communtiy of Mark*, p. 97. See also Jacob Neusner, *The Idea of Purity in Ancient Judaism* (Leiden, Netherlands E. J. Brill, 1973).
69. Mark 140:45; 7:24–31; 11:17.
70. Mark 1:41–42.
71. See F. W. Danker, "Mark 1:45 and the Secrecy Motif," *Concordia Theological Monthly* 37 (1966): 492–99 for an explanation of this activity. Danker thinks that the leper's reaction to Jesus points out the Marcan hostility toward the religious leaders in Jerusalem.
72. Mark 15:45.
73. Mark 15:47.
74. Leviticus 11:31.
75. Achtemier, "Toward the Isolation of Catena," pp. 265–91, and "Origin of Miracle Catena," pp. 198–221.
76. Mark 7:26.
77. Mark 7:27; W. Storch, "Zur Perikope von der Syrophönizierin. Mk. 7, 28 und Re. 1.7," *Biblische Zeitschrift* 14 (1970): 256–57.
78. T. A. Burkill, "The Syrophoenician Woman: The Congruence of Mark 7:24–31," *Zeitschrift für die Neutestamentliche Wissenschaft* 57 (1966): 35. See also A. Dermience, "Tradition et rédaction dans la pericope de la Syrophénicienne: Marc 7, 24–30," *Revue Théólogique de Louvain* 8 (1977): 15–29 who sees the story as expressing the tensions that result from the integration of non-Jews into the Christian community.
79. Ibid.
80. Kee, *Community of Mark*, p. 92.
81. Ibid.
82. See chap. 3.

83. Charles Guignerbert, *The Jewish World in the Time of Jesus* (New York: New York University Books, 1959), p. 60.

84. Mark 11 : 17.

85. Kee, *Community of Mark*, p. 150

86. Guignerbert, *Jewish World*, p. 61.

87. Mark 13 : 1 ναός. The apparent destruction of the temple is mentioned twice: Mark 14 : 58, 15 : 29.

88. Kee, *Community of Mark*, p. 115.

89. Mark 2 : 17.

90. Mark 14 : 41.

91. Mark 2 : 17.

92. Mark 2 : 19–20.

93. Mark 5 : 27, 28, 30, 31.

94. Mark 1 : 41; 3 : 10; 6 : 56; 7 : 33; 8 : 22; 10 : 13.

95. Mark 3 : 10; 6 : 56.

96. *Theological Dictionary of the New Testament*, 1965 ed., s.v. ἱμάτιον.

97. Matthew 9 : 20; Luke 8 : 44. See also Numbers 15 : 38.

98. *Theological Dictionary of the New Testament*, 1965 ed., s.v. ἰάομαι.

99. Leviticus 14 : 3, 48.

100. Johannes Weiss, *Earliest Christianity: A History of the Period A.D. 30–A.D. 150*, 2 vols., trans. F. C. Grant (Magnolia, Mass.: Peter Smith, 1970), 1 : 226–27.

101. Mark 3 : 1.

102. Mark 4 : 5; 11 : 20–21.

103. Matthew 9 : 21–22.

104. Luke 8 : 44–45.

105. Irene Brennan, "Women in the Gospels," *New Blackfriars* 52 (1971): 296. She bases her assumptions on Aboth. 1.5.12a, b, which reads: "Jose B. Johanan (a man) of Jerusalem used to say: Engage not in too much conversation with women. They said this with regard to one's own wife, how much more [does the rule apply] with regard to another man's wife. Hence have the sages said: As long as a man engages in too much conversation with women, he causes evil to himself, [for] he goes idle from [the study of] the words of the Torah, so that his end will be that he will inherit gehinnom." This translation is found in: *The Babylonian Talmud*, ed. I. Epstein, trans. Israel W. Slotki, vol. 28, *Hodayoth* (New York: Rebecca Bennet Publishing Co., 1959), p. 4.

106. Brennan, "Women in the Gospels," p. 294.

107. Exodus 22 : 16–17. See also Exodus 21 : 7–11.

108. Deuteronomy 22 : 13–21; 22 : 28–29.

109. See chap. 2, p. 41.

110. Hugh Anderson, *The Gospel of Mark*, The New Century Bible (Greenwood, S.C.: Attic Press, Inc., 1976), p. 153; and Bowman, *Gospel of Mark*, p. 147.

111. *Theological Dictionary of the New Testament*, 1965 ed., s.v. ἰάομαι.

112. Judges 18 : 6; I Samuel 1 : 17; 2 Samuel 15 : 9, I Kings 22 : 17; Luke 7 : 50; Acts 16 : 36; James 2 : 17.

113. *Theological Dictionary of the New Testament*, 1964 ed., s.v. ἐιρήνη. See also Proverbs 17 : 1 and Isaiah 14 : 30.

114. Ibid.

115. Ibid.

116. Ibid., Hans Windisch, "Friedensbringer-Gottessöhne Eine religiongeschichtliche Interpretation der 7. Seligpreisung," *Zeitschrift für die Neutestamentliche Wissenschaft* 24 (1925): 245–260.

117. Mark 10:52.
118. Mark 7:25. See also Mark 3:11.
119. Mark 1:1; 15:39.
120. Mark 13:1–36.
121. Lane, *Gospel According to Mark*, p. 193.
122. Bowman, *Gospel of Mark*, p. 146.
123. Origen, *Commentary on Matthew*, 10.9. For the text see *Origenis: Commentaria in Evangelium Secundum Matthaem* in *Patrolgae Graeca*, ed. J. P. Migne (Paris: Excudebat Vrayet, 1857), 13:883–84; D. E. Nineham, *The Gospel of Mark* (Baltimore: Penguin Books, 1963), pp. 155–62; L. Sabourin, "The Miracles of Jesus III: Healings, Resuscitations, Nature Miracles," *Biblical Theology Bulletin* 5 (1975): 146–200; V. Taylor, *The Gospel According to St. Mark* (London: Macmillan & Co., 1952), pp. 289–93; Ernst Haenchen, *Der Weg Jesu* (Berlin: Alfred Töpelmann 1966), p. 205.
124. Ephraim *Hymns and Homilies*. For the text see E. *Ephroem Syri Hymni et Sermones* (Malines, Belgium: n.p., 1882–1902). For the English translation see Philip Schaff and Henry Wace, *A Select Library of Nicene and Post Nicene Fathers of the Christian Church*. second series. 14 vols. (Grand Rapids, Mich.: Eerdmans, 1979), 13:310.
125. Chrysostom *Homilies on the Gospel of Matthew*, 52.3 and 31. For the text see *Joannis Chrysostomi* in *Patrologae Graeca*, ed. J. P. Migne (Paris: Excudebat Vrayet, 1859), 57:454.
126. Ibid.
127. Mark 10:46–52.
128. Chrysostom, *Homilies on the Gospel of Matthew*, 31.
129. Mark 6:45–50.
130. Mark 6:1, 4.
131. Matthew 9:22; Luke 8:48.
132. Mark 13:1–36.
133. Mark 11:22.
134. Mark 1:15.
135. Mark 13:1–36.
136. Bundy, *Jesus and the First Three Gospels*, p. 245.
137. Allan Menzies, *The Earliest Gospel: A Historical Study of the Gospel According to Mark* (London: Macmillan & Co., 1901), pp. 125–29. See also J. M. Hull, *Hellenistic Magic and the Synoptic Tradition* (Geneva, Ill.: Allenson, 1974); Thomas W. Davies, *Magic Divination and Demonology Among the Hebrew and their Neighbors* (New York: KTAV, 1969); Anderson, *Gospel of Mark*, p. 153.
138. Irenaeus *Against Heresies*, 3.1.2. For the text see *Sancti Irenaei: Contra Haereses* in *Patrologae Graeca*, ed. J. P. Migne (Paris: Sue-Petit Montrouge, 1857), 6:243–46.
139. Mark 6:2, 5, 14.
140. Mark 9:1.
141. Mark 13:26; 14:62.
142. Matthew seeks to correct the notion that power went out from Jesus unknowingly by omitting this section (Matthew 9:22).
143. *Theological Dictionary of the New Testament*, 1965 ed., s.v. δύναμις.
144. Mark 6:2, 5, 14.
145. Leviticus 2:7, 8, 11; 8:4, 5, 34, 36; 9:7, 16.
146. Van der Loos, *Miracles of Jesus*, pp. 509–19.
147. Weeden, *Traditions in Conflict*, pp. 27–28.
148. Marie J. Lagrange, *Evangile selon Saint Marc* (Paris: Librairie Lecoffre, 1929), p. 141.
149. Mark 9:38.

150. See chap. 2.

151. I Corinthians 12:9, 28, 30.

152. Matthew 10:8.

153. Mark 6–13. See also James 5:13ff.

154. Mark 9:17ff.

155. Mark 1:41; 7:33; 8:22; 10:13.

156. ἅπτομαι and women are linked four times in this pericope for obvious reasons.

157. Mark 14:43–45.

158. Mark 14:71.

159. Some scholars view ἀναθεματίζειν as reflexive. So Peter is really cursing himself. T. A. Burkill, "Blasphemy: St. Mark's Gospel as Damnation History," in *Christianity, Judaism, and Other Greco-Roman Studies for Morton Smith at 60.* 2 vols., ed. J. Neusner (Leiden, Netherlands: E. J. Brill, 1975), 1:68.

160. Ibid., p. 70.

161. Mark 10:35–37.

162. Mark 10:35–37.

163. Mark 10:40; Weeden, *Traditions in Conflict*, p. 63.

164. Mark 13:8.

165. Mark 1:40; 16:1–8.

166. Mark 1:4ff, 10:46ff; Sabourin, "Miracles of Jesus," p. 174.

167. Kee, *Community of Mark*, p. 117.

168. Mark 2:13; 4:1, 2; 6:2, 6, 30, 37; 7:7.

169. Some manuscripts omit the name.

170. C. E. B. Cranfield, *The Gospel According to St. Mark: The Cambridge Greek New Testament Commentary* (Cambridge: Cambridge University Press, 1959), p. 183.

171. Achtemeier, *Mark*, p. 50.

172. It is also true that Mark adds specific details to the miracle stories in order to heighten their affect on the audience. B. Bornkamm, B. Barth, and H. J. Held, *Tradition and Interpretation in Matthew* (Philadelphia: Westminster Press, 1963), pp. 215–19.

173. E. Schweizer, *The Good News According to Mark*, trans. D. H. Madvig (Atlanta: John Knox Press, 1966), p. 178; Lohmeyer, *Des Evangelium des Markus*, pp. 102–5.

174. Swidler, *Woman in Judaism, pp.* 115–17.

175. Matthew 9:18–26.

176. Mark 12:32.

177. Ephesians 4:20–21.

178. *Theological Dictionary of the New Testament*, 1964 ed., s.v. ἀλήθεια.

179. Deuteronomy 22:20; 13:14; 17:4.

180. Psalms 15:2; 51:6.

181. Hosea 4:1.

182. *Theological Dictionary of the New Testament*, 1964 ed., s.v. ἀλήθεια.

183. Ibid.

184. Ibid.

185. John 14:6.

186. Mark 1:1; 15:39.

187. Mark 14:66–72.

188. Constance F. Parvey, "The Theology and Leadership of Women in the New Testament," in *Religion and Sexism*, ed. R. R. Reuther (New York: Simon & Schuster, 1974), p. 123.

189. Mark 1:41; 10:45; 15:41.

190. Mark 10:45.

191. Mark 8 : 34–38.
192. Mark 10 : 45 and also 8 : 34.
193. Kee, *Community of Mark*, p. 93.
194. Mark 10 : 51, 10 : 36.
195. *A Greek-English Lexicon of the New Testament and Other Early Christian Literature,* 1979 ed., s.v. κατακυριεύω.
196. *Theological Dictionary of the New Testament*, 1964 ed., s.v. διάκονος.
197. Ibid.
198. Mark 3 : 15; 6 : 5.
199. Mark 3 : 12–13.
200. Matthew 27 : 55. See also Luke 8 : 3.
201. Luke 22 : 27.
202. Matthew 23 : 11.
203. Kee, *Community of Mark*, p. 152.
204. αὐτῳ is found in variants in all three Gospels.
205. Romand 15 : 31.
206. Acts 19 : 22.
207. Romans 17 : 7.
208. Matthew 25 : 42–44.
209. *Theological Dictionary of the New Testament*, 1964 ed., s.v. διάκονος.
210. Mark 1 : 13; F. W. Danker, "The Demonic Secret in Mark," *Zeitschrift für Neutestamentliche Wissenschaft* 61 (1970): 48–69.
211. Mark 1 : 2–8.
212. Mark 12 : 25; 13 : 32.
213. Mark 13 : 32.
214. Mark 13 : 27.
215. Mark 1 : 18; 2 : 14.
216. Mark 5 : 24; 3 : 7.
217. Mark 10 : 32.
218. Mark 10 : 52.
219. Mark 2 : 15.
220. Mark 10 : 28.
221. Mark 10 : 17–22.
222. Mark 10 : 32.
223. Mark 14 : 54.
224. Mark 8 : 31; 9 : 12 and it is used five times in chap. 14 of the Passover.
225. αἷμα is used twice in the miracle story; Mark 5 : 25, 29; 14 : 24.
226. Mark 5 : 29; 14 : 8, 22; 15 : 43.
227. Mark 10 : 34.
228. Mark 3 : 10.
229. Mark 14 : 30, 31, 72.
230. Mark 12 : 41–44.
231. *Theological Dictionary of the New Testament*, 1964, s.v. ζαώ. ζωη or ζαώ is used in the sense of eternal life (10 : 17) and the idea that God is the god of the living (12 : 27).
232. Kee, *Community of Mark*, p. 149.
233. Mark 10 : 17–22.
234. Mark 8 : 34.
235. Mark 14 : 3. See also Mark 1 : 41.
236. John 12 : 3.
237. Luke 7 : 47.
238. Mark 14 : 5.

239. Matthew 26:9.
240. John 12:4.
241. Luke 7:39.
242. Mark 10:13–16.
243. Mark 8:34.
244. Mark 12:41–44.
245. Mark 15:41.
246. Mark 15:43, 47; 16:1–3.
247. Austin M. Farrer, *A Study in St. Mark* (New York: Oxford University Press, 1952), p. 167.
248. Mark 7:24–31 and possibly Bartimaeus in 10:46–52.
249. Achtemeier, "Toward the Isolation of Catena," pp. 265–91 and "Origin and Function of the Catena," pp. 198–221.
250. Mark 5:27; 7:25.
251. Mark 5:33; 7:25.
252. Mark 5:32–34; 7:27ff.
253. Mark 5:32–34; 7:27–28; T. A. Burkill, "The Syrophoenician Woman: The Congruence of Mark 7:24–31," *Zeitschrift für Neutestamentliche Wissenchaft* 52 (1966): 31.
254. Mark 5:34; 7:29.
255. Mark 5:30; 7:27–30.
256. Mark 7:26.
257. Burkill, "Syrophoenician Woman," pp. 23–37. See also Erich Klostermann, *Das Markusevangelium* (Tübingen, W. Germany: Mohr, 1950), pp. 58–62.; Bundy, *Jesus and the First Three Gospels*, p. 278.
258. Mark 7:28–30.
259. Mark 7:27.
260. Mark 15:41.
261. Mark 16:1, 15:47.
262. Stagg, *Woman in the World of Jesus*, p. 138.
263. Kee, *Community of Mark*, p. 156.
264. Paul K. Jewett, *Man as Male and Female* (Grand Rapids, Mich.: Eerdmans, 1975), p. 34.
265. Augustine, *City of God*, 23.17. For the text see *Sancti Averlii Augustini de Civitate Dei. Libri XI–XXII, Corpus Christianorum, Series Latina,* ed. Benardus Dombart and Alphonsus Kalb (Turnholti: Typographi Brepols Editores Pontificii, 1955), pp. 814–15. See also Jewett, *Man as Male and Female*, p. 41; Rosemary R. Ruether, "Misogynism and Virginal Feminism in the Fathers of the Church," in *Religion and Sexism,* ed. R. R. Reuther (New York: Simon & Schuster, 1974), p. 160.
266. Mark 12:23; Bruce M. Metzger, *A Textual Commentary on the Greek New Testament* (London: United Bible Societies, 1971), pp. 110–11. The translation used in the text is from *The New International Version of the New Testament,* ed. A. Marshall (Grand Rapids, Mich.: Zondervan, 1976).
267. Mark 12:27; ζαώ is used only here and with reference to the healing of Jarius' daughter in 5:23.
268. *Oxford Classical Dictionary*, 1970 ed., s.v. "Oracles" and "Delphic Oracles."
269. H. B. Swete, *The Gospel According to St. Mark* (London: Macmillan & Co., 1908), p. 34; A. M. Hunter, *The Gospel According to St. Mark* (London: SCM Press, 1948), p. 65.
270. Brennan, "Women in the Gospels," p. 299. See also *Yerushalmi Sanhedrin* 3.9. in *The Babylonian Talmud,* ed. I. Epstein.

271. Oxford Classical Dictionary, 1970 ed., s.v. "Delphic Oracles," and W. C. Allen, "St. Mark XVI: 8: 'They were Afraid' Why?" *Journal of Theological Studies* 47 (1946): 46–49 says, "Their fear was not fright or terror but a solemn awe of human beings who felt they stood at the gate of heaven. . . ."

272. *Theological Dictionary of the New Testament*, 1974 ed., s.v. φόβος.

273. Mark 4 : 41.

274. Mark 4 : 41; 5 : 15; 6 : 50; 9 : 32; 11 : 18, etc.

275. Luke 1 : 50; 18 : 2, 4; Acts 10 : 35; I Peter 2 : 17; Revelation 14 : 7.

276. *Theological Dictionary of the New Testament*, 1965 ed., s.v. θάμβος.

277. Mark 4 : 41; 6 : 50.

278. *Theological Dictionary of the New Testament*, 1964 ed., s.v. εἰρήνη.

279. My own translation.

280. Mark 16 : 8; R. H. Smith, "New and Old in Mark 16 : 1–8," *Concordia Theological Monthly* 48 (1972): 518–27.

281. Mark 16 : 7.

282. Burkill, "Syrophoenician Woman," p. 33.

283. Mark 8 : 9.

284. Mark 7 : 28.

285. Burkill, "Syrophoenician Woman," p. 35.

286. F. W. Danker, "Postscript to the Markan Secrecy Motif," *Concordia Theological Monthly* 38 (1967): 26.

287. Mark 16 : 8. See γυνή in *A Greek–English Lexicon of the New Testament and Other Early Christian Literature*, 1979 ed.

Bibliography

Primary Sources

Aelian. *On the Characteristics of Animals.* Translated by A. F. Scholfield and edited by T. E. Page. 3 vols. The Loeb Classical Library. Cambridge: Harvard University Press, 1959.

Aland, Kurt, ed. *Synopsis Quattuor Evangeliorum* (Symposium of the Four Evangelists). Stuttgart, W. Germany: Württembergische Bibelanstalt Stuttgart, 1964.

Aland, Kurt, Matthew Black, Carlo M. Martini, Bruce M. Metzger, and Allen Wikgren. *The Greek New Testament.* 3d ed. W. Germany: United Bible Societies, 1975.

Ancilla to the Pre-Socratic Philosophers. A translation of *Die Fragmente der Vorsokratiker.* Translated by Kathleen Freeman. Oxford: Basil Blackwell, 1946.

Aquinas, Thomas. *Catena Aurea in Quatuor Evangelia.* Vol. 1, *Expositio in Matthaeum et Marcum.* Translated by Angelici Guarienti. Rome: Marietti, 1953.

Aristotle. *Generations of Animals.* Translated by A. L. Peck and edited by T. E. Page. The Loeb Classical Library. Cambridge: Harvard University Press, 1943.

The Babylonian Talmud. Translated and edited by I. Epstein. London: The Soncino Press, 1936–59.

Bedae, Venerabilis. *Opera Exegetica: In Lucae Evangelium Expositio* (Expositions of St. Luke). Translated by D. Hurst. Turnholti: Brepols, 1960.

Beveridge, William. Συνοδίκον *sive Padectae Canonum SS. Apostolorum, et Conciliorum ab Ecclesia Graeca Receptorum.* 2 vols. Oxonii: E. Theatro Sheldoniano, 1877.

Charles, R. H., ed. *The Apocrypha and Pseudepigrapha of the Old Testament in English.* 2 vols. Oxford: Clarendon Press, 1963.

Charles, R. H. *The Book of Enoch.* London: S.P.C.K., 1974. Columella, Lucius Junius Moderatus. *On Agriculture and Trees.* Vol 3, *Res Rustica X-XII: De Arboribus.* Translated E. S. Forster and E. H. Heffner and edited by T. E. Page. The Loeb Classical Library. Cambridge: Harvard University Press, 1955.

Demosthenes. *Demosthenes Prooemia.* Edited by F. Blass. Leipzig, E. Germany: n.p., 1888–92.

Denis, Albert-Marie. *Introduction aux Pseude'pigraphes d'Ancien Testament.* Leiden, Netherlands: n.p., 1970.

Diodorus Siculus. *Diodori Bibliotheca Historica.* Edited by I. Bekker; L. Dindorf; and F. Vogel. 2 vols. Stuttgart, W. Germany: B. G. Teubner, 1964.

Dittenberger, Wilhelm. *Syllöge Inscriptionum Graecarum.* Leipzig, Germany: S. Hirzel, 1915–24.

Eusebius. *The Ecclesiastical History.* Edited by J. E. Oulton and H. J. Lawlor. 2 vols. The Loeb Classical Library. New York: C. P. Putnam's Sons, 1932.

Ewald, Marie Liguori. *The Homilies of Saint Jerome.* vol. 2, *Homilies 60–96.* Washington, D.C.: The Catholic University Press, 1966.

A General Biographical Dictionary, 1851 ed. S. v. "Balsamon."

A Greek-English Lexicon of the New Testament and Other Early Christian Literature, 1979 ed. s. v. κατακυριεύω, γυνή.

Hippocrates. *Airs, Waters, Places.* Translated by W. H. S. Jones and edited by T. E. Page. The Loeb Classical Library. Cambridge: Harvard University Press, 1923.

Hippocrates. *Heracleitus on the Universe.* Translated by W. H. S. Jones and edited by T. E. Page. The Loeb Classical Library. Cambridge: Harvard University Press, 1953.

The Jerusalem Bible. Edited by Alexander Jones. New York: Doubleday & Company, Inc., 1966.

Josephus. *Jewish Antiquities.* Translated by H. St. J. Thackeray and edited by T. E. Page. The Loeb Classical Library. London: William Heinemann, 1930.

Josephus. *The Jewish War.* Translated by H. St. J. Thackeray and edited by T. E. Page. 8 vols. The Loeb Classical Library. London: William Heinemann, 1928.

Josephus. *The Life Against Apion.* Translated by H. St. J. Thackeray and edited by E. Capps. The Loeb Classical Library. London: William Heinemann, 1926.

Klosterman, E., ed. *Die Griechisch Erhaltenen Tomoi.* Vol 10, *Origenes Werke. Origenes Matthäuserlärung.* Leipzig, Germany: J. C. Hinrichs Verlag, 1935.

Lambot, Cyrillus, ed. *Sancti Aureluii Augustine Sermones* (Sermons of St. Augustine). *De Vetere Testamento.* Turnholti: Typographi Brepols Editores Pontificii, 1961.

Lamy, J., ed. *S. Ephroem syri Hymni et sermones.* 4 vols. Malines, Belgium: n.p., 1882–1902.

Menzies, Allan, ed. *The Ante-Nicene Fathers: Translations of the Fathers down to A.D. 325.* Vol. 10, *Origen's Commentary on Matthew.* New York: Charles Scribner's Sons, 1925.

Metzger, Bruce M. *A Textual Commentary of the Greek New Testament.* New York: United Bible Societies, 1971.

Migne, Jacques Paul, ed. *Patrologiae cursus Completus: Series Graeca.* Paris: Excudebat Vrayet, 1845–87. Vol. 2, *Euthymii Zigabeni Commenatrius in Quatuor Evangelia.* Vol. 6, *Sancti Irenaei. Contra Haereses.* Vol. 7, *Origenis: Commentaria in Evangelium Secundum Matthaeum.* Vol. 16, *Sancti Ambrosii Mediolonesis Episcopi: De Poententia.* Vol. 25, *S. Athanasius Alexandrinus Archiepiscopus.* Vol. 26, *Vista S. Antoni.* Vol. 57, *Joannis Chrysostomi.* Vol. 123, *Theophylact: Bulgariae Archiepiscopi.*

The Misnah. Translated by Herbert Danby. London: Oxford University Press, 1933.

Montefiore, C. G., and H. Loewe, eds. *A Rabbinic Anthology.* Philadelphia: Jewish Publication Society, 1960.

Nestle, Eberhard. *Introduction to the Textual Criticism of the Greek New Testament.* London: Williams and Norgate, 1901.

The New International Version: Interlinear Greek-English New Testament. Edited by Alfred Marshall. Grand Rapids, Mich.: Zondervan Publishing House, 1976.

Oxford Classical Dictionary, 1970 ed. S. v. "Oracles," and "Delphic Oracle."

Philo. *Special Laws.* Translated by F. H. Colson and G. H. Whitaker and edited by T. E. Page. The Loeb Classical Library. London: William Heinemann, 1930.

Philo. *Unchangeableness of God.* Edited by T. E. Page. The Loeb Classical Library. London: William Heinemann, 1930.

Pliny and Elder. *Natural History.* Translated by H. Rackham and edited by T. E. Page. The Loeb Classical Library. Cambridge: Harvard University Press, 1950.

Plutarch. *Moralia.* Vol. 6, *439a–523b.* Translated by W. C. Helmbold and edited by T. E. Page. The Loeb Classical Library. Cambridge: Harvard University Press, 1957.

Rahlfs, Alfred, ed. *Septuaginta: Id est Vetus Testamentum Graece iuxta LXX Interpretes.* Vol. 1, *Leges et Historiae.* Stuttgart, Germany: Bibelstiftung Stuttgart, 1935.

Roberts, Alexander, and James Donaldson, eds. *The Ante-Nicene Fathers: Translations of the Writings of the Fathers down to A.D. 325.* Grand Rapids, Mich.: William B. Eerdmans, 1926, 1973, 1978, and 1979. Vol. 1, *Justin Martyr and Irenaeus.* Vol. 3, *Latin Christianity: Its Founder, Tertullian.* Vol. 8, *The Gospel of Nicodemus.*

Ruiz, Daniel, ed. *Obras de San Juan Crisostomo: Homilias sobre el Evangelio de San Mateo* (Sermons of St. John Chrysostom: Sermons of St. Matthew) (46–90). Madrid: Biblioteca de Autores Cristianos, 1952.

Sancti Aurelii Augustine. *Sancti Aurelii Augustini de Civitate Dei: Libri XI–XXII: Corpus Christianorum. Series Latina.* Edited by Bernardus Dombart and Alphonsus Kalb. Turnholti: Typographi Brepols Editores Pontificii, 1955.

Schaff, Philip, Henry Wace, eds. *A Select Library of the Nicene and Post-Nicene Fathers of the Christian Churches.* Grand Rapids, Mich.: William B. Eerdmans, 1956, 1978, and 1979. Vol. 10, *Saint Ambrose: Selected Works and Letters Concerning Repentance.* Vol. 3, *Saint Augustine.* Vol. 10, *Saint Anthanasius: The Life of Saint Anthony.* Vol. 10, *Saint Chrysostom: Homilies of the Gospel of Saint Matthew.* Vol. 13, *Ephraim: Hymns and Homilies.* Vol. 14, *The Seven Ecumenical Councils.*

Sorani Gynaeciorum. Ioannes Ilberg, ed. Lipsiae et Berolini: B. G. Teubneri, 1927.

Soranus' Gynecology. Translated by Owsei Temkin. Baltimore: The John Hopkins University Press, 1956.

Tertullian. *Tertullian: Opera.* 2 vols. Corpus Christianorum: Series Latina. Turnholti: Tyographi Brepols Editores Pontificii, 1954.

Theological Dictionary of the New Testament, 1964–1970. ed. S. v. ἀλήθεια, διάκονος, δύναμις, ἐιρηνη, ζαώ, θάμβος, ἰάομαι μαστίξ, φόβος, ἱμάτιον.

Weimar, Johannes, ed. *D. Martin Luthers Werk.* Berlin: Bohlaus Nachfolger, 1910.

Woman: Old Testament/Hebrew Bible

Batten, L. W. "The Social Life of the Hebrews from Josiah to Ezra." *Biblical World* 11 (1898): 397–409.

Beer, Georg. *Die soziale und religiöse Stellung der Frau im israelitischen Altertum.* Tübingen, Germany: J. C. B. Mohr, 1919.

Berman, Saul. "The Status of Women in Halachic Judaism." *Tradition* 14 (1973): 5–27.

Bertholet, A. *A History of Hebrew Civilization.* London: n.p., 1926.

Bird, Phyllis. "Images of Women in the Old Testament." In *Religion and Sexism,* edited by, Rosemary Radford Ruether, pp. 41–88. New York: Simon & Schuster, Inc. 1974.

Blackman, A. M. "On the Position of Women in Ancient Egyptian Hierarchy." *Journal of Egyptian Archaeology* 7 (1921): 8–20.

Breyfogle, C. M. "The Religious Status of Women in the Old Testament." *Biblical World* 35 (1910): 405–419.

Brooten, Bernadette J. *Women Leaders in the Ancient Synagogue*. Brown Judaic Studies, 36. Chicago: Scholars Press, 1977.

Cohen, Boaz. *Jewish and Roman Law. A Comparative Study*. 2 vols. New York: The Jewish Theological Seminary, 1966.

Culpepper, Emily E. "Zoroastrian Menstruation Taboos: A Woman's Studies Perspective." In *Women and Religion*, edited by Judith Plaskow and Joan Arnold Romero. Missoula, Mont.: The Scholars Press, 1974.

Douglas, Mary. *Purity and Danger*. London: Routledge and Kegan Paul, 1966.

Encyclopedia Judaica, 1971 ed. S. v. "Daughter," "Purity," and "Niddah."

Foldes, Riv-Ellen Prell. "Coming of Age of Kelton: The Constraints on Gender Symbolism in Jewish Ritual." In *Women in Ritual and Symbolic Roles*, edited by Judith Hock-Smith and Anita Spring. New York: Plenum Publishing Corporation, 1978.

Freund, L. "Zum semitischen Ehegüterrecht bei Auflosung der Ehe." *Wiener Zeitschrift für Kunde des Morganlandes* 30 (1917–18): 163–76.

Kahane, Kalman. *Daughter of Israel*. Jerusalem: Feldheim, 1973.

Loewe, Raphael. *The Position of Women in Judaism*. London: S.P.C.K., 1966.

Löhr, M. *Die Stellung des Weibes zu Jahweh-Cult und Religion*. Leipzig, Germany: J. C. Hinrich's, 1908.

MacDonald, Elizabeth Mary. *The Position of Women as Reflected in Semitic Codes of Law*. Tornoto: The University of Toronto, 1931.

Neusner, Jacob. "From Scripture to Mishnah: The Origins of Tractate Niddah." *Journal of Jewish Studies* 39 (1978): 137–48.

Neusner, Jacob. *The Idea of Purity in Ancient Judaism*. The Haskill Lectures, 1972–73. Leiden, Netherlands: E. J. Brill, 1973.

Nock, A. D. "Eunuchs in Ancient Israel." *Archiv für Religionwissenschaft* 23 (1925): 27–37.

Oesterley, W. O. E. *The Sacred Dance: A Study in Comparative Folklore*. New York: Macmillan Publishing Co., Inc., 1923.

Peritz, Ismar J. "Women in the Ancient Hebrew Cult." *Journal of Biblical Literature* 17 (1898): 111–48.

Phipps, William E., "The Menstrual Taboo in Judeo-Christian Tradition." *Journal of Religion and Health*. 19 (1980): 293–303.

Segal, J. B. "Popular Religion in Ancient Israel." *Journal of Jewish Studies* 27 (1976): 1–22.

Seibert, Ilse. *Women in the Ancient Near East*. Translated by Marianne Herzfeld. New York: A. Schram, 1974.

Shulman, Gail B. "View from the back of the Synagogue: Woman in Judaism." In *Sexist Religion and Women in the Church: No More Silence*, edited by Alice L. Hageman, pp. 143–65. New York: Association Press, 1974.

Stephens, William N. "A Cross-Cultural Study of Menstrual Taboos." *Gentic Psychology Monographs* 64 (1961): 385–416.

Swidler, Leonard. *Women in Judaism: The Status of Women in Formative Judaism*. Metuchen, N. J.: The Scarecrow Press, 1976.

Vaux, Roland de. *Ancient Israel: Its Life and Institutions*. Translated by John McHugh. New York: McGraw-Hill Book Company, 1961.

Vos, Clarence J. *Woman in Old Testament Worship*. Delft, Netherlands: Verenigde Drukkerijen Judels and Brinkman, 1978.

Woman: New Testament Times

Balsdon, J. P. V. *Roman Women, Their History and Habits*. London: Badley Head, 1962.

Barrois, Georges. "Women and the Priestly Office According to the Scriptures." *St. Vladimir's Theological Quarterly* 19 (1975): 174–92.

Bennett, Anne McGrew. "Overcoming the Biblical and Traditional Subordination of Women." *Radical Religion* 1 (1974): 28–38.

Brennan, Irene. "Women in the Gospels." *New Blackfriars* 52 (1971): 291–99.

Brown, Raymond E. "Roles of Women in the Fourth Gospel." *Theological Studies* 36 (1975): 688–99.

Burkill, T. A. "The Syrophoenician Woman: The Congruence of Mark 7 : 24–31." *Zeitschrift für die Neutestamentliche Wissenschaft* 57 (1966): 23–37.

Case, Shirley Jackson. *The Social Origins of Christianity*. Chicago: University of Chicago Press, 1923.

Catchpole, D. "The Fearful Silence of the Women at the Tomb: A Study in Markan Theology." *Journal of Theology for Southern Africa* 18 (1977): 3–10.

Clark, Elizabeth, and Herbert Warren Richardson, *Women and Religion: A Feminist Sourcebook of Christian Thought*. New York: Harper & Row Publishers, 1977.

Cox, Janice Nunnally. *Foremothers: Women of the Bible*. New York: Seabury Press, 1981.

Cross, E. B. *The Hebrew Family*. Chicago: n.p., 1927.

Danielou, Jean. *Ministry of Women in the Early Church*. London: Faith Press, 1961.

Descamps, A. L. "Les textes evangeliques sur le mariage." *Revue Theologique de Louvain* 9 (1978): 259–86.

Faxon, Alicia C. *Women and Jesus*. Philadelphia: United Church Press, 1973.

Feuillet, A. "Les temoignages de saint Paul, saint Marc et saint Matthieu relatifs a la Vierge Marie." *Bible et Vie Chretienne* 30 (1959: 45–54.

Fiorenza, E. S. "The Study of Women in Early Christianity." *Proceedings of the College Theology Society's 1977 Annual Meeting*.

Fiorenza, E. S. "Women in the Pre-Pauline and Pauline Churches." *Union Seminary Quarterly Review* 33 (1978): 153–66.

Fiorenza, E. S. *In Memory of Her: A Feminist Reconstruction of Christian Origins*. New York: Crossroads Press, 1984.

Fiorenza, E. S. "The Apostleship of Women in Early Christianity." In *Women Priests: A Catholic Commentary on the Vatican Declaration*, edited by Leonard the Arlene Swidler, pp. 132–34. New York: Paulist Press, 1977.

Ford, J. Massyngberde. "Social Consciousness in the New Testament: Jesus and Paul, a Contrast." *New Blackfriars* 57 (1976): 244–54.

Fowler, W. Warde. *The Roman Festivals*. London: Macmillan & Co. Ltd., 1925.

Genest, Olivette. "Evangiles et femmes." *Science et ésprit* 37 (1985): 275–95.

Harding, M. Esther. *Woman's Mysteries*. London: Longmans, Green and Co., 1935.

Hepding, Hugo. *Attis: seine Mythen und seine Kult: Religionsgeschictliche Versuche und Vorarbeiten 1*. Gresen: Richer, 1903.

Jewett, Paul K. *Man as Male and Female: A Study in Sexual Relationships from a Theological Point of View*. Grand Rapids, Mich.: William B. Eerdmans, 1975.

Ketter, Peter. *Christ and Womankind*. Translated by Isabel McHugh. Westminster, Md.: The Newman Press, 1952.

Lane, Alice Buchanan. "The Significance of the Thirteen Women in the Gospel of Mark." *Unitarian Universalist Christian* 38 (1983): 18–27.

Leipoldt, Johannes. *Die Frau in der Antiken Welt und im ur Christentum*. Leipzig, E. Germany: Koehler and Amelong, 1955.

Malaise, Michel. *Les conditions de pénétration et de diffusion des cultes e'gyptiens en Italie*. Leiden, Netherlands: E. J. Brill, 1972.

Meeks, W. A. "The Image of the Androgyne: Some Uses of a Symbol in Earliest Christianity." *History of Religion* 13 (1974): 169–74.

Munro, Winsom. "Women Disciples in Mark." *Catholic Biblical Quarterly* 44 (1982): 225–41.

Ochs, Carol. *Behind the Sex of God: Toward a New Consciousness-transcending Matriarchy and Patriarchy*. Boston: Beacon Press, 1978.

Parvey, Constance F. "The Theology and Leadership of Women in the New Testament." In *Religion and Sexism*, edited by Rosemary Radford Ruether, pp. 117–50. New York: Simon & Schuster, Inc., 1974.

Pomeroy, S. B. *Goddesses, Whores, Wives and Slaves: Women in Classical Antiquity*. New York: Schocken Books, Inc., 1975.

Ruether, Rosemary Radford. "Misogynism and Virginal Feminism in the Fathers of the Church." In *Religion and Sexism*, edited by R. R. Ruether, pp. 150–84. New York: Simon & Schuster, Inc., 1974.

Sabourin, L. "The Miracles of Jesus III: Healings, Resuscitations, Nature Miracles." *Biblical Theology Bulletin*, 5 (1975): 146–200.

Sanders, Jack T. "Dionysius, Cybele, and the 'Madness' of Women." In *Beyond Androcentrism: New Essays on Women and Religion*, edited by Rita M. Gross, pp. 125–37. Missoula, Mont.: Scholars Press, 1977.

Scanzoni, Letha, and Hardesty, Nancy. *All We're Meant To Be: A Biblical Approach to Women's Liberation*. Waco, Tex.: Word, 1974.

Selvidge, Marla J. "Mark 5 : 24–34 and Leviticus 15: A Reaction to Restrictive Purity Regulations." *Journal of Biblical Literature* 103 (1984): 619–23.

Selvidge, Marla J. *Daughters of Jerusalem*. Scottsdale, Pa.: Herald Press, 1986.

Smith, Judith H., and Anita, Spring, eds. *Women in Ritual and Symbolic Roles*. New York: Plenum Press, 1978.

Stagg, Evelyn, and Frank Stagg, *Woman in the World of Jesus*. Philadelphia: Westminster Press, 1978.

Stauffer, E. "Jeschu ben Mirjam: Kontroversgeschichtliche Anmerkungen zu Mark 6 : 3." In *Neo Testamentica et Semitica: Studies in Honor of Matthew Black*, edited by E. Earle Ellis and Max Wilcox, pp. 119–28. Edinburgh: Clark, 1969.

Storch, W. "Zür Pericope von der Syrophönizierin: Mk. 7 : 28 und Re. 1,7." *Biblishce Zeitschrift* 14 (1970): 256–57.

Struthers, Elizabeth Malbon. "Fallible Followers: Women and Men in the Gospel of Mark." *Semeia* 28 (1983): 29–48.

Swidler, Leonard. "Greco-Roman Feminism and the Reception of the Gospel." In *Traditio-Krisis-Renovatio aus theologischer Sicht: Festschrift für Winfried Zeller zum 65. Geburtstag*. ed. Bernd Jaspert and Rudolph Mohr. Marburg, W. Germany: N. G. Elwert, 1976, pp. 41–55.

Swidler, Leonard. "Jesus and His Encounter with Women." *African Ecclesiastical Review* 13 (1971): 290–300.

Swidler, Leonard. "Jesus Was a Feminist." *Southeast Asia Journal of Theology* 13 (1971): 102–10.

Trible, Phyllis. "Depatriarchalizing in Biblical Interpretation." *Journal of the American Academy of Religion* 41 (1973): 30–47.

Witherington III, Ben. *Jesus and the ministry of Women. A Study of Jesus' Attitude to Women and Their Roles as Reflected in His Early Life*. Cambridge: Cambridge University Press, 1984.

The Gospel of Mark

Abbott, Lyman. *The New Testament with Notes and Comments: Matthew and Mark*. New York: A. S. Barnes & Co., Inc., 1875.

Achtemeier, Paul J. "Gospel Miracle Tradition and the Divine Man." *Interpretation* 26 (1972): 174–97.

Archtemeier, Paul J. *Mark. Proclamation Commentaries*. Edited by Gerhard Krodel. Philadelphia: Fortress Press, 1975.

Achtemeier, Paul J. "The Origin and Function of the Pre-Markan Miracle Catenae." *Journal of Biblical Literature* 91 (1972): 198–221.

Achtemeier, Paul J. "Toward the Isolation of Pre-Markan Miracle Catanae." *Journal of Biblical Literature* 89 (1970): 265–91.

Allen, W. C. "St. Mark XVI : 8: 'They were Afraid' Why?" *Journal of Theological Studies* 47 (1946): 46–49.

Ambrozic, Aloysius M. *The Hidden Kingdom: A Redactioncritical Study of the References to the Kingdom of God in Mark's Gospel*. Washington, D.C.: C. B. Associates of America, 1972.

Anderson, Hugh. *The Gospel of Mark*. The New Century Bible. Greenwood, S.C.: Attic Press, Inc., 1976.

Bacon, B. W. *The Beginnings of the Gospel Story*. New Haven: Yale University Press, 1909.

Barclay, William. *The Gospel of Mark*. Philadelphia: The Westminster Press, 1975.

Best, Ernest. "The Role of the Disciples in Mark." *New Testament Studies*. 23 (1977): 377–40.

Best, Ernest. "Peter in the Gospel According to Mark." *Journal of Biblical Literature* 40 (1978): 547–58.

Best, Ernest. "The Twelve in Mark." *Zeitschrift für die Neutestamentliche Wissenschaft* 69 (1978): 11–35.

Betz, H. D. "Jesus as Divine Man." In *Jesus and the Historian*, edited by F. F. Trotter, pp. 114–33. Philadelphia: Westminster Press, 1968.

Bowman, John. *The Gospel of Mark: The New Christian Jewish Passover Haggadah*. Leiden, Netherlands: E. J. Brill, 1965.

Burkill, T. A. "Blasphemy: St. Mark's Gospel as Damnation History." In *Christianity, Judaism, and other Greco-Roman Cults*. 2 vols, pp. 51–74. Studies for Morton Smith at 60, edited by J. Neusner. Leiden, Netherlands: E. J. Brill, 1975.

Burkill, T. A. *New Light on the Earliest Gospel: Seven Marcan Studies*. Ithaca and London: Cornell University Press, 1972.

Calvin, John. *Calvin's Commentaries: A Harmony of the Gospels: Matthew, Mark, and Luke*. Vol. 1, *Matthew and Mark*. Grand Rapids, Mich.: William B. Eerdmans, 1972.

Carrington, Philip. *The Primitive Christian Calendar: A Study in the Making of the Marcan Gospel.* Cambridge: Cambridge University Press, 1952.

Cook, Michael J. *Mark's Treatment of the Jewish Leaders.* Novum Testamentum. Supplement 5. Leiden, Netherlands: E. J. Brill, 1978.

Coults, J. "The Authority of Jesus and the 12 in St. Mark's Gospel." *Journal of Theological Studies* 8 (1957): 111–18.

Cranfield, C. E. B. *The Gospel According to St. Mark.* Cambridge: Cambridge University Press, 1959.

Danker, Frederick W. "The Demonic Secret in Mark: A Reexamination of the Cry of Dereliction." *Zeitschrift fur die Neutestamentliche Wissenschaft* 61 (1970): 48–69.

Danker, Frederick W. "Mark 1 : 45 and the Secrecy Motif." *Concordia Theological Monthly* 37 (1966): 492–99.

Danker, Frederick W. "Mark 8 : 3." *Journal of Biblical Literature* 82 (1963): 215–16.

Danker, Frederick W. "Postscript to the Markan Secrecy Motif." *Concordia Theological Monthly* 38 (1967): 24–27.

Dermience, A. "Tradition et redaction dans le pericope de la Syrophénicienne. Marc 7, 24–30." *Revue Théologique de Louvain* 8 (1977): 15–29.

Derrett, J. Duncan. "Mark's Technique: The Haemorrhaging Woman and Jairus' Daughter." *Biblica* 4 (1982): 474–505.

Dinkler, E. "Peter's Confession and the Satan Saying: The Problem of Jesus' Messiahship." In *The Future of Our Religious Past*, edited by J. M. Robinson, pp. 169–202. London: SCM Press, 1971.

Ebeling, H. J. *Das Messiageheimnis und die Bötschaft des Markusevangeliums.* Berlin: n.p., 1939.

Farrer, Austin M. *A Study in St. Mark.* New York: Oxford University Press, Inc., 1952.

Faw, C. E. "The Outline of Mark." *Journal of Bible and Religion* 25 (1957): 19–23.

Fledderman, Harry. "The Discipleship Discourse (Mark 9 : 33–50)." *The Catholic Biblical Quarterly* 43 (1981): 57–75.

Focant, C. "L'incompréhension des disciples dans le deuxiemè évangile: Tradition et Rédaction." *Revue Biblique* 82 (1975): 161–85.

Gnilka, Joachim. *Das Evangelium nach Markus.* Ensiedeln: Benzigner, 1978; distributed by Glencoe, Mission Hills, Calif.

Gould, Ezra P. *A Critical and Exegetical Commentary on the Gospel According to St. Mark.* New York: Charles Scribner's Sons, 1896.

Grant, F. C. *The Earliest Gospel: Studies of the Evangelic Traditions at Its Point of Crystallization in Writing.* New York: Abingdon, 1943.

Guy, Harold A. *The Origin of the Gospel of Mark.* London: Hodder and Stoughton Ltd., 1954.

Haas, J. A. W. *Annotations on the Gospel According to Mark.* New York: The Christian Literature Society, 1895.

Haenchen, Ernst. *Der Weg Jesu: Eine Erklärung des Markus Evangeliums und der kanonischen Parallelln.* Berlin: Alfred Topelmann, 1966.

Hamilton, N. Q. "Resurrection Tradition and the Composition of Mark." *Journal of Biblical Literature* 84 (1965): 415–21.

Harrisville, R. A. *The Miracle of Mark: A Study in the Gospel.* Minneapolis, Minn.: Augsburg, 1967.

Harrington, D. J. "A Map of Books on Mark (1975–1984)." *Biblical Theology Bulletin* 15 (1985): 12–16.

Hartman, Lars. *Prophecy Interpreted: The Formation of Some Jewish Apocalyptic Texts and of the Eschatological Discourse Mark 13.* Lund, Sweden: Gleerup, 1966.

Hawkin, David J. "The Incomprehension of the Disciples in the Marcan Redaction." *Journal of Biblical Literature* 91 (1972): 491–500.

Henry, Matthew. *Matthew Henry's Commentary on the Whole Bible.* Vol. 5, *Matthew to John.* Old Tappan, N. J.: Fleming H. Revell Company, 1974.

Hooker, Morna D. *The Son of Man in Mark.* London: S.P.C.K., 1967.

Hunter, A. M. *The Gospel According to St. Mark.* London: SCM Press, 1948.

Johnson, Sherman E. *A Commentary on the Gospel According to St. Mark.* London: Adam and Charles Black, 1960.

Kee, Howard C. *Aretalogies, Hellenistic Lives, and the Sources of Mark.* Colloquy 12. Edited by W. Wuellner, Berkeley, Calif.: The Center for Hermeneutical Studies in Hellenistic and Modern Culture, 1975.

Kee, Howard C. *Community of the New Age: Studies in Mark's Gospel.* Philadelphia: The Westminster Press, 1977.

Kertelge, K. "Die Funktion der Zwölf im Markusevangelium." *Trier Theologishe Zeitschrift* 78 (1969): 193–206.

Klostermann, E. *Das Markusevangelium.* Handbuch zum Neuen Testamentum. Tübingen, W. Germany: Mohr, 1950.

Kopas, Jane. "Jesus and Women in Mark's Gospel." *Review for Religious* 6 (1985): 912–20.

Lagrange, Marie-Joseph. *Evangile selon Saint Marc.* Paris: Librairie Lecoffre, 1929.

Lane, William L. *The Gospel According to Mark.* The New International Commentary on the New Testament. Grand Rapids, Mich.: William B. Eerdmans, 1974.

Lane, William L. "The Gospel of Mark in Current Study." *Southwestern Journal of Theology* 21 (1978): 7–23.

Lightfoot, Robert H. *The Gospel of St. Mark.* Oxford: Clarendon Press, 1950.

Lohmeyer, E. *Das Evangelium des Markus.* Göttingen, Germany: Vanderhoeck and Ruprecht, 1937.

Lohmeyer, E. *Galiläa und Jerusalem.* Göttingen, Germany: Vanderhoeck and Ruprecht, 1936.

Martin, Ralph P. *Mark. Evangelist and Theologian.* Grand Rapids, Mich.: Zondervan, 1973.

Marxsen, Willie. *Mark the Evangelist.* Translated by Roy A. Harrisville. Nashville, Tenn.: Abingdon Press, 1969.

Menzies, Allan. *The Earliest Gospel: A Historical Study of the Gospel According to Mark.* London: Macmillan and Company Ltd., 1901.

Meye, R. P. *Jesus and the Twelve: Discipleship and Revelation in Mark's Gospel.* Grand Rapids, Mich.: William B. Eerdmans, 1968.

Meyer, A. *Die Enstehung des Markusefvangeliums.* Tübingen, Germany: Mohr, 1927.

Micklem, E. R. *Miracles and the New Psychology.* London: n.p., 1922.

Minear, Paul S. *The Gospel According to Mark.* The Layman's Bible Commentary. Atlanta: John Knox Press, 1962.

Nineham, D. E. *The Gospel of Mark.* The Pelican Gospel Commentaries. Baltimore: Penguin Books, 1963.

Parker, P. *The Gospel Before Mark.* Chicago: University of Chicago Press, 1953.

Pilch, John J. "Healing in Mark: A Social Science Analysis." *Biblical Theology Bulletin* 4 (1985): 142–50.

Pudussery, Paul Savio. "The Meanings of Discipleship in the Gospel of Mark." *Jeevadhara: A Journal of Christian Interpretation* 10 (1980): 93–110.

Rawlinson, A. E. J. *St. Mark.* London: Methuen Press, 1925.

Rhoades, David, and Donald Michie. *Mark as Story: An Introduction to the Narrative of a Gospel.* Philadelphia: Fortress Press, 1982.

Riddle, Matthew B. *The Gospel According to Mark.* New York: Charles Scribner's Sons, 1881.

Riesenfeld, Harald. *The Gospel Tradition.* Translated by E. M. Rowley and Robert A. Kraft. Philadelphia: Fortress Press, 1970.

Roth, C. "The Cleansing of the Temple and Zechariah 14:21." *Novum Testamentum* 4 (1960): 174–81.

Sandmel, S. "Prolegomena to a Commentary on Mark." *Journal of Biblical Literature* 31 (1963): 294–300.

Schmahl, G. "Die Zwölf in Markusevangelium." *Trier Theologisch Studien* 30 (1974): 20–30.

Schmidt, John J. "Women in Mark's Gospel." *Bible Today* 19 (1981): 228–33.

Schmidt, K. L. *Der Rahmen der Geschichte Jesu: Literarkritische Untersuchungen zur Ältesten Jesusüberlieferung.* Berlin: Trowitsch and Sohn, 1919.

Schreiber, Johannes. "Die Christologie des Markusevangeliums." *Zeitschrift für Theologie und Kirche* 58 (1961): 175–83.

Schweizer, Eduard. *The Good News According to Mark.* Translated by Donald H. Madvig. Atlanta: John Knox Press, 1966.

Schweizer, Eduard. "Neuere Markus-Forshung in U.S.A." *Evangelische Theologie* 33 (1973): 533–37.

Scroggs, Robin. "The Earliest Christian Communities as Sectarian Movement." In *Christianity, Judaism, and other Greco-Roman Cults*, edited by Jacob Neusner, 2:1–23. Studies for Morton Smith at 60. 2 vols. Leiden, Netherlands: E. J. Brill, 1975.

Scroggs, Robin. "The Exaltation of the Spirit by Some Early Christians." *Journal of Biblical Literature* 84 (1965): 359–73.

Slusser, Dorothy M., and Gerald H. Slusser, *The Jesus of Mark's Gospel.* Philadelphia: The Westminster Press, 1967.

Stagg, Frank. "Reassessing the Gospels." *Review and Expositior* 78 (1981): 187–203.

Stein, R. H. "The Proper Methodology of Ascertaining a Markan Redaction History." *Novum Testamentum* 13 (1971): 181–98.

Swete, Henry B. *The Gospel According to St. Mark.* London: Macmillan and Company Ltd., 1908.

Taylor, Vincent. *The Gospel According to St. Mark.* 1st ed. 1952. Reprint. London: Macmillan & Co., 1966–69.

Tiede, D. L. *The Charismatic Figure as Miracle Worker.* SBL Dissertation Series 1. Missoula, Mont.: Scholars Press, 1972.

Tolbert, Mary A. "Defining the Problem: The Bible and Feminist Hermeneutics." *Semeia* 28 (1983): 113–26.

Trocmé, Etienne. *The Formation of the Gospel According to Mark.* Translated by Palmela Gaughan. Philadelphia: The Westminster Press, 1975.

Trocmé, Etienne. *La Formation de l'évangile selon Marc.* Paris: Universitaires de France, 1963.

Tyson, J. B. "The Blindness of the Disciples in Mark." *Journal of Biblical Literature* 80 (1961): 261–68.

Vielhauer, Philipp. "Erwägungen zür Christologie des Markusevangeliums." Im *Zeit und Geschichte*. Edited by Bultmann Festschrist, pp. 155–69. Erich Dinkler. Tübingen, W. Germany: Mohr, 1964.

Weeden, Theodore J. "The Heresy that Necessitated Mark's Gospel." Zeitschrift für Neutestamentliche Wissenschaft 59 (1968): 145–58.

Weeden, Theodore J. *Mark: Traditions in Conflict*. Philadelphia: Fortress Press, 1971.

Weiss, B. *Das Evangelium des Markus*. Kritisch exegetischer Kommentar. Göttingen, W. Germany: Vanderhoeck and Ruprecht, 1892.

Welhausen, Julius. *Das Evangelium Marci. Ubersetzt und Erklart*. Berlin: Reimer, 1909.

Wendling, E. *Die Entstehung des Marcus-evangeliums*. Tübingen, Germany: Mohr, 1908. 1908.

Windisch, Hans. "Friedensbringer-Gottessöhne: Eine religionsgeschichtliche Interpretation der 7 Seligpreisung." *Zeitschrift für die Neutestamentliche Wissenschaft* 24 (1925): 240–60.

Wrede, William. *The Messianic Secret*. Translated by J.C.G. Gerig. Greenwood, S.C.: Attic Press, 1971.

Miscellaneous

Allport, G. W., and L. J. Postman: "The Basic Psychology of Rumor." In *Basic Studies in Social Psychology*, edited by H. Proshansky and B. Seedenberg. New York: H. Holt, 1965.

Bornkamm, Gunther; Gerhard Barth; and Heinz Joachim Held. *Tradition and Interpretation in Matthew*. Philadelphia: The Westminster Press, 1963.

Brown, R. E.; K. P. Donfried; and J. Reuman, *Peter in the New Testament*. Augsburg, W. Germany: Paulist Press, 1973.

Brown, S. "Review of T. J. Weeden. *Traditions in Conflict*." *Theological Studies* 33 (1972): 754–56.

Bultmann, R. *The History of the Synoptic Tradition*. Translated by John Marsh. Oxford: Basil Blackwell, 1963.

Bundy, Walter E. *Jesus and the First Three Gospels: An Introduction to the Synoptic Tradition*. Cambridge: Harvard University Press, 1955.

Cadoux, C. J. *The Early Church and the World*. Edinburgh: Clark, 1925.

Childs, Brevard S. *The Book of Exodus: A Critical Theological Commentary*. Philadelphia: The Westminster Press, 1974.

Cullmann, O. *Peter. Disciple, Apostle, Matryr*. London: SCM Press, 1953.

Davies, Thomas W. *Magic, Divination, and Demonology Among the Hebrews and their Neighbors*. New York: KTAV, 1969.

Deissmann, A. *Light from the Ancient East*. New York: Hodder and Stoughton, 1909.

Dibelius, Martin. *From Tradition to Gospel*. Translated by Bertram Lee Woolf. New York: Charles Scribner's Sons, 1965.

Edersheim, Alfred. *The Life and Times of Jesus the Messiah*. 2 vols. New York: Longmans, Green, and Co., 1912.

Enslein, M. S. "A New Apocalyptic." *Religion in Life* 44 (1975): 105–10.

Farmer, W. R. *The Synoptic Problem*. New York: Macmillan Publishing Co., Inc., 1964.

Fitzmyer, J. A.; Raymond E. Brown; and Roland E. Murphy, eds. *The Jerome Biblical Commentary*. Englewood Cliffs, N.J.: Prentice-Hall, Inc., 1968.

Frazer, J. G. *The Golden Bough*. Vol. 10, *Balder the Beautiful*. Vol. 3, *Taboo and the Perils of the Soul*. New York: Macmillan Publishing Co., Inc., 1935.

Gager, John C. *Kingdom and Community: The Social World of Early Christianity*. Englewood Cliffs, N.J.: Prentice-Hall, 1975.

Gaster, Theodore H. *The Dead Sea Scriptures, With Introduction and Notes*. New York: Anchor Press, 1976.

Gerhardsson, Birger. *Tradition and Transmission in Early Christianity*. Lund, Sweden: Gleerup, 1964.

Grant, F. C. *The Economic Background of the Gospels*. New York: Russell and Russell Publishers, 1973.

Gray, G. B. *Sacrifice in the Old Testament: Its Theory and Practice*. New York: KTAV, 1971.

Guignerbert, Charles. *The Jewish World in the Time of Jesus*. New York: New York University Press, 1959.

Hanson, Paul D. *The Dawn of the Apocalyptic*. Philadelphia: Fortress Press, 1975.

Holloday, C. H. *Theios Aner in Hellenistic-Judaism: A Critique of the Use of this Category in New Testament Christology*. SBL Dissertation Series 40. Missoula, Mont.: Scholars Press, 1977.

Holtzmann, H. J. *Commentar zum Neuen Testament*. Vol. 1, *Die Synoptiker: Die Apostelgeschichte (The Synoptics Acts of the Apostles)*. Freiburg, Switzerland: Mohr, 1889.

Holtzman, H. J. *Die Synoptischen Evangelien: Ihr Ursprung und ihr geschichlicher*. Leipzig: Germany: Mohr, 1863.

Hull, John M. *Hellenistic Magic and the Synoptic Problem*. Studies in Biblical Theology. second series. London: SCM Press, 1974.

Hultgren, A. J. "Review: T. J. Weeden, Traditions in Conflict." *Lutheran World* 20 (1973): 71–74.

Jayne, Walter A. *The Healing Gods of Ancient Civilizations*. New York: New York University Press, 1962.

Jepsen, A. "De Nebiah in Jes. 8 : 3." Zeitschrift fur die Altestamentliche Wissenschaft 72 (1960): 267–70.

Jeremias, Joachim. *Jerusalem in the Time of Jesus: An Investigation into Economic and Social Conditions During the New Testament Period*. Translated by F. H. Cave and C. H. Cave. Philadelphia: Fortress Press, 1969.

Kelber, Werner H. *The Oral and Written Gospel*. Philadelphia: Fortress Press, 1983.

Kümmel, Werner G. *Introduction to the New Testament*. Translated by Howard C. Kee. New York: Abington Press, 1973.

Leon, Harry J. *The Jews of Ancient Rome*. Philadelphia: Jewish Publication Society, 1960.

Lightfoot, R. H. *Locality and Doctrine in the Gospels*. London: Clarendon Press, 1938.

Löhse, Eduard. *Die Texte aus Qumran: Hebräisch und Deutsch mit Masoretischer Punktation Übersetzung, Einführung und Anmerkungen*. Germany: Satz und Druck, 1964, 1971, 1984.

Loos, H. Van der. *The Miracles of Jesus*. Leiden, Netherlands: E. J. Brill, 1965.

Maertens, J. T. "La structure des récits de miracle dans les Synoptiques." *Sciences Religieuses* 6 (1977): 253–66.

McKinley, Laurence J. *Form Criticism of the Synoptic Healing Narratives: A Study in the Theories of Martin Dibelius and Rudolph Bultmann.* Maryland: Woodstock College Press, 1944.

Moore, G. F. *Judaism in the First Centuries of the Christian Era.* 2 vols. Cambridge: Harvard University Press, 1927.

Noth, Martin. *Leviticus: A Commentary.* Philadelphia: The Westminster Press, 1977.

Oppenheimer, A. *The AM Ha-Aretz: A Study in the Social History of the Jewish People in the Hellenistic-Roman Period.* Translated by I. H. Levine. Leiden, Netherlands: E. J. Brill, 1977.

Otto, Rudolph. *The Idea of the Holy.* New York: Oxford University Press, Inc., 1923.

Otto, Walter F. *Dionysius: Myth and Cult.* Translated by Robert B. Palmer. Bloomington: University of Indiana Press, 1965.

Pederson, J. *Israel.* Copenhagen: n.p., 1933.

Perrin, Norman. *A Modern Pilgrimage in New Testament Christology.* Philadelphia: Fortress Press, 1974.

Pesch, R. "Peter in the Church of the New Testament." *Concilium* 4(1971): 21–35.

Preuss, Julius. *Biblisch-talmudische Medizin: Beitrage zur Geschichte der Heilkunde und der Kultur uberhaupt.* Hoboken, N.J.: KTAV, 1971.

Richardson, A. *The Miracle Stories of the Gospels.* London: SCM Press, 1941 and 1952.

Riesenfeld, Harald. *The Gospel Tradition.* Translated by E. M. Rowley and R. A. Kraft. Philadelphia: Fortress Press, 1970.

Rohde, J. *Rediscovering the Teaching of the Evangelists.* Translated by D. M. Barton. London: SCM Press, 1968.

Sabourin, L. *The Divine Miracles Discussed and Defended.* Rome: Catholic Book Agency, 1977.

Schmithals, Walter. *The Apocalyptic Movement. Introduction and Interpretation.* Translated by J. E. Steeley. Nashville, Tenn.: Abingdon Press, 1975.

Smith, Joathan Z. "The Social Description of Early Christianity." *Religious Studies Review* 1 (1975): 19–25.

Snaith, N. H., ed. *Leviticus and Numbers.* The Century Bible. London: Thomas Nelson, 1967.

Stark, Werner. *The Sociology of Religion. A Study of Christendom.* Vol. 2, *Sectarian Religion.* New York: Fordham University Press, 1967.

Strack, Hermann L., and Paul Billerbeck, *Kommentar zum Neuen Testament aus Talmud und Midrasch.* 6 vols. Munich: Beck, 1922–28.

Sukenik, Eliezer. *Ancient Synagogues in Palestine and Greece.* London: Oxford University Press, 1934.

Sutcliffe, Edmund F. *The Monks of Qumran as Depicted in the Dead Sea Scrolls With translation in English.* Westminster, Md.: The Newman Press, 1960.

Theissen, Gerd. *Sociology of Early Palestinian Christianity.* Translated by John Bowden. Philadelphia: Fortress Press, 1978.

Theissen, Gerd. *The Miracle Stories of the Early Christian Tradition.* Translated by John Riches. Edinburg: T & T Clark, 1983.

Tödt, Heinz E. *The Son of Man in Synoptic Tradition.* Translated by Dorothea M. Barton. Philadelphia: The Westminster Press, 1965.

Torrey, C. C. *Our Translated Gospels.* London: Hodder and Stoughton Ltd., n.d.

Troeltsch, E. *The Social Teaching of the Christian Churches.* Translated by Olive Wynon. 2 vols. London: George Allen & Unwin Ltd., 1931.

Weiss, Johannes. *Earliest Christianity: A History of the Period A.D. 30–A.D. 150.* Translated by F. C. Grant. 2 vols. Magnolia, Mass.: Peter Smith, 1970.

Wikenhauser, Alfred. *New Testament Introduction.* Translated by Joseph Cunningham. W. Germany: Herder and Druck, 1958.

Index